ADVANCE PRAISE FOR

Researching the Writing Center

"This is the first book in our field to examine the hard evidence undergirding writing center theory and practice. Synthesizing research from writing center studies and related disciplines, Babcock and Thonus gather evidence that sometimes supports and often challenges our beliefs. Their analysis opens new vistas and is sure to invigorate the field. Directors, researchers, graduate students, and tutors will learn a good deal in these pages and be inspired to conduct their own research."

—Ben Rafoth, Professor of English; Director,
Indiana University of Pennsylvania Writing Center

"*Researching the Writing Center* is what the field has been waiting for—an overall review of the research and methodologies employed by writing center theorists and practitioners. This volume becomes a history, a guide, and call to action. In this comprehensive overview of the nature of writing center publication and inquiry, the authors demonstrate clearly the initial focus of writing centers on research-as-program development, the growth of a sub-discipline determining what stands for writing center research, and the eventual coming of age as the field increases its engagement in qualitative and quantitative replicable, aggregatable data-driven research. This is an essential guide not only to writing center scholars but to anyone interested in how a field develops and how one might develop a field."

—Joan Mullin, Professor, Illinois State; co-designer, the Research Exchange
(database of writing research)

Researching the Writing Center

This book is part of the Peter Lang Education list.
Every volume is peer reviewed and meets
the highest quality standards for content and production.

PETER LANG
New York • Washington, D.C./Baltimore • Bern
Frankfurt • Berlin • Brussels • Vienna • Oxford

Rebecca Day Babcock and Terese Thonus

Researching the Writing Center

Towards an Evidence-Based Practice

PETER LANG
New York • Washington, D.C./Baltimore • Bern
Frankfurt • Berlin • Brussels • Vienna • Oxford

Library of Congress Cataloging-in-Publication Data

Babcock, Rebecca Day.
Researching the writing center: towards an evidence-based
practice / Rebecca Day Babcock, Terese Thonus.
p. cm.
Includes bibliographical references.
1. English language—Rhetoric—Study and teaching—Research.
2. Report writing—Study and teaching (Higher)—Research.
3. Writing centers—Administration. 4. Tutors and tutoring.
I. Thonus, Terese. II. Title.
PE1404.B223   808'.04207—dc23   2012010388
ISBN 978-1-4331-1924-8 (hardcover)
ISBN 978-1-4331-1923-1 (paperback)
ISBN 978-1-4539-0869-3 (e-book)

Bibliographic information published by **Die Deutsche Nationalbibliothek.**
Die Deutsche Nationalbibliothek lists this publication in the "Deutsche
Nationalbibliografie"; detailed bibliographic data is available
on the Internet at http://dnb.d-nb.de/.

The paper in this book meets the guidelines for permanence and durability
of the Committee on Production Guidelines for Book Longevity
of the Council of Library Resources.

© 2012 Peter Lang Publishing, Inc., New York
29 Broadway, 18th floor, New York, NY 10006
www.peterlang.com

Printed in the United States of America

Acknowledgments

Thanks to the following people for making this book possible: Sue Doyle, for introducing us to the concept of evidence-based practice; Michael Spooner for his helpful feedback on our proposal and letting us know that this was a viable project; Neal Lerner for his thorough reading of the manuscript and excellent suggestions for revision; Charles Barkley, Ashley Meadows, Amber Norris, Marie Schmitz, and Somorah Smith from KU and Katie Groneman and Sarah Banschbach from UTPB for assisting with the index; Chris Myers, Stephen Mazur, Bernadette Shade and Patty Mulrane at Peter Lang for seeing the book through from idea to reality. Of course it couldn't have been done without the help and support of our family and friends.

Contents

CHAPTER ONE

Theory, Practice, and What's in Between: Writing Center Scholarship

If Darwin were to teach us anything about writing centers, he would probably urge us to adopt a materialist model, complete with rich, thick descriptions of our own pedagogical Galapagos, out of which patterns and revelations will emerge. He would tell us to write them down, not lock them away in a desk and wait for our world to catch up. We must relinquish our faith, stop *believing* in writing centers and start convincing ourselves, and others, by the *evidence*. (Boquet, in Griffin, Mattingly, & Eodice, 2007, p. 11)

Overview of the Book and Chapter 1

Writing Center Research: Towards an Evidence-based Practice is the first book-length treatment of the research base for academic writing tutoring. With a 100-year history in secondary schools, colleges, and universities in the U.S. and, increasingly, across the globe, writing centers have become a staple in the teaching of writing. They serve populations of high school, undergraduate and graduate students, basic writers and faculty. They are located in departments of English, are affiliated with university- or school-wide entities or departments of writing, rhetoric and communication, or are supported by private endowments. Tutors in these centers are peers (secondary students, undergraduates, and graduate students) or professionals (*Writing Centers Research Project*, 2004). With the growing importance of writing centers to education since the late 1970s, writing center scholarship has emerged with the express purpose of mediating theory and practice in writing center work.

In "Preparing to Sit at the Head Table: Maintaining Writing Center Viability in the Twenty-First Century," Muriel Harris (2000) employed a banquet analogy to urge writing centers to aspire to be ever more central to the academic mission of universities:

> What will writing centers need to do to be viable parts of our academic community? We have some serious thinking and testing and researching to do. But it will be in areas we already know are important. We just need to realize how vital it is to keep moving forward—to ask ourselves some hard questions; to explore and surface principles for some areas that we have tended to leave unarticulated because we "know" them ... (pp. 10–11)

Harris' call for "serious researching" was, for us, reinforced by Johanek's (2000) *Composing Research: A Contextualist Paradigm for Rhetoric and Composition* as well as Haswell's (2005) polemic, "NCTE/CCCC's Recent War on Scholarship." Surveying National Council of Teachers of English and Conference on College Composition and Communication publications between 1980 and 2000, Haswell noted that journal pages devoted to replicable, aggregable, and data-supported (RAD) scholarship had been declining:

> More and more, the two organizations are letting others do their hard research for them....That labor is turned over to the work hands—to unlicensed apprentices in masters' theses or dissertations, to ERIC freelancers who are not peer reviewed, to novices in "Research Net Forums" ancillary to the main CCCC convention, or to laborers in the surrounding disciplines presumably at lower altitudes—in discourse and communication studies, technical communication, second-language writing, social sciences, professional schools, and schools of education. (p. 217)

Haswell's observation has been echoed in writing center circles. At the 2010 International Writing Centers Association conference, Dana Driscoll and Sherry Wynn-Perdue argued that while writing center scholars yearn for more empirical research to support theory-practice in the field, we lack the knowledge and skill to carry out such research. Citing Haswell (2005), the authors proposed a rubric for "RAD Research in the Center." Their analysis of *Writing Center Journal* articles (1980-2009) found that only 5% qualified as "RAD research."

The unified message of these authors is that composition/rhetoric and writing center researchers need to do some "serious researching" before we can sit at the head table and be taken seriously by our academic colleagues. In our view, writing center scholarship has been largely *artistic* or *humanistic*, rather than *scientific*, in a field where *both* perspectives can and must inform our practice. While theoretical investigations build the foundation for writing center studies, and anecdotal experience points in the direction of best practices, empirical research will create a credible link between the two.

The purpose of this book is first to argue for RAD research, qualitative and quantitative scholarship that engages empirical evidence as mediating theory and practice. In chapter 2, we examine fields outside of composition and writing center studies in which empirical research has yielded reputable evidence-based practice, taking lessons we can apply to our own field. In chapter 3, we explain and exemplify qualitative and quantitative methods we believe are applicable in writing center research. In chapters 4–7, we explore the institutional contexts of academic writing centers and present research-based studies that offer some answers to a host of practical questions asked by writing center administrators and tutors on a daily basis. We mine not only the published literature but also the unpublished voices of thesis and dissertation writers who have chosen writing center theory and practice as their topics yet may never be employed as writing center professionals (Babcock et al., forthcoming). We end the book with a chapter focused on a specific research question: What is a "successful" writing center consultation? We survey the research literature to answer this question and then pose additional questions to be answered regarding success and suggest ways that these can be investigated empirically.

We make what we believe are important observations about the nature of inquiry, evidence, and argumentation in writing center scholarship. Writing center scholarship is a young field, and the direction(s) in which we will grow depend upon the decisions we make today about the definitions of and the connections among theory, inquiry, and practice.

In this first chapter, we propose that recommendations for practice be based on evidence in the form of observations, recordings, microanalyses of actual tutoring sessions; analyses of session feedback forms and textual revisions; and interviews with participants when feasible. We examine published articles such as those by Blau, Hall, and Sparks (2002), Thonus (1999a, 1999b, 2001, 2002, 2004, 2008), and Williams (2004), which have demonstrated that empirical research findings offer important insights for both theory and principled practice. We mine the large number of unpublished dissertations (e.g., Anglada, 1999; Babcock, 2005; Levin, 2006; Ritter, 2002), produced by what Haswell (2005) termed "work hands," to show how vital this research, much of which qualifies as RAD, can become to evidence-based practice in the writing center.

Assessment and Research and Assessment Again

What is *writing center assessment*, and how does it compare with writing center *research*? Harris (1999b), in "Diverse Research Methodologies at Work for Diverse Audiences: Shaping the Writing Center to the Institution," explained the necessity of "exploring knowledge locally produced for local use in the administration of a writing center" (p. 3), which she termed *local research*. She explored institutional research methodologies in order to "shape the writing center to the institution," including "methodologies familiar to composition researchers: interviews, ethnographies, questionnaires, data and textual analyses, case studies, participant observation, and so on" (pp. 9–10).

Although it employs some familiar research methods, we would argue that what Harris described as *local research* is better termed *assessment*. According to the *American Heritage Dictionary*, to *assess* is "to estimate or judge the value, character, etc., of; to evaluate," from the Latin *assesāre*, "to assess a tax," a derivative of *assēssus*, "seated beside a judge." *Research*, on the other hand, is defined as "diligent and systematic inquiry or investigation into a subject in order to discover or revise facts, theories, applications," from the Middle French *recercher*, "to seek or to search." Research, then, does not necessarily involve evaluation or judgment. Nor does it seek immediate application to a local context; rather, it opens inquiry beyond the local context (the individual writing center) to global contexts and applications.

In writing center work, both assessment and research are necessary, and they share at least three characteristics: First, both assessment and research should be based on *empirical data*, be they qualitative or quantitative, including narratives, numbers, and anything noticed. Second, both assessment and research involve *inquiry*, the seeking of knowledge, operationalized as the request for data. Third, both assessment and research drive what Joan Hawthorne termed an "evidence-based approach to our work" (2006, p. 244). And assessment, just like research, Hawthorne noted, qualifies as *scholarly activity* because it involves setting goals, framing questions, selecting methods, and using what we learn. It is at the point of use that assessment and research diverge.

To illustrate, we present Neal Lerner's work, which has demonstrated how writing center assessment can develop into writing center research. In "Counting Beans and Making Beans Count" (1997), Lerner reported a quantitative study in which he investigated writing center use compared to course grade in first-year composition at his home institution. He learned that writing center use made no difference in course grades for most students, although those with the lowest SAT verbal scores showed a benefit from writing center use. In the follow-up to this study, Lerner (2001) explained why this methodology was flawed. He had used SAT verbal scores, noting the lack of correlation between SAT verbal scores and freshman course grades. (In fact, the correlation between SAT math scores and composition grades was closer!) Also, he had neither recognized that course grades may fail to indicate actual writing skill nor accounted for the variation in course grades among instructors. (Enders [2005] also described the pitfalls of using numbers, especially student grades, to measure the success of the writing center's services.) Lerner concluded that a better way to investigate this question would be to do longitudinal research on the effects of writing center attendance on students' overall GPA or on retention rates. Here we see the author extending assessment projects to a more global inquiry, inviting others to participate in a comprehensive research project across local sites.

In Lerner's process, we see that assessment can easily pave the way to research. And we don't want to suggest that assessment is only an exercise, or that it only takes place at the bidding of one's superiors. As Chris Gallagher, in "Being There: (Re)Making the Assessment Scene" (2011), argued, *"being there matters"* (emphasis the author's); meaningful assessment is always locally contextualized, not carried out by "experts" remote from the setting. Writing center professionals have begun to understand the importance of assessment not only to the survival but also to the growth of their endeavors. To this end, Lerner and Kail prepared an excellent bibliography for the 2004 IWCA Summer Institute. They included methodological treatments such as Lamb's "Evaluation Procedures for Writing Centers: Defining Ourselves through Accountability" (1981); Bell's "When Hard Questions Are Asked: Evaluating Writing Centers" (2000); and Thompson's "Writing Center Assessment: Why and a Little How" (2006).

An excellent (and recent) example of locally contextualized assessment that produced valuable research questions is Thompson et al.'s "Examining Our Lore: A Survey of Students' and Tutors' Satisfaction with Writing Center Conferences" (2009). The authors collected post-consultation surveys from writers and their tutors in the Auburn University English Center to assess ratings of their satisfaction with those consultations. Coding was based upon seven attributes the authors drew from what they call "writing center lore": students' questions answered, students' comfort, positive feedback, how much students talked, tutors as peers more than instructors, tutors' expertise, and tutors' non-directiveness. Their finding? "Our surveys supported only those lore-based mandates about the tutors' responsibility to provide a comfortable place for students to ask questions" (p. 95). This finding resulted in immediate application to the local context: "In our training practicums for new tutors, we should discontinue describing lore-based mandates for dialogic collaboration" (p. 100). Thompson and colleagues also suggested future research directions to investigate satisfaction: analysis of asymmetrical collaborations and scaffolding as the primary move in "expert tutoring" (see Chapter 8).

Overlooked in this writing assessment bibliography was "Forms and Functions of Formative Assessment," a 1997 *Clearing House* special edition edited by Eric

Hobson. In "Formative Assessment and the Paradigms of Writing Center Practice," Law and Murphy noted as "surprising, if not disturbing" that a search of the ERIC database for the combined terms *writing center* and *formative assessment* yielded not a single hit (p. 106). Tracing the concept of formative assessment through writing center work from process-oriented pedagogy to the shift to social constructivist theory and practice, the authors found that the second wave of social constructivism delegitimized assessment. They quote from Grimm's 1996 article, "Rearticulating the Work of the Writing Center," as support for the notion that assessment need not be inimical to social constructivism; it can be used to show exactly how "the writing center took on an oppositional stance to classroom practices of the homogenization of student voices ... Student empowerment became a central goal of formative assessment along with the transformative power of the writing center for academic reform" (p. 208).

Of additional interest in the writing center assessment/research discussion is the fact that the International Writing Centers Association currently hosts two separate special interest groups: the Research SIG (led by Neal Lerner at the 2010 IWCA; SIGs on Qualitative and Quantitative research were held at the 2006 and 2008 IWCAs) and the Assessment SIG (most recently led by Kim Ballard, Frances Crawford, and Jill Reglin). This binary suggests that writing center studies is beginning to make the distinction between the two terms and their associated methods/applications. We view this as an extremely positive, though difficult, transition that will yield more credible scholarship.

Who Are Writing Center Scholars?

Let's return to the quote by Beth Boquet that opened this chapter. Her reference to Darwin and the Galapagos Islands reminds us of a key evolutionary tenet: the survival of the fittest. If anything, writing center professionals are survivors, amassing "the numbers" and student and faculty feedback to demonstrate anew each academic year the reason for their existence. Between running their centers and fighting for funding, we have little time to think beyond the immediate, a feature basic to all research.

In "Writing Center Work: An Ongoing Challenge" (2000), Harvey Kail personalized the struggle:

> It is late in my day when I get around to thinking of the writing center director as the writing center researcher—very late in the day. Why? Because research is something we have added on after the original writing center creation myth was well established in our minds and embedded in our job

descriptions....as Writing Center Director my priorities are teaching, service, service, service, and then research—on our service. (pp. 27–28)

Kail's lament still resounds today. Perhaps the most cogent exegesis of the professionalization-research issue is Marshall (2001), "Sites for (Invisible) Intellectual Work." While we agree with Marshall's analysis of the institutional marginalization of writing center work, we disagree with her conclusion that until writing center administration is accorded the same institutional status as faculty work, engagement in "intellectual projects" for scholarly publication (a.k.a. *research*) is not worth it:

> An assignment to direct a writing center could be a particularly enriching site for faculty to work with writers, teachers, disciplinary issues, and institutional priorities they might otherwise never encounter. But what faculty member can afford to take on these responsibilities without the assurance that the work will be valued and evaluated in keeping with their other intellectual projects? (p. 83)

What Marshall reminds us is that it is impossible to describe and evaluate writing center scholarship outside of its institutional contexts. Who *does* writing center scholarship? What is the perceived *value* of this scholarship to the institutions that employ writing center scholars? And most important, how many writing center professionals actually *think* of themselves as scholars?

Two studies of alumni of the yearly International Writing Center Summer Institutes take a stab at answering these questions. In "The Summer Institute for Writing Center Directors and Professionals: A Narrative Bibliography," Babcock, Ferrel, and Ozias (2011) detailed how the writing groups formed at each Institute created a "community of practice" that fostered on-site and future scholarly collaborations. Much of the resulting collaborative work appeared online, in conference presentations, and in newsletter articles:

> While a presentation at a regional writing center conference or an article in *IWCA Update* (the IWCA's biannual newsletter) may not hold the cachet of a Conference on College Composition and Communication (CCCC) presentation or an article in a peer-reviewed journal, for some scholars these publication venues begin the intellectual conversation, increase the scholarly presence of the individual, and provide a needed line on a vita, yet they all belong to the same discursive formation.

The second study was less encouraging: Salem and Eodice (2010) reported the results of a survey administered to 75 attendees during the 2009 and 2010 Institutes.

Using factor analysis, the authors searched for beliefs underlying patterns of answers to attitudinal and demographic questions on a Likert scale. Factors that emerged were (a) long- vs. short-term commitment to writing center work; (b) doing writing-related analysis themselves; and (c) everyday administrative concerns, especially training tutors. Salem and Eodice realized that 50% of those surveyed did not anticipate a long-term commitment to writing center work; rather, they viewed their current positions as "temporary service gigs." The other 50% of respondents fell into two groups: 25% who assumed "writing center director" as their primary professional identity, and 25% who professed a long-term commitment to writing center work and to research, though not necessarily writing center research. The authors concluded that the primary orientation Summer Institute attendees had towards writing center research was that of consumers, not producers.

These studies convince us that writing center professionals are eager to share their experiences, anecdotes, and research findings with their local and global professional communities, but they face institutional, time, and even disciplinary barriers to doing so. All have learned to assess their practice; some have written theses and dissertations in other fields; and some have done valuable theoretical reflection in writing center contexts (Babcock, Carter-Tod, & Thonus, forthcoming). Even if writing center scholars secure institutional backing and the time to address a research agenda, we hazard a guess that the majority of our colleagues lack training in research methodologies, be they qualitative or quantitative. We can only begin to address this need in Chapter 2 of this volume.

We owe a debt of gratitude to those writing center administrators who pursued intellectual work despite institutional and personal hurdles; without them, writing center scholarship would still be in its infancy, and we would have no base from which to launch our call for empirical research.

A Brief Overview of Writing Center Scholarship

In this section, we summarize writing center scholarship since 1984. In particular, we focus on anthologies and edited volumes, what we term "canonical collections," which, by printing and reprinting key articles, have set the tone for explorations along the theory-practice continuum. Several works of writing center scholarship, beginning with *Weaving Knowledge Together: Writing Centers and Collaboration* (Haviland, Notarangelo, Whitley-Putz, & Wolf, 1998), the now-canonical *Good Intentions: Writing Center Work for Postmodern Times* (Grimm, 1999), and *Noise from the Writing Center* (Boquet, 2002), merit our attention here. Although they do not qualify as *research* in the sense we are using the term in this book, these volumes have created a contemporary theoretical framework for writing center endeavors. More recent (and popular) additions to this theoretical literature are the collaboratively authored *The Everyday Writing Center* (Geller et al., 2006) and *Facing the Center: Toward an Identity Politics of One-to-One Mentoring* (Denny, 2010). Lerner's *The Idea of a Writing Laboratory* (2009a) reported a history of the laboratory method in writing and science in the academy and theorized from those findings. These six volumes are possibly the most widely read of all writing center publications, and because they speak for themselves, we see no need to analyze them further here. We will refer to them again in subsequent chapters since they frame much of what is currently denominated "writing center scholarship," and emergent research.

We discuss how writing center research can move towards a new definition of *evidence*, that which is empirically definable and can be generalized in practice across multiple sites. Along with the acceptance and significance of *research* as a term in writing center scholarship, we continue to advocate interest in the conceptual and historical roots of our field; the value of both theory and knowledge production; and openness to self-reflective, qualitative, and quantitative methodologies as data sources. Excluded are publications specifically for a writing *tutor* audience, most often used for tutor training. These include excellent volumes by Harris (1986); Meyer and Smith (1987); Rafoth (2005); Gillespie and Lerner (2008); Rafoth and Bruce (2009); and Ryan and Zimmerelli (2010).

Key Journal Articles and Book Chapters

Writing center scholars enjoy an array of periodicals dedicated to our work (see DeCiccio et al., 2007), though only two have achieved "journal" status. First among these is the *Writing Lab Newsletter*, founded by Muriel Harris at Purdue University in 1976. *WLN* continues to blend tutor reflections and mini-research reports with pithy commentary on the state of the art of tutoring along with professional networking opportunities, and a recent departure from the norm with publication of Lerner's valuable bibliography of theses and dissertations on writing center work and tutoring since 1924 (2009b). *The Writing Center Journal* has appeared in 31 volumes and is now an official publication of the International Writing Centers Association, an assembly of NCTE. It has become the preferred venue for publishing in-depth writing center scholarship, although the former editors of the journal, Boquet and Lerner (2008), lamented that it has been, at times, the *only* place to do so. *Praxis: A Writing Center Journal* has been published online by the University of Texas since 2003. This twice-yearly themed journal covers theory, practice, and administration of writing centers. Two additional online publications, *The Dangling Modifier* from the National Conference on Peer Tutoring in Writing (Texas A&M University), and the blog PeerCentered (hosted by Clint Gardner at Salt Lake Community College), publish writing tutor reflections on their practice. Finally, the *IWCA Update* (available at http://www.writingcenters.org) and regional affiliate newsletters keep members up to date with news and announcements of writing center events.

In this chapter, we limit our review of journal articles and book chapters to those that survey the state of *research* in the field. The continued novelty of this term emerged in our perusal of the *MLA Bibliography* (1 July 2010). We performed a search using the term *writing center*, which yielded 852 results. A Boolean search using *writing center* AND *research* yielded only 24 results. These included all of the chapters in Gillespie and colleagues' 2002 volume *Writing Center Research: Extending the Conversation* as well as several articles published in the *Writing Center Journal*. Only one of the articles contained the term *research* in its title: Carol Severino's "The Writing Center as Site for Cross-Language Research" (1994). After discussing the difficulties of moving from *research* (with a lower-case *r*) to *Research* (with a capital *R*) in writing center work, Severino asserted: "The writing center has the potential to become a truly multicultural, twenty-first century research site where first language writing (composition) and second language writing (ESL) research intersect, each enriching the other with its strengths" (p. 53). Given Severino's considerable output, we think she might have capitalized *Research*, as the bulk of her writing center scholarship has reported findings from empirical data analysis (Severino, 1993b, 1994, 2002, 2009; Severino, Swensen, & Zhu, 2009; Williams & Severino, 2004).

Since writing center professionals may also wear the hat of faculty in university departments, they often publish outside of specialized writing center journals. For example, Stephen North (1985) published a piece on case study research methodology ("a prelude to research") in the *Rhetoric Review*. And in *Education*, Jones (2001) lamented how little empirical research on the effectiveness of specific tutoring practices has been conducted. As an assessment of the literature, though, Jones did not present new research findings. And the assertion that "hard, concrete evidence for [writing consulting's] efficacy may be minimal" and that because of this, "the writing center movement may be viewed as the intellectual cousin to the self-help movement" (p. 18) certainly fails to encourage future empirical research in the writing center context. Maxwell (1994) asked a more fundamental question: Why has so little research been published on the topic of peer tutoring in general? We find her reflections valid even today:

1. Tutor coordinators rarely have the research skills and almost never the incentive to undertake research projects with the exception of those individuals who are pursuing doctoral degrees. Research and evaluation studies take money, time, and resources that are rarely available to the tutoring program.

2. Tutoring takes many forms—individual, group, in-class, etc., and is offered in many types of courses. This makes it difficult to find large enough numbers to find significant differences and to generalize the results. Furthermore, researchers rarely describe the amount of experience and training of the tutors.

3. Tutoring represents just one part of programs designed to help underachieving students. There is often staff resistance to attempting to measure the effects of complex, interpersonal interactions. (p. 114)

The (under)professionalization of tutoring Maxwell alluded to is a topic we have touched on elsewhere (Babcock, Carter-Tod, & Thonus, forthcoming), and we will do so in this volume as we examine reasons why empirical research is undervalued in our discipline.

We were surprised that the *MLA International Bibliography* failed to list the special issue of the *Journal of Second Language Writing* (2004) edited by Williams and Severino on L2 writing center research, even though that is a journal they index. In the lead article, the editors reported that they had rejected many submissions for the special issue because "the research questions were not articulated clearly enough" (p. 170). Even case study and survey research, they argued, should include "explicit research questions, a thorough description of methods, and detailed results that respond to the research questions" (p. 170). These and the "rich, thick descriptions" that Boquet advocated can only serve to promote writing center scholarship to the head table.

The Anthologies

Preferred sources for writing center scholarship include anthologies containing mostly reprinted and some original articles assembled under loose chapter headings alluding to history, theory, practice, and administration of writing centers. Three widely-read writing center collections, several in multiple editions, have compiled previously published writing center scholarship from *The Writing Lab Newsletter*, the *Writing Center Journal*, and various composition-related journals. We call these "canonical collections" because they have for so long been essential reading for prospective and current writing center professionals.

Among these anthologies, the three best sellers at the time we completed this manuscript (according to Amazon.com sales rankings) were (in this order): Murphy and Sherwood's *The St. Martin's Sourcebook for Writing Tutors* (4th ed., 2011); Barnett and Blummer's *The Longman Guide to Writing Center Theory and Practice* (2008); and Murphy and Law's *Landmark Essays on Writing Centers* (1995). Eleven of the articles reprinted in *The Longman Guide* appear in one or both of the other edited volumes, and three are anthologized in all three: North's "The Idea of a Writing Center" (1984a); Lunsford's "Collaboration, Control, and the Idea of a Writing Center" (1991); and DiPardo's "Whispers of Coming and Going: Lessons from Fannie" (1992). The North and Lunsford articles provide a theoretical foundation for the field (Murphy and Law, 1995); and DiPardo's offers an "on the ground" example of work in tutor-led small groups. The obvious overlaps between Murphy and Law (1995) and Murphy and Sherwood (2011) might be explained by their common editor, but we believe that they have less to do with that than the emerging thematic consensus developing in the field of writing center scholarship.

Murphy and Law's volume (1995), less available originally because of its publication by a small press (Hermagoras), is now distributed by Routledge. Nine of its 21 chapters also appear in either Barnett and Blumner (2008), Murphy and Sherwood (2008), or both. Its seven chapters on historical perspectives, detailing the history of writing center work through 1990, created it as an important landmark in the developing field. Its multidisciplinary grounding in writing across the curriculum (Wallace), writing to learn (Leahy), Bakhtinian dialogism (Gillam), sociocultural theory (Bruffee, Ede) and feminist pedagogy (Woolbright) announced that writing center work had "achieved a kind of legitimacy: writing centers have become academically respectable programs" (p. xi). None of its essays, however, qualifies as a RAD research study.

Barnett and Blumner's (2008) volume, formerly known as *The Allyn & Bacon Guide to Writing Center Theory and Practice* (2001), is a compilation of previously published articles with an introduction. It begins with a reprint of Robert Moore's 1950 *College English* article, "The Writing Clinic and the Writing Laboratory." The same article had also been reprinted in Murphy and Law (1995). Barnett and Blumner included sections on history, theory, administration, tutoring practice, diversity, writing across the curriculum, and technology. There is no section on empirical research, and the only articles of the 45 included that could be considered reports of research studies are Jean Kiedaisch and Sue Dinitz' "Look Back and Say 'So What': The Limitations of the Generalist Tutor" and DiPardo's "Whispers." This one highly anthologized article is an actual research study, but, as we have come to learn, its context was not a writing center but rather an "adjunct" developmental writing course, consisting of a small-group out-of-class meeting with an undergraduate student in addition to regular class meetings, similar to the program described by Marie Wilson Nelson in *At the Point of Need*.

In *The St. Martin's Sourcebook for Writing Tutors* (4th ed.), editors Murphy and Sherwood reviewed writing pedagogies and advocated an informed, reflective practice for tutors. The articles themselves are grouped into sections titled "Theoretical Constructs," "What We Talk about When We Talk about Tutoring," "Affirming Diversity," and "Explorations: the Multimodal Writing Center." Three of the reprinted articles, Corbett's, DiPardo's, and Thonus's, meet the criteria for empirical research. We view this is an improvement over earlier editions of the anthology. These "canonical collections" have made an important contribution to the field of writing center studies. It is our hope that future editions of these anthologies or their successors will include even more data-driven research.

The Edited Volumes

In contrast to the three anthologies, eleven other volumes have collected articles written "from scratch": Olsen (1984); Wallace and Simpson (1991); Kinkead and Harris (1993); Mullin and Wallace (1994); Stay, Murphy, and Hobson (1995); Hobson (1998); Silk (1998, 2002); Inman and Sewell (2000); Gillespie (2002); Murphy and Stay (2006); Pemberton and Kinkead (2003); Macauley and Mauriello (2007); and Griffin, Mattingly, and Eodice (2007). We would be remiss in excluding Murphy, Law, and Sherwood's *Writing Centers: An Annotated Bibliography* (1996), in the Greenwood Press series *Bibliographies and Indexes in Education*. This compilation of previously published work and the simultaneous generation of novel content in writing center scholarship demonstrate to us two things: (a) The writing center movement is still new enough that appeals to the founders are seen as both necessary and, at times, sufficient to win institutional legitimacy; and (b) as the movement develops over time and expands in membership, diversity in approaches to theory, research, and practice will keep us alive and maturing.

Olsen, editor of *Writing Centers: Theory and Administration* (1984), concluded, echoing North ("In all the writing center literature to date, *there is not a single published study of what happens in writing center tutorials,*" 1984b, p. 28), that writing centers "don't know what we are doing" (p. xii). Composition scholars, he lamented, had bypassed writing centers as sites of inquiry, but while writing centers had a great deal to offer to research on writing, "their practice outstrips their theoretical grasp of principles behind their work" (p. xii). As the earliest thematic volumes in writing center scholarship, these titles reflected the contemporary state of the art: "*Writing Centers: Theory and Administration* is in fact the first book to examine the pedagogical theories of tutorial services and to relate them to actual center practices" (p. viii). We see in this description the inklings of a yearning for generalizability expressed in the theory-(administrative) practice connection. Olsen's volume is divided into three sections: (1) "Writing Center Theory," (2) "Writing Center Administration," and "Special Concerns." The last section is fascinating both in its topics (e.g., prewriting, technical writing, foreign students) and in its separation from the theory and administration sections as a sort of "junk" category. We see in this separation the inability of the writing center scholarship of that time to create a synthesis of either theory or of practice. Too much critical work remained, from defining terms and the place of writing centers in the academy, to acknowledging epistemological foundations, to finding time to move beyond assessment to research.

Wallace and Simpson's *The Writing Center: New Directions* (1991) begins with a dedication to "all the Writing Center staffs across the United States who struggle every day to have their achievements acknowledged, their expertise rewarded, and their Centers adequately funded." The editors acknowledged that writing centers were poised to enter "a second generation," so important themes were "pedagogical issues involving theory and methods for writing center instruction, administrative issues involving the planning and organization of writing centers, and assessment issues involving the study of how well writing centers do their jobs" (p. xiii). To our knowledge, the first time the term *writing center researcher* appeared in print was in Donald Bushman's chapter "Past Accomplishments and Current Trends in Writing Center Research" (p. 33). The remaining chapters in the volume examined practical issues from the role of writing centers in student retention programs (Simpson), to portfolio evaluation (Keene), to group tutoring for graduate students (Fitzgerald, Mulvihill, and Dobson), the last being what we believe to be the first mention of writing center graduate student support in the literature. Olsen's final chapter in the volume is Christina Murphy's "Writing Centers in Context: Responding to Current Educational Theory," later reprised in Murphy and Law (1995). The positioning of this chapter at the end of the collection suggests to us that even as recently as 20 years ago, writing center scholarship was still urgently seeking a theoretical home. We see this search as a necessary prequel to what would eventually be called "writing center *research*," since legitimate inquiry and selection of research methodology cannot be sustained outside of a theoretical framework.

A different take on writing center scholarship is Kinkead and Harris's *Writing Centers in Context: Twelve Case Studies* (1993). The chapters are not technically case studies[1] but rather eleven writing center directors' self-reports on their work in diverse institutional contexts. Kinkead's final bibliographical essay, "The Scholarly Context: A Look at Themes," is touted as "the most comprehensive overview to date of writing center research" (p. xviii). And Kinkead was successful at providing "the big picture" of writing center scholarship of the time, citing such themes as collaborative learning, writing across the curriculum, work with "special-interest groups" (p. 244), and incipient forays into computing and the Internet. Looking to the future, Kinkead foresaw the need for scholarship on the inherent tensions between writing center and composition pedagogies; on cultural, gender, and linguistic diversity; and on textual rhetoric. The most basic question she posed, however, was this: "Should research in the writing center be restricted to qualitative and quantitative studies or should it include the 'stories' of tutoring?" (p. 247). We suggest that the construction of this question as an alternative misses the point:

Research questions almost always begin as stories about our own experience in the writing center, but our stories are not enough to constitute research.

Mullin and Wallace's (1995) *Intersections: Theory-Practice in the Writing Center* opens with an essay by Eric Hobson, "Writing Center Practice Often Counters Its Theory. So What?" Addressing "this theory/practice disjunction" in writing center work, Hobson argued that the writing center community's "insecurity" in its valuing of practice-based "lore" makes sense because

> Writing Center theory has problems keeping up with writing center practice because writing center theory, to a large extent, is not based on the same foundations as the practice it is most often called upon to justify...writing center theory grew out of practice because no theory called Writing Center Theory existed. (pp. 2–3)

Hobson proposed critical praxis in order to fulfill writing center studies' "theory hope" (a term original to Stanley Fish). Missing from the proposal, however, was a call for empirical research. The remaining chapters in the volume invoked theoretical frameworks ranging from the by-now-expected social constructivism and collaborative learning theory (Murphy; Gillam) as well as unexpected theoretical excursions into whole language, text linguistics, medical ethics, Buberian thought, and the translation theory of Gadamer. In the midst of these are articles referencing practitioner knowledge (lore) on learning disabilities, peer tutoring, and individualized instruction.

Stay, Murphy, and Hobson (1995), the first volume published by the National Writing Centers Association Press (now IWCA Press), is a loosely-organized collection of essays that "attest to the vibrancy of writing centers in postmodern times" (p. 8). Several themes emerge among the chapters, including "situational and demographic forces that shape writing centers and their missions" (p. 4); "tensions between the ideological demands placed upon the writing center and the practical realities of everyday operations" (p. 5); and "explorations of the writing center's potential as a research site" (p. 7). In the latter category, we find Hagemann's "Writing Centers as Sites for Writing Transfer Research," which reported a case study of a Taiwanese student writing in five courses in three separate academic disciplines and argued that the writing center is an ideal site for "interdisciplinary writing transfer" (p. 122). Werder and Buck's "Assessing Writing Conference Talk: An Ethnographic Method" began as a means of *assessing* tutor performance, which "responds to the need that writing centers...be accountable" (p. 174). Historically, their chapter foreshadowed ethnographic research such as Lerner's "Insider as Outsider: Participant Observation as Writing Center Research" (in Gillespie et al., 2002).

The Writing Center Resource Manual (edited by Bobbie Bayliss Silk) appeared from NWCA Press in first edition in 1998 and in a second edition in 2002. Published in manual format (loose-leaf pages to be placed in a three-ring binder), its purpose was to offer novice writing center directors "accumulated and varied experience," ranging from "Starting a Writing Center" and "Managing a Writing Center" to "Special Needs and Opportunities." Bird's "Program Assessment and Reporting," Hawthorne's "Assessment and the Writing Center (Not a Horror Story)," and Lerner's "Research in the Writing Center" complement one another, though Silk placed them in separate sections: Bird's and Hawthorne's in "Managing a Writing Center" and Lerner's in "Special Needs and Opportunities." On the surface, this placement suggests that the editor viewed assessment as essential to writing center survival while research was optional (along with serving clients with learning disabilities, working with second-language writers, and participating in WAC initiatives). In his chapter, Lerner decried a moment at a conference when a speaker referred to research as "a luxury," what he labeled *research,* however, more exactly qualifies as localized *assessment,* prompted by questions such as "How many students are using my writing center and who are they?" and "What effect does the writing center have on students' grades?" What all three articles have in common is information about data collection—a key step in both assessment and research (as we have defined the terms).

The Writing Center Resource Manual was re-envisioned in 2006 as *The Writing Center Director's Resource Book.* It includes a section on "case studies," but as in Kinkead and Harris, these are more like narratives than true case studies, which we define as having a specific research question and bounded data collection. Four of the 39 chapters in the volume were based on research studies, two on focus groups and surveys, and two on textual research. Neal Lerner began the volume with a historical study relying heavily on primary documents, and Brad Peters also provided a historical study in which he analyzed primary documents. The two chapters that conceive of research in a qualitative and quantitative vein are "Writing a Sustainable History: Mapping Writing Center Ethos," based on a survey of 65 writing centers about their concepts of writing centers, and Carol Haviland and Marcy Trianosky's "Tutors Speak: 'What Do We Want from Our Writing Center Directors?'," based on a survey of tutors via the WCenter listserv and interviews of tutors at conference venues. Their results are presented in thematic groups, rich with participants' voices. These chapters provide some balance to the others in the collection, which continue the tradition of using anecdote and personal experience as data and content.

Two edited volumes on electronic writing center work (Hobson, 1998; Inman & Sewell, 2000) contain chapters touching the theory-practice continuum and the need for further research. In a selected bibliography at the end of Hobson (1998),

Steve Sherwood listed three publications under "research," unfortunately, one of these is itself a bibliography of "scholarly research on online writing labs" while the others report survey results on funding, training, and services. Peter Carino's chapter, "Computers in the Writing Center: A Cautionary History," though not a research study, has merit as a historical overview of scholarship, much like Neal Lerner's later works (2006, 2009a, b). In Inman & Sewell (2000), Beebe and Bonevelle examined the role of technology in "the theory-practice debate" in writing center work, though the chapter conflated *research* with *assessment*.

Gillespie, Gillam, Brown, and Stay's *Writing Center Research: Extending the Conversation* (2002) used the term *research* to describe all writing center scholarship. Their volume is divided into three sections: (1) "Writing Center as Sites of Self-Reflective Inquiry;" (2) "Writing Centers as Sites of Institutional Critique and Contextual Inquiry;" and (3) "Writing Centers as Sites of Inquiry into Practice." In the Preface, the editors confessed to four different motivations for starting the project: Brown, to "explain research methodology used in composition studies;" Gillespie, to continue her interest in "scientifically based empirical research and the statistical interpretations of data, with new interest in qualitative research methods"; Gillam, to understand the development of "what counts as research in the writing center community" (p. xi); and Stay, to create "a book in which contributors would define their methodologies" (p. xii). Of these motivations, Stay's is the one that intrigues us most. It implied that previous writing center scholarship under the rubric "research" had been critically lacking in discussions of methodology.

In the introduction to the volume, Gillespie and colleagues mulled over various terms used in composition studies to describe *research* and *scholarship*. They settled on *empirical inquiry* and *conceptual inquiry* as superordinates for "two types of research that have dominated writing center knowledge production" (p. xvi): practitioner inquiry vs. theoretical or conceptual inquiry. The editors cited as groundbreaking the terminological debate in North's "Writing Center Research: Testing Our Assumptions" (1984b), followed by his 1987 volume *The Making of Knowledge in Composition*, in which *researchers* pursue empirical inquiry and *scholars* pursue conceptual inquiry. Gillespie and colleagues also engaged their readers in the debate over the value of "informal practitioner inquiry" or "lore" in writing center knowledge production, which Hobson had argued was central to "postmodern, postdisciplinary knowledge making" (p. xxi). North (1987) had explained that practitioner knowledge was essential to a growing intellectual endeavor: "[Lore is] concerned with what has worked, is working, or might work in teaching, doing, or learning writing" (p. 23). According to James Sosnoski (1991):

> [Lore] count[s] as understanding for teachers of writing. It is not, however, formed in the way that disciplines paradigmatically produce knowledge. It

is contradictory. It disobeys the law of noncontradiction. It is eclectic. It takes feeling into account. It is subjective and nonreplicable. It is not binary. It counts as knowing only in a postdisciplinary context. (p. 204)

Writing center scholarship must value lore, but lore is limiting. Scholars need to talk about what they know, what they have experienced (locally produced knowledge), but they also need to move beyond that step and problematize writing center issues more broadly. How can lore be generalized to inform practice beyond the immediate context of its creation? How does informal practitioner inquiry compare to or interact with qualitative research methods? Harris (1999b), for example, wrote of the "hazy borderlines" between "the interplay of knowledge for local use and knowledge for the profession" (p. 3). Is it possible, however, that "knowledge for the profession" (= writing center work) can find application beyond the profession to composition studies and to literacy studies as a whole? These questions are woven throughout the volume, particularly in chapters by Lerner (participant observation) and Neff (grounded theory). As a whole, *Writing Center Research: Extending the Conversation* posed important questions about inquiry that the field has yet to answer.

Pemberton and Kinkead (2003) was written as a *festschrift* for Muriel Harris, undeniably the most important figure in writing center work over the past forty years. The articles in it, from Pemberton's "*The Writing Lab Newsletter* as History: Tracing the Growth of a Scholarly Community" to Kail's "Separation, Initiation, and Return: Tutor Training Manuals and Writing Center Lore," reflected on Harris's voluminous contribution to writing center theory, practice, administration, and scholarship. Chapter touched on areas as diverse as collaboration (Eodice), space design (Hadfield et al.), and online writing labs (Inman & Sewell). Grimm ("In the Spirit of Service: Making Writing Center Research a 'Featured Character'") and Lerner ("Writing Center Assessment: Searching for the 'Proof' of Our Effectiveness") nicely contrasted *conceptual inquiry* into how writing centers can shift from an autonomous to an ideological understanding of literacy (p. 50) to *empirical inquiry* into how writing centers "measure up" in linking student needs to student outcomes, among other measures (p. 67). Here we see the application of the terminology developed by North (1987) and a growing awareness of the need for and value of different types of scholarship along the theory-practice continuum in writing center studies.

Maccauley and Mauriello's edited volume, *Marginal Words, Marginal Work? Tutoring the Academy in the Work of Writing Centers* (2007), is an elegant collection of writing center scholarship with a clear purpose: connecting writing centers to the academic contexts that sustain them. The publisher's blurb states, "Based on the premise that writing centers know how to guide learners toward more productive and successful work, this volume includes scholarship that provides historical, theoretical, and practical guidance for both writing centers and their campus communities." In terms of empirical research, the most valuable contribution to the volume is Gillespie, Hughes, and Kail's "Nothing Marginal about This Writing Center Experience: Using Research about Peer Tutor Alumni to Educate Others." The Peer Tutor Alumni Research Project (http://www.writing.wisc.edu/pwtarp/) is an excellent example of empirical research based on survey and focus-group data. In contrast, Melissa Nicolas' "Why There Is No 'Happily Ever-After': A Look at the Stories and Images that Sustain Us," though inspiring and beautifully written, is a telling example of writing center scholars' reliance on lore and anecdote.

Finally, Griffin, Mattingly, and Eodice's compact disk (2007) reports proceedings from the 2004 Watson Conference. The authors sought to answer the following question: In the context of writing centers becoming "institutions within an institution...to what extent can we support student retention, writing as learning, and writing for empowerment?" This question speaks more to assessment than specifically to either conceptual or empirical inquiry. Nevertheless, two papers in the collection, by Lerner and Russell respectively, explored the notion of evidence in writing center research.

In "Seeking Knowledge about the Writing Center in Numbers, Talk, and Archives," Lerner offered one of the few exhaustive sources on published and unpublished (including thesis and dissertation) research studies carried out in a writing center (and previously, "writing lab") context since 1910. The title of the paper, however, is misleading. Numbers? Talk? Archives? We wish Lerner had grouped the scholarship he listed historically into these three categories, and performed a critical analysis of each study. We were pleased to read his 2009 *The Idea of a Writing Laboratory* (2009a), in which these concerns were addressed.

Lerner noted that "The Idea of a Writing Center" was not the only piece Stephen North had published in 1984. In fact, "The Idea" was paired with an article on writing center research in which North stated, "In all the writing center literature to date, *there is not a single published study of what happens in writing center tutorials*" (North, 1984b, p. 28). Lerner set 1995 as the beginning of a third wave in writing center research, prompted by Christina Murphy's declaration of the "bankruptcy" of writing center scholarship, a scholarship that failed to "go beyond what's easy and what's known" (p. 69). The difficulty writing center scholars face "tapping into the power and breadth of writing center research" depends not only on a lack of resources and a reliance on "lore" but also "a lack of larger disciplinary notions of writing centers as entities with accepted research methodologies, controlling theories, and an ever-renewing supply of graduate students to explore questions of interest" (p. 56). This inability to conceptualize the writing center as a research site is unfortunate, in our view, given the power of writing center work as a window into the values and beliefs about literacy and education that our institutions, our society, and we, ourselves, hold. Writing centers are complex places and, as such, bring forth a wide variety of questions for us to explore. And those questions, in turn, give rise to a wide variety of research methods, a sort of big cross-disciplinary tent, equally comfortable for the linguist, the historian, the anthropologist, the composition scholar, and others. The true potential for writing center research, according to Lerner, is yet to be fulfilled—quantitative (numbers?), qualitative (talk?), and historical (archival?) studies of our work:

> Our current time is not without barriers to writing center research, but the opportunities are many to create new knowledge about the one-to-one teaching of writing, about the literacy practices of higher education, and about the ways that writing center work can be a model for successful teaching and learning in any subject. (p. 76)

The second notable contribution to *Writing at the Center* was "How to Keep from Getting Stuffed" (as in museum specimens, harkening back to Boquet's natural history metaphor). In this piece, David Russell lamented how humanities-trained composition scholars "turn away" from data-driven research, which he described as "trying to be like lit, not to be like education" (p. 93). Like Lerner, he promoted all types of research, "whether quantitative, qualitative, textual, or otherwise" (p. 93), and supplied research questions and example studies suitable to each. Why? "We, as professional writing teachers and program administrators, have an obligation to provide the most *effective* writing instruction we can" (p. 107, our emphasis). In particular, Russell argued for research comparisons and meta-analyses: "It's o.k. to (systematically) talk with other researchers about stuff" (p. 103). The risks of not doing so, in his view, were dire:

> By not talking to one another more systematically—and not talking with people who do writing research in other fields, especially education—we are not only losing a chance to expand our understanding of writing and our effectiveness as writing teachers, WPAs and WCDs, we are also losing a chance to amplify our political influence through organization, and—let me emphasize this—losing out on major funding. (p. 106)

So it all comes down to funding—and we should not be surprised. The need to prove our worth in difficult financial times, however, has largely propelled writing center directors to do more (local) *assessment*, not more (generalizable) *research*. This explains why so much empirical inquiry is undertaken by graduate students rather than full-time professionals. In fact, as Maxwell (1994) pointed out, perhaps the only writing center workers who have the time or even the skills to attempt research studies are those "pursuing doctoral degrees" (p. 113). Their dissertations are often available only through limited-access databases or interlibrary loan. One of our missions in this book is to make these unpublished works known because they enhance our understanding of the connections between writing center theory and informed practice. And while grant monies are far from significant in the humanities and social sciences, the writing center focus on assessment to the exclusion of empirical research bypasses even these minor sources of funding. Yet how much more convincing an argument for funding rooted in research is than any local assessment might be!

A Call for Empirical Research

While writing center scholars and practitioners are beginning to value empirical research, output remains scarce. Because many writing center directors and staff are not required to publish, much empirical work goes unknown and unreported.

Liggett, Jordan, and Price's (2011) proposal of a taxonomy of writing center research methodologies is an exciting development in the field. And two presentations at the 2010 International Writing Centers Association conference reported surveys of the past 20 years of *Writing Center Journal* articles through research-focused lenses. In "Whose Ideas Count the Most?" Neal Lerner (2010) examined citation practices in the *WCJ* as a means of understanding how our field "regulates and displays knowledge." Driscoll and Wynn-Perdue (2010), in their rubric of "RAD Research in the Center," offered three recommendations to researchers:

1. Work locally but envision broadly (which creates aggregable research).
2. Seek transparency (e.g., clear exposition of methods, which creates replicable research).
3. Focus on connections among studies, seeing research as a continuing conversation (in which one study builds upon another to create a reputable research foundation).

There is a fascinating postscript to this chapter: In the introduction to the 30th anniversary issue of the *Writing Center Journal* ("An Alternative History"), Ianetta and Fitzgerald (2010) described it as "essays that draw our collective gaze to *research* [emphasis ours] published during *WCJ*'s first three decades" (p. 9). Davis, Hayward, Hunter, and Wallace's "The Function of Talk in the Writing Conference: A Study of Tutorial Conversation" (1988) was introduced by Michael Pemberton as following "the standard format of conventional scientific research articles"

(p. 24). Pemberton argued that "the number and frequency of such studies are too few and too far between...if talk, conversation, and teaching are the center of a writing center's practice and pedagogy, then it only makes sense that we should continue using every technique in our methodological toolkit to study and understand them" (p. 24).

This chapter's brief overview of writing center scholarship suggests some promising directions: a continued interest in the conceptual and historical roots of our field; the valuing of both theory and knowledge production; openness to self-reflective, qualitative, and quantitative methodologies and to data sources; and growing acceptance of the significance of *research* as a term in the writing center scholarly vocabulary. We have begun to move away from what Boquet (2007) termed "believing" to "convincing ourselves, and others, by the *evidence*." Since 2007, the International Writing Centers Association has offered small but significant grants for research projects, several of which have gone beyond local assessment to qualitative inquiry and reported results that can be further examined in the full range of writing center contexts.

Perhaps as writing center professionals we have come some way towards fulfilling Neuleib's vision in "Research in the Writing Center: What to Do and Where to Go to Become Research Oriented" (1984). We offer this work to collect and display research that has been done and also to encourage further research and writing center practice based on that research. In the next chapter, we mine research in fields with strong "practice" components, including medicine, social work, and education, and monitor the growth of evidence-based practice (EBP) in those fields. We are convinced there are lessons for us to be discovered there.

Note

1. See chapter 2 for a detailed discussion of case-study research.

CHAPTER TWO

Research Basics in Evidence-Based Practice

Research. [1604]. Systematic investigation or inquiry aimed at contributing to knowledge of a theory, topics, etc., by careful consideration, observation, or study of a subject … Original critical or scientific
investigation carried out under the auspices of an academic or other
institution. (*Oxford English Dictionary*)

Evidence-Based Practice across the Disciplines

The title of this book includes the term *evidence-based practice (EBP)*, which iden-
tifies a specific research orientation across a wide variety of disciplines. In the spirit
of "not reinventing the wheel," we seek to learn from the development of EBP in
these fields and reflect on how we might apply these insights to writing center research. Our goal is to understand the way these scholars struggle along the theory-
inquiry-practice continuum, particularly with the nature of evidence. Once we have
done this, we will argue that writing center scholarship is not all that different. The
scholarly struggles we engage in today mirror those of other fields. We, too, must
come to some consensus if our field is to move forward.

Although we use health care fields as examples, in no way do we intend to imply
or reinforce the "writing center as hospital" metaphor. If there were such a thing as

EBP in auto mechanics, we could just as easily have used that as an example, without trying to reinforce the "fix it shop" metaphor for the writing center.

Medicine, Nursing, and Health Professions

Evidence-based practice first appeared as the term *evidence-based medicine* (EBM) in 1992 at McMaster University in Canada (Sackett et al, 2000). It arose from the circumstances of medical clinicians, who needed real-time, up-to-date information to inform their clinical judgment. Clinicians argued that most sources for such information were voluminous yet difficult to access. Sadly, they had discovered that this state of affairs inevitably led to a growing gap between physician's increasing "diagnostic skills and clinical judgment," on the one hand, and decreasing "up-to-date knowledge and clinical performance" (p. 2). In response, Sackett and colleagues introduced EBM, which they described as

> The conscientious, explicit, and judicious use of current best evidence in making decisions about the care of individual patients. The practice of evidence based medicine means integrating individual clinical expertise with the best available external clinical evidence from systematic research…External clinical evidence can inform, but can never replace, individual clinical expertise, and it is this expertise that decides whether the external evidence applies to an individual patient at all and, if so, how it should be integrated into a clinical decision. (Sackett et al, 1996, pp. 71-72)

The step-by-step practice of EBM, as set out below, has been co-opted by other health care professions:

1. Convert the need for information into an answerable question.
2. Track down the best evidence with which to answer that question.
3. Critically appraise that evidence for its validity, impact, and applicability.
4. Integrate the critical appraisal with our clinical expertise and our patient's unique biology, values, and circumstances.
5. Evaluate effectiveness and efficiency in executing steps 1-4 and seek ways to improve them both for next time. (Sackett et al., 2000, pp. 3-4)

Where, then, were physicians and health professionals to easily and quickly find systematic reviews of the research literature in their fields? The Cochrane Collaboration, culminating in the Cochrane Database of Systematic Reviews (CDSR), was instigated in 1974 by British physician Archie Cochrane, who observed that physicians lacked access to relevant summaries of "relevant randomized controlled trials" upon which to base their practice (Starr & Chalmers, 2003, p. 2) Therefore, Sackett argued, clinical decision-making was often flawed. As collaborators pooled their research, rapid progress in computer technology permitted electronic publication of syntheses and real-time updates, to the point where the CDSR (Cochrane.org) is now the primary knowledge source for evidence-based practice in medicine and health professions.

EBP has, not surprisingly, also made inroads in nursing (Blomfield & Hardy, 2000). The EBP movement is particularly strong in nursing education, in which increased demands for accountability, higher teacher-student ratios, and cost-cutting measures in nursing education are underpinnings for the movement towards evidence-based practice in their field. Nursing educators must not only fully grasp nursing theory and practice; they must also excel in the scholarship of teaching or evidence-based education, enabling them to fulfill societal mandates, set priorities for funding, and instigate cultural change within the academy (Emerson & Records, 2008, p. 362).

Some in these fields have criticized the philosophical foundation of EBM/EBP. Trinder (2000) examined EBM/EBP's epistemological stance, noting its firm foundation in modernist principles: "Evidence-based practice remains firmly committed therefore to the modernist promise that risk can be assessed and controlled by expert knowledge, meaning in this context that the potential harm of interventions is minimized and potential benefits maximized" (pp. 7-8). In a postmodern world, where theory is pervasive and non-empirical understanding valued, Trinder argued that EBP must answer three questions:

1. Can "evidence" be trusted?
2. Does evidence-based practice produce knowledge that is useful to practitioners?
3. Can evidence-based practice incorporate, or do justice to, other forms of knowledge, including practitioner experience and consumer perspectives? (p. 226)

In answer to (1), EBP critics argue that meta-analyses can produce misleading results, results very different from large-scale randomized controlled studies; that empirical studies are not without bias; and that underlying biases and values often go unacknowledged. Aggregate data analyses do not always generate conclusions suitable for application to individuals, critics argue in response to (2). Because professionals and patients may be un- or under-representative of the broader population, and because treatments may be atypical, empirical studies "provide an indication of the *efficacy* of an intervention under the most favorable circumstances, rather than its *effectiveness* in everyday situations" (p. 230, italics the author's).

However, empirical studies, particularly those conducted in social situations, cannot always explain why an intervention works. In Trinder's words, "Although useful, they offer limited purchase on what the precise mechanisms are that generate effects" (2000, p. 231). In response to (3) above, critics of EBP have argued that it denies the value of theory, overlooks the "art" of practice, and ignores the patient/consumer's individualized story and experiences. For example, Giacomini (2009) reasoned that practitioners would do well to revert to theory as mediation between evidence and practice. The crux of her critique was that there are no panaceas for the dilemmas that arise in clinical practice, only better or worse ways of managing them. Current writing center research's reliance on anecdote and lore speaks to this dilemma, since it recognizes and honors individual variability in writers, our clients.

Psychology and Psychotherapy

The American Psychological Association policy on EBP resembles that of EBM:

> Researchers and practitioners should join together to ensure that the research available on psychological practice is both clinically relevant and internally valid. It is important not to assume that interventions that have not yet been studied in controlled trials are ineffective. However, widely used psychological practices as well as innovations developed in the field or laboratory should be rigorously evaluated, and barriers to conducting this research should be identified and addressed. (APA, pp. 1–2)

Interestingly, the language of the statement suggests that APA continues to view researchers and practitioners as distinct, with practitioners as instigators for research studies. As researchers became valued over clinicians in training programs, clinicians felt marginalized and undervalued. Fortunately, in the current generation, researchers and practitioners have come together in a common belief in "the place of the therapeutic relationship as central to all our work with patients" (Alonso, 2009, p. 388). As writing center practitioners *and* researchers, we can agree with Alonso that the primary goal of our work is to better serve our clients, the writers who visit our centers for support and instruction.

In psychology/psychotherapy, just as in the health professions, critics of EBP have examined its philosophical bases. Ramey and Grubb (2009), for example, cited the open debate in psychological circles regarding what constitutes evidence, whether EBP applies to all cultures and minority individuals, and even whether therapies supported by empirical findings fare better than those that do not. They constituted the paradigm framing this debate as modernist, one that ignores the "powerful and constitutive" role of language. To avoid the pitfalls of modernism, Ramey and Grubb urged collaborative inquiry, mutual critique, and a strong ethical frame for clinical reasoning, all fruits of postmodern ontology and epistemology. This fuels our hope that writing center professionals, known for their practical eclecticism, can find a way to marry the modernist frame of EBP to the postmodern application of research outcomes.

Speech Therapy and Communication Disorders

Like writing center work, speech therapy is a fairly new field, and, according to Reilly (2004), the impact of very limited history and anecdote can be enormous. She argued that EBP's guidelines for clinical decision-making are "explicit and accountable rather than being based on history and anecdote" (p. 7). It was necessary to resort to this framework, she asserted, for the same reasons medical practitioners had turned to EBP: Research evidence is burgeoning; new evidence is difficult to access, and this new evidence should effect changes in clinical decision-making, which has often developed from practice without recourse to academic research (pp. 8-11).

Not surprisingly, EBP also has its critics in this field. The logical-positivist underpinnings of EBP, maintained Kovarsky (2008), clashed with the phenomenological evidence of client experiences. Models in speech therapy "marginalize and even silence the voices of those who are the potential beneficiaries of assessment and intervention" (p. 47). The addition of ethnographic and discourse-analytical methods, she contended, would "undoubtedly be useful in constructing more ecologically valid chains of evidence" (p. 56). Here, again, we see arguments in favor of *qualitative* data as valid empirical evidence in support of clinical decision making within a postmodern frame.

Social Work

Scholars supporting EBP in the field of social work have argued that the framework would aid social work in maintaining its legitimacy as a field of practice. According to O'Hare (2005), "the qualifier 'evidence-based' becomes superfluous when defining competent and caring social work practice" (2005, p. 547). O'Hare called for quantitative and qualitative practitioner evaluations of clients and their environments, guided by systematic examination of research meta-syntheses. EBP is "a naturally evolving convergence of social work's pragmatic person-in-environment mission, the applied psychosocial sciences, and the growing demands for ethical, legal, and fiscal accountability" (p. x). Like the Cochrane Collaboration, the Campbell Collaboration (campbellcollaboration.org) aims to provide a resource where practitioners in social welfare, criminal justice, and education can find research syntheses and meta-analyses of important topics.

Postmodern critics of EBP are also active in the field of social work. Blom (2009) questioned whether EBP ignored the need for reflection, or what he termed "deliberate partial un-knowing" (p. 165). While acknowledging that syntheses of quantitative and qualitative research studies could develop "knowledge concerning the effects of interventions and programmes that are possible to standardize" (p. 159), Blom argued that this knowledge was not contextualized and therefore impossible to apply to novel interventions. Supporters of EBP in social work continue to disagree.

Education

EBP has enjoyed wide acceptance and application in fields such as educational policy (Hedges, 2000; Hood, 2003); school social work (Kelly et al., 2010; Woolley, G. L. Bowen, & N.K. Bowen, 2004); special education (Council for Exceptional Children, 2008; Horner et al., 2005); and developmental education (Boylan, 2002). According to the Wing Institute (2011),

> Evidence-based education is a paradigm by which education stakeholders use empirical evidence to make informed decisions about education interventions (policies, practices, and programs). "Evidence-based" decision making is emphasized over "opinion-based" decision making.

EPB in education springs from the action research movement of the 1950s-1970s, which empowered "teacher-researchers" in the use of formative classroom assessment and follow-up interventions in developing "actionable knowledge" (Torrance, 2004, p. 191). Behaviorist educators have created programs such as CABAS (Comprehensive Application of Behavior Analysis to Schooling; Greer & Keohane, 2004) and Precision Teaching (Merbitz et al., 2004) that qualify, at least on the surface, as EBP. Writing center researchers will recall that advocacy for the educational practice of tutoring derived from behaviorist theories and research in education. From an applied behavioral analysis perspective, tutoring is one of the best researched and effective pedagogies extant in both education and psychology (Greer, 2002).

Other writers have taken a more nuanced view of EPB. For example, Cordingley (2004) claimed that teachers would have to be be convinced that using evidence-informed practice in their profession would help them work "smarter" rather than "harder" (p. 86). Eraut (2004) coined the useful term "practice-based evidence" (PBE), defined as "information generated by oneself or others … treated as evidence when it is cited either as evidence *of* the validity of an analysis or diagnosis or as evidence *for* or *against* an argument, conclusion, or decision option" (p. 92, italics original).

Some education scholars are even more critical of EPB. Hammersley (2004), for example, maintained that relying on "transparent accountability," the belief that "research can 'ensure' that the best is being done" (p. 142) created "a climate in which clients demand that their needs and wants be fully met, while practitioners are increasingly concerned simply with protecting themselves from likely criticism" (p. 145). Such is the climate in which much educational reform is proposed and carried out; see, for example, Moran and Malott's (2004) commentary on the "research" behind the No Child Left Behind Act of 2001. The variety of approaches to EBP in education reflects a unity of opinion that practice must be informed by empirical inquiry. The form of that inquiry, nonetheless, continues to be hotly debated, just as it is in writing center research.

Human Resources Management

The relatively new field of coaching and mentoring has also experimented with applying principles of EBP (Stalinski, 2003). To prove its worth to clients, coaching has become "an intervention subject to increasing scrutiny and research" (Stober, Wildflower, & Drake, 2006, p. 3). Briner (2000) saw the research component of EBP as applying to employee selection, job redesign, team building, performance management, and assessment. The fourth volume of the *International Journal of Evidence Based Coaching* (2006) featured an article on the *potential* of EBP as applied to that field. By 2009, however, the journal was publishing more elaborated discussions of the "artistry" of coaches "who blend science and practice to meet client needs through the questions we form, the evidence we choose, and the reflexive evaluation of our performance" (Drake, 2009, p. 10). Drake wisely pointed out that the concept of "evidence" is inevitability political:

1. What types of evidence should be developed and how should they be weighted? How restrictive should the definition of "evidence" be?
2. Who gets to decide what counts as evidence? What is effective in examining the evidence?

3. What discourse and treatments are privileged by our evidence? Does the drive for standards put at risk the needs of individual clients and actions at the local level?
4. What are the implications of Evidence Based Practice (EBP)? What will be gained and lost?
5. Will the adoption of EBP methods be used by other stakeholders to increase the quality and credibility of coaching or to limit the choices available for coaches and clients? How do we balance the need for accountability with the need for further innovation and the exploration of potentially effective techniques and methods? (2009, p. 8)

Masterful coaches, argued Drake, "move beyond thinking of evidence as only a tool or label to be brought from the outside into their practice" (p. 1). Rather, they can seek evidence in the "multiple streams" of foundational, professional, contextual, and self-knowledge to be applied to individual interactions with clients.

A (Cautious) Argument for EBP Research in Writing Center Inquiry

To paraphrase Sackett and colleagues (2000), it is the nature of practice-focused fields to become disconnected from both theory and empirical research. In the writing center context this will not be due to any conscious decision on our part; for some, lore has proven to be enough. It allows us to train writing consultants, to pass on important insights about writing and writing tutoring, and to be proud of the results of our practice. The major insight of evidence-based practice researchers is that practitioners can focus on all three (theory, research, and practice) while interacting with their patients, clients, or students.

The modernist principles underlying EBP cannot be denied, and it is clear that current writing center scholarship is based on postmodernist epistemology that values individual experience and interpretations above other types of data. The meta-analyses central to EBP research must always be scrutinized for principled applicability to individual writing center contexts and problems. Just as the application of theory to practice must be mediated by research inquiry, so must application of research findings to further practice be mediated by theory.

One of the best ways to mitigate the weaknesses of theory-evidence-practice links in EBP is to recognize the value of qualitative data as a source of empirical evidence:

> To date, evidence-based practice has largely consigned qualitative research into a preliminary hypothesis-generating role or into identifying consumer

perspectives...It may now be time to incorporate qualitative...studies into research on the *process* of effectiveness, particularly where the interventions are themselves processes. (Trinder, 2000, p. 231, italics original)

EBP's incorporation of qualitative as well as quantitative methodologies means that despite its modernist roots, it also qualifies as a valid epistemological stance from a postmodern perspective. In its valuing of individual experience as well as aggregate research results, it meets postmodern criteria as well, a stance spelled out by Nancy Grimm's *Good Intentions: Writing Center Work for Postmodern Times* (1999).

We foresee one major obstacle in incorporating EBP into writing center inquiry, and that is our scholars' predilection to isolate and view ourselves as unique. Recognition of writing centers as institutions and of writing center practitioners as scholars in the academy has been hard won. A plethora of publications in our field distances writing centers from metaphors such as *clinic, hospital, prison, church, gas station, storehouse, parlor, garret,* and even *center* (Fischer & Harris, 2001; Lunsford, 2003). Attempts to apply insights from other fields have been few—see, for example, Jay Jacoby's "The Use of Force: Medical Ethics and Center Practice" (1994). The temptation, therefore, is to distance ourselves not only from the nomenclature of other disciplines but from their research practices as well. We ignore these to our own peril, for two reasons: First, we delegitimize writing center studies as a research discipline, and second, we marginalize writing center scholarship that could be of value to researchers and practitioners in other fields. We would do well to learn from the research journeys of other fields.

For writing center researchers, there is no shame in borrowing epistemologies, methodologies, and perspectives from research traditions in other fields as we develop a coherent tradition of our own. Evidence-based practice is one cross-disciplinary research tradition we believe is highly applicable to studying what goes on in writing centers, because its outcome is informed practitioner decision-making.

Approaches and Methods

The material in this book shows that although many fields base their practice on evidence generated from empirical research, only some in the field of writing center studies have engaged in this type of inquiry. Yet we are heartened by some new developments. We reflect on a taxonomy of research methods appropriate to writing center studies (Liggett, Price, & Jordan, 2011) and a survey of *Writing Center Journal* articles for RAD (replicable, aggregable, data-based) research (Driscoll & Wynn-Perdue, 2010, after Haswell, 2005).

Earlier in this chapter, we introduced the work of coaching researcher Drake (2009) and a series of questions he asked about evidence-based practice in that field. Here, we ask several of these questions (adapted to the writing center context) to examine the pros and cons of this broad approach to research for writing center studies.

1. **What types of evidence should be developed and how should they be weighted? How restrictive should the definition of "evidence" be?**

   As shown in our overview of writing center scholarship in Chapter 1, writing center practice has been based largely on lore and application of theories from related fields rather than on research results. It may be useful to define the differences among *lore, anecdote,* and *research* as types of evidence (Thompson et al., 2009).We define *lore* as common sense, common knowledge, and common practice, based on experience and observations of others. *Anecdotes* are personal experiences, but because anecdotes are remembered, not systematically collected, memory and desire can alter them. In contrast to *lore* and *anecdote, data* are accessible to both the researcher and others and are collected to answer a specific research question. Data are generally classified as either quantitative (numerical) or qualitative (descriptive). While lore and anecdote have their place in writing center studies, it is research based on *data* evidence that we highlight here and in the following chapters.

2. **Who gets to decide what counts as evidence?**

   The short answer to Drake's second question (2009) is "whoever controls conferences and publications in the field."The long answer, as suggested in Chapter 1, involves writing center researchers' professional identities and time and financial support for scholarship. Writing center dissertation authors have done most of the empirical research in the field yet are rarely published. On the other hand, the majority of influential scholars in writing center studies, those who publish and vet the work of others for presentation and publication, have neither conducted empirical research themselves nor privileged empirical research in their roles as disciplinary decision-makers. One of us (Thonus) recalls being barred from presenting research at a regional writing center conference in California in the 1990s because she did not work as a writing center professional. In hindsight, this makes perfect sense: If credible scholarship is based on lore and anecdote, it is unthinkable that someone without current day-to-day experience in a writing center could produce it. Fortunately, writing center conferences and publications are becoming more inclusive of a variety of research approaches.

Since many writing center professionals have been trained in humanities disciplines in which research takes the form of critical and archival inquiry, we offer a broad overview of some applicable research techniques from the social sciences and education. While this chapter is neither a "how-to" manifesto nor a research guide, we anticipate that after having read it, some will be interested in evaluating empirical research studies and conducting their own data-driven research.

Research Ethics

Before starting any research program, it is important to consult with colleagues about the proper procedure to acquire permission to do your research. Most writing center research, since it follows standard educational practices, will be exempt from human subjects review by Institutional Review Boards (IRBs). However, researchers cannot declare their own studies exempt from review. If working with live humans in any capacity, investigators must receive either an exemption or a review from an IRB officer. In some cases, the department chair or dean can declare a study exempt from Human Subjects review, and in other cases it may be a vice president, head of the graduate school, or head of the IRB who can declare a study exempt.

In rare cases, writing center research proposals may be required to go through the entire Human Subjects review process, especially if research participants are members of protected classes, such as minors or those with certain disabilities. Or perhaps the researcher wants to test the effects of ingestion of certain substances on participants in the tutoring session. While the chances of this occurring in writing center research are quite slim, it is important to realize that actual studies have been done on the effects of ingestion of alcohol on learner's pronunciation of foreign languages (i.e., Guiora, Beit-Hallahmi, Brannon, Dull, & Scovel, 1972); and other studies have focused on the effects of Valium (Guiora, Acton, Erard, & Strickland, 1980) and hypnosis (Schumann, Holroyd, Campbell, & Ward, 1978). Recall that protection of human subjects became an international priority after Nazi experimentation (which very definitely did not involve informed consent!) during World War II. To prevent further abuses, the Nuremberg Code was developed and is still in use to guide research involving human subjects (see box on next page).

It is essential that researchers follow protocols even if the educational institution or other study site does not require them. Some community colleges, for example,

The Nuremberg Code

1. The voluntary consent of the human subject is absolutely essential. This means that the person involved should have legal capacity to give consent; should be so situated as to be able to exercise free power of choice, without the intervention of any element of force, fraud, deceit, duress, over-reaching, or other ulterior form of constraint or coercion; and should have sufficient knowledge and comprehension of the elements of the subject matter involved as to enable him to make an understanding and enlightened decision. This latter element requires that before the acceptance of an affirmative decision by the experimental subject there should be made known to him the nature, duration, and purpose of the experiment; the method and means by which it is to be conducted; all inconveniences and hazards reasonable to be expected; and the effects upon his health or person which may possibly come from his participation in the experiment. The duty and responsibility for ascertaining the quality of the consent rests upon each individual who initiates, directs or engages in the experiment. It is a personal duty and responsibility which may not be delegated to another with impunity.
2. The experiment should be such as to yield fruitful results for the good of society, unprocurable by other methods or means of study, and not random and unnecessary in nature.
3. The experiment should be so designed and based on the results of animal experimentation and a knowledge of the natural history of the disease or other problem under study that the anticipated results will justify the performance of the experiment.

do not have IRBs responsible for approving (or exempting) research projects. In this case, we suggest researchers obtain informed consent from participants directly, especially if they plan to submit the study findings for class credit or publication. (See Appendix A for a sample informed consent form.) If researchers plan to audio- or video-record sessions, or to collect student work, they should ask participants if the data may be shared with colleagues through professional meetings and publications. It is important to note that increasingly, publishers are asking for evidence of participant informed consent.

If the research site has an IRB, there are probably forms to be filled out on its website. (See Appendix B for a sample IRB form.) Although procedure for the protection of human subjects may seem time-consuming and unnecessary, an understanding of the history behind the protections can make their necessity clear to the researcher. In the past, researchers took chances with risky procedures that may have been harmful to their participants either mentally or physically. In Massachusetts, residents of the Fernald School were exposed to radiation in milk and

4. The experiment should be so conducted as to avoid all unnecessary physical and mental suffering and injury.
5. No experiment should be conducted where there is an a priori reason to believe that death or disabling injury will occur; except, perhaps, in those experiments where the experimental physicians also serve as subjects.
6. The degree of risk to be taken should never exceed that determined by the humanitarian importance of the problem to be solved by the experiment.
7. Proper preparations should be made and adequate facilities provided to protect the experimental subject against even remote possibilities of injury, disability, or death.
8. The experiment should be conducted only by scientifically qualified persons. The highest degree of skill and care should be required through all stages of the experiment of those who conduct or engage in the experiment.
9. During the course of the experiment the human subject should be at liberty to bring the experiment to an end if he has reached the physical or mental state where continuation of the experiment seems to him to be impossible.

During the course of the experiment the scientist in charge must be prepared to terminate the experiment at any stage, if he has probable cause to believe, in the exercise of the good faith, superior skill and careful judgment required of him that a continuation of the experiment is likely to result in injury, disability, or death to the experimental subject. (*Directives*)

oatmeal and also by injection as part of an experiment funded by MIT and Quaker Oats, who in 1998 had to pay a settlement because proper informed consent was not obtained ("Settlement Reached").

Although it might not seem that tutors or writing center directors have the potential to harm subjects, more nuanced ethical issues are involved. For instance, a supervisor asked one of us to perform a study that assessed student writing. He had a difficult time understanding why she could not simultaneously engage a writer in a confidential tutoring session in the writing center and then ask to assess that writing as part of a research study.

Research Approaches and Data-Gathering Techniques

Broadly viewed, empirical research approaches are *quantitative* or *qualitative*, or a combination of the two. *Quantitative* research looks at numerical data,. These data are usually gathered through surveys, although analysis can be conducted on exist-ing data collected for another purpose, such as comparing writing center visits to grades in courses (Lerner, 1997, 2001). Quantitative analysis can also be conducted by counting tokens of the items under investigation from naturalistic data, such as types of questions used by tutors, or timing the talk ratios of students and tutors in the tutorial.

In contrast, the main *qualitative* data gathering techniques are observation, in-terview, and collection of documents. These documents can be created as part of a study, such as journals kept by the researcher or participants, or related documents, such as student papers or writing center teaching materials. One of the best gen-eral sources on qualitative research is *The Sage Handbook of Qualitative Research* (Denzin & Lincoln, 2005), especially part IV, "Methods of Collecting and Analyz-ing Empirical Materials."

When approvals have been received and the researcher is ready to conduct a study, observation of tutoring sessions of self or others or the general context of the writing center or institution is a great way to begin. Observation can be done by taking notes or by video and audio recording. Recording devices are becoming smaller and less obtrusive, although sometimes the use of older technology can be less intimidating and even a source of interest or humor. In self-observation of tutoring sessions, note-taking may not be practical, although when doing teacher research many tutor-researchers take reflective notes over each session immediately after the session concludes. This practice blurs the line between observation and journaling. Other researchers prefer to have a permanent record of the data, which can be done by recording sessions electronically and storing data on a computer hard drive or by printing out transcripts. Audio and video recordings can be stored, manipulated, and analyzed by computer, making the researcher's job both more in-teresting and more challenging. Audio transcripts can be created by hand or through the use of computer software. Since this technology is constantly chang-ing, we will not mention any specifics here, but we encourage our readers to speak with their institutional technology office to inquire about relevant software avail-able. Occasionally, institutions purchase licenses for software (e.g., Statistical Pack-age for the Social Sciences, SPSS, or speech-to-text interface Dragon Naturally Speaking) and make it available to all employees.

Experiment

As the most empirically based of all research approaches, experimentation involves establishing experimental and control groups in order to confirm or disconfirm a hy-pothesis. When writing center researchers use the term *experiment*, we typically mean *experience*. Take, for example, Wilson and LaBouff's (1986) description of "one writing center's recent experiment in offering more than 'some extra help down the hall'" (p. 20), this is, trying something new. Experiments are often motivated by the null hypothesis, which states that there is no direct relationship between the variables to be examined. The null hypothesis is rejected if there is found to be a connection between variables. In actual experiments, researchers exert control over all conceivable variables in order to attribute causality to one they have targeted. Writing center researchers have, rightly, resisted this kind of control over the tutoring process. The only example of experimentation we uncovered in the writing center literature was Cumming and So (1996), though we did find some experimental studies in dissertations looking at peer review of student writing over the past several decades (Patchan, 2011; Mausehund, 1993; Swift, 1986).

In our view, the only way to conceivably conduct an experiment in a writing center context is to ask an extremely narrow research question. Cumming and So compared the language used in the tutorial and specific tutoring techniques in a 2 x 2 study, in which both groups got both treatments (language and tutoring technique). One of us (Thonus, collaborating with Beth Hewett) has recently embarked on a quasi-experimental research project examining the effects of online metaphorical tutor response on the revisions of writers in a first-year composition class. In this case, both tutors and writers have been assigned to either experimental or control groups, while the instructor for both groups remains the same. In constructing this study, we are fully aware of the possibility that this approach may affect both classroom instruction and writing consultation for good or for ill; we have obtained IRB approval and been especially careful to request informed consent from all participants.

Experimentation as a research method remains both difficult and suspect. Since writing center tutoring is based on talk, it is extremely hard to manipulate factors such as types of questions asked, use of questions vs. imperatives, etc. Writing center researchers are more likely, we believe, to select empirical research approaches that are more intimately integrated with their daily practice of tutoring writers and less intrusive into those techniques and practices.

Teacher Research

In the writing center context, the reflective tutor is constantly looking back on successful and unsuccessful sessions; the writing center director is seeking patterns in the experiences of tutors and writers. *Teacher Researchers at Work* (MacLean & Mohr, 1999) and *What Works? A Practical Guide for Teacher Research* (Chiseri-Strater & Sunstein, 2006) are useful sources about this research approach for tutors and administrators. The process of teacher research, or in this case, tutor research, is simple and intuitive. The practitioner keeps a detailed log or journal of all tutoring sessions, noting practices and situations and reflecting on their effectiveness. Noting a successful practice, the practitioner continues it in subsequent sessions and notes the situations and populations for which this technique seems productive. When reflective tutor-researchers experience sessions that "just don't feel right," they note the circumstances and the details in their logs and attempt to determine a different approach that may work better next time. When the tutor meets this student again, or when a student with similar background and needs attends the writing center, the tutor implements the new approach and then reflects on its effectiveness by journaling. Enhancements to this practice can occur in group debriefing sessions where tutors get together and share successful and unsuccessful approaches.

Tutor research has found its way into a few writing center publications. Grimm (1999) wrote of a tutor whose experience of discomfort with a student's unconventional literacy practices inspired her dissertation research. Kirsch (1992) also mentioned unease or embarrassment in a classroom or tutoring session as a prompt to work toward a better understanding of different ways to help student writers. In addition to sharing individual research with a group, tutor-research can also be undertaken by groups. Nelson (1991), in the only book-length report of writing center tutor-research, reported on groups of tutors who got together to reflect on their practice and determine future directions they would take. Tutors built on the findings of previous semesters, refining and revamping their practices along the way. Group tutor-research can also be enhanced by audio- and video-recording sessions for later reflection. Results can be shared with tutors in subsequent semesters, at conferences, or in publications so that knowledge is built collectively. That way, each new tutor need not reinvent the wheel.

Action Research

According to most sources, the term *Action Research* was coined by Kurt Lewin in a 1946 paper (Leitch & Day, 2000). Action research is similar to teacher research in that it is data driven. However, practitioner-researchers do not attempt to hide the social and political goals of their research, which, ultimately, are liberation and equality. In action research, the researcher and participants are partners in the process, and research goals are mutually determined and relevant. Even though teacher research is sometimes referred to as *action research*, the latter must involve the full participation of the research participants all the way from developing research questions to analyzing and writing up data. The authors of the original Action Research Manifesto stated:

> We acknowledge the complexity of social phenomena and the non-linearity of cause and effect and see that the best response to such complexity is

to abandon the notion of understanding as a product of the enterprise of a lone researcher, and to engage local stakeholders, particularly those traditionally excluded from being part of the research process, in problem definition, research processes, interpretation of results, design for action, and evaluation of outcomes. ("Action Research," 2009)

Those interested in doing action research should look at *The Sage Handbook of Action Research* (Reason & Bradbury-Huang, 2007). *Action Research Essentials* (Craig, 2009) is an excellent guide through an entire action research project from conception to write-up.

In the writing center context, an action research project ideally involves tutors, tutees, faculty, and administrators working together to solve a mutually recognized problem. The earliest action research study performed in a writing center we could find is Horner and Jacobson (1985), who conducted the first phase of an action research project and published the results as an ERIC document. In order to improve their college's writing lab, the authors surveyed instructors and students at their institution and conducted follow-up interviews with students. From these data, they compiled a list of issues and problems to explore in further research. A weakness of their method was that it excluded writing center tutors. In addition, the report only described the first phase of the research. Subsequent phases (which were not published) were to attempt a remedy for the problems found and then to assess the results. A more recent study labeled as action research is that of Hutchings (2006), conducted in a multiracial, multicultural South African university writing center. However, Hutchings did not indicate whether the participants were involved in the choice of research questions, the analysis, or the interpretation of results, thus weakening it as verifiable action research inquiry.

Ethnography

Ethnography is a broad category of research, typically involving *participant observation* or *immersion*. In this approach, the researcher spends long periods of time (anywhere from a few months to several years) living and working among the research participants, "establishing a place in some natural setting on a relatively long-term basis in order to investigate, experience and represent the social life and social processes that occur in that setting" (Emerson, Fretz, & Shaw, 2007, p. 352). In workplace and educational studies, the ethnographer typically spends time with the participants in that setting alone, although research results can be enhanced by spending time with workers at home or during leisure activities (Smith, 2007). Educational ethnographies are usually based on theoretical frameworks such as social interaction, feminism, or cultural studies (Gordon, Holland, & Lahelma, 2007).

Van Maanen (1988) is a classic text on writing ethnography, while Fetterman (2009) is a more recent how-to work on the approach.

Some examples of ethnographic studies that have been done in a writing center context are McInerney (1998), who studied a Midwestern writing center over an academic year, and Thonus (2001), "Triangulation in the Writing Center: Tutor, Tutee, and Instructor Perceptions of the Tutor's Role," in which the researcher engaged in participant observation and interviews. *Triangulation* (using several data sources to confirm hypotheses) occurred because the perspectives of instructors, tutors, and tutees about the role of the tutor were all represented. Neuleib and Scharton (1995) also used triangulation in investigating their own writing center. They collected tutor session notes, observations, student papers, introspection (their own perspectives as administrators), and tutor evaluations of students. Jordan (2003) did an ethnographic study centered on the theme of empowerment in writing tutorials. She collected data by following two beginning tutors through three semesters: their semester-long training course and their first year of tutoring. Mota de Cabrera (2004) conducted an ethnographic study of ESL students in a rhetoric class and in their tutoring sessions. Her study lasted one semester and resulted in a case study (see below for a discussion of this method). In her dissertation, Levin (2007) also used ethnographic methods, interviewing writing center administrators, observing the writing center context and specific tutoring sessions, recording and transcribing tutorials, and interviewing tutors. The multiple data sources and rich descriptions of the ethnographic approach provide compelling data for close analysis.

Case Study

A case study is an in-depth look at a single person or situation. A multiple case study in which the researcher discusses, compares, and contrasts several cases side by side is also viable. Case studies differ from other types of qualitative research in that there must be limits to the case, which are specific boundaries created by setting or participant type. Informal anecdotes and reports in the writing center literature in the form of "I tutored a student and here's what happened," are sometimes incorrectly referred to as case studies. Rather than a simple description of a past event, a case study must begin with a research question such as, "How do first-generation college students navigate academic discourse conventions?" Then, the case-study researcher gathers data from a variety of different sources. For instance, a writing center case-study researcher observes tutoring sessions, interviews participants (student, tutor, writing center director, instructor), and looks at relevant written documents, such as student papers, teacher assignments, writing center handouts, or tutor training materials. A case study is usually written up as a narrative, using ample detail and evidence for the writer's conclusions. Stake's *The Art of*

Case Study Research (1995) is the classic how-to text in the genre. Another more recent text is *Doing Case Study Research: A Practical Guide for Beginning Researchers* by Hancock and Algozzine (2006).

In "Designing a Case Study Method for Tutorials: A Prelude to Research," North (1985) blazed a trail for this approach to writing center research:

> [The case study] derives its validity externally, from the resemblance of the description it creates to its chunk of the "'real" world as perceived by the people involved—an emphasis which delights the practitioner in me. And yet, unlike the "clinical" study, it has a great reverence for context; rather than prompting or isolating certain behaviors, it consults with all participants to determine what they think were the significant features of the tutorial; it insistently tries to reduce and account for the "alien" presence of the researcher; and, ideally at least, it is deeply interested in considering the tutorial relationship over time—to treat it, let's say, as an evanescent language and knowledge community, and explore it from cradle to grave and beyond in both directions. (p. 95)

Since North's call, which in 1985 claimed that there had been no formal case studies of writing center tutoring, several such studies have been conducted.

Perhaps the best-known case study in the writing center literature is DiPardo's (2003) "'Whispers of Coming and Going': Lessons from Fannie," first published in the *Writing Center Journal* in 1992. (In actuality, this is not a study of writing center tutoring, so we find it ironic that it has become so iconic in the literature.) In this study, DiPardo presented a "story" using Fannie's writing, tutoring sessions, and interviews with her and her tutor as evidence. Fannie and her tutor, Morgan, were both minority women: Fannie was Navajo and Morgan, African American. DiPardo explored Fannie's difficulties with producing academic discourse and Morgan's inability to reach and understand her. Morgan had attended some sessions on collaborative tutoring at the Conference on College Composition and Communication, and DiPardo saw that Morgan thoughtlessly pursued the techniques she had learned to the detriment of true communication with Fannie. DiPardo concluded that tutors needed more training about how to work with language-minority students. They should also be "respectfully curious" and "attentive to whatever clues [the tutee] might...offer, ever poised to revise old understandings in the light of fresh evidence" (p. 115).

Another well-known case study is Bell's investigation of a basic writer and her graduate-student tutor (1999). Bell collected data by observing and transcribing the tutoring session, looking at the student's essay, and interviewing the tutor. He presented his findings beginning with a portrait of the tutor, told in her own words from the interview. He then reproduced a copy of the student's essay and a copy of the tutorial transcript. Previously, Bell (1989) had produced a multiple case study for his dissertation project, in which he recorded three tutorials each for all eight graduate student tutors working in a particular writing center. He analyzed the consultations through phases, type of consultation, and topics covered.

Other lesser-known but exemplary case studies are those of Briggs (1991), who examined a long-term writer/consultant relationship; Cook-Gumperz (1993), who analyzed a single consultation with an African American basic writing student; Callaway (1993), who studied one tutor and two of her tutees in depth; Rodby (2002), who investigated a single tutorial on the topic of recreation studies; and Mota de Cabrera (2004), who looked at the experiences of two ESL students, both in class and in their tutoring sessions. Case study appears to be the most pervasive empirical research approach in writing center scholarship (Driscoll & Wynn-Perdue, 2010), and we expect that as the acceptance of empirical research approaches grows in our field, this, along with teacher research and action research, will become more widespread.

Analytical Methods: Quantitative and Qualitative

> What is effective in examining the evidence? (Drake, 2009)

Having completed our overview of research approaches and data collection, we turn to data analysis methods. For writing center research, we argue for two cross-cutting categories for analyzing data: *qualitative* versus *quantitative*, and *talk* versus *text*. In the rest of the chapter, we attempt to answer these questions: What qualitative and quantitative techniques can systematize and reveal patterns in our talk and text data? Table 1 displays a matrix of analytical methods by category.

Quantitative analysis is performed on numerical data gathered in an attempt to answer a particular research question. Those interested in quantitative analysis should take a statistics course or collaborate with a colleague in the field of sociology, psychology or education. Purely quantitative analysis is fairly rare in writing center studies, and these have been criticized for methodological weaknesses (Lerner, 1997, 2001). One such study is that of Davis, Hayward, Hunter and Wallace (1988). The researchers coded the tutorial transcripts according to Fanselow's "conversation moves" (*structure, solicit, respond,* and *react)*, and added two more moves, interruptions that were successful and those that were not. These were quantified and compared with Fanselow's results on teaching and non-teaching contexts, yielding the finding that these features of tutorial conversation fell somewhere in between those of the other contexts. However, Davis and colleagues only used four tutoring sessions in their analysis, so their results cannot be reliably generalized.

Table 1: Examples of Analytical Methods by Category

ANALYTICAL METHODS	TALK	TEXT
Quantitative	Number of words/turn (volubility)	Number of error-free T-units
Qualitative	Question types	Holistic scoring of written revisions

Qualitative data analysis, predictably, focuses on qualities, non-numerical patterns in the data. Much qualitative data analysis is rooted in *grounded theory*, first codified by the sociologists Glaser and Strauss in 1967. Researchers examine their data iteratively, coding them, and allowing theory to emerge from the data. There are no preconceived categories for coding; rather, the researcher notes tentative codes and writes coding memos describing the issues rising to the surface. From this coding emerges theory, contrary to the post-theoretical coding common in quantitative analysis. One of the best comprehensive introductions to grounded theory is *Basics of Qualitative Research*, 3rd edition (Corbin & Strauss, 2008).

We know of four writing center studies, all of them dissertations, which have used grounded theory to analyze qualitative data. Roswell (1992) and Magnotto (1991) are early examples. More recently, Levin (2007) used what she called a "modified version" of grounded theory in her writing center study. Levin explained her process this way:

> I repeatedly examined my data (taped tutorials, observation notes, transcripts, and interviews), making notes and adding informal codes for patterns of phenomena that I observed, and reviewing and revising these notes and codes several times. The concepts I eventually generated contribute to my explanation of the kinds of tutoring and tutors in operation at [her research site]. (p. 27)

Babcock (2005) used grounded theory in her study of tutoring deaf college students in the writing center. After conducting observations and interviews, she transcribed the data and then read through it looking for emergent codes. She coded the data and recorded these codes in a code book. These open codes were further represented textually and graphically in the form of coding memos, graphs, tables, and charts. She then engaged in axial coding, looking for categories and attempting to demonstrate the relationships and interplay among several categories. The result was a narrative based on a matrix that described the entire tutoring process.

Often, writing center researchers opt to use both qualitative and quantitative analyses in their studies. Johanek's (2000) *Composing Research: A Contextualist Paradigm for Rhetoric and Composition* is an excellent text for humanists willing to expand their inquiry into the empirical realm. Several studies have used mixed qualitative and quantitative analysis, most recently Brown (2008), which looked at tutor strategies; Griffin (2008), which investigated distance-learning technologies; Vasquez (2008), which studied motivational factors involved with writing center use and course performance; and Barnett (2007), which researched the challenges to viability of writing centers through use of questionnaires and interviews with writing center directors.

The data artifacts produced by experimentation, ethnography, case study, teacher research, and action research typically fall into two categories: *talk* (i.e., tutoring and interview transcripts) and *texts* (i.e., written observations, journals, and student writing). Some analytical methods, such as discourse analysis, are appropriate for both talk and texts; some, such as conversation analysis, are specific to talk, while others, such as text analysis, are specific to text.

The Analysis of Text

Although the object of discussion in many writing center consultations is writing, the majority of writing center research in the empirical vein has focused on talk *about* writing. What goes on between tutor and writer is a topic of intense interest; less important have been studies looking at changes in student's texts as an outcome of writing center consultations. Therefore, it is not surprising that no particular textual analytic method has taken root in writing center studies. We will cite three studies to make this abundantly clear.

Anglada (1999) looked at written tutor comments in an online writing center interface and second-language writer revisions based on them. She analyzed tutor comments using a taxonomy based on Ferris and colleagues' (1997) rubric, and then created a taxonomy of writer revisions based on these comments:

1. Change made by the student in response to comment, effect negative or negligible...the student has incorporated, replaced, deleted, and/or rearranged words, phrases and/or sentences producing only a minimal, slight, or imperceptible effect.
2. Change made by the student in response to comment, effect mixed... student has incorporated, replaced, deleted, and/or rearranged words, phrases and/or sentences, and the effect of any of these changes is mixed

because in the final product, even if the content is clear to the reader than it was in the original (after the consultant pointed out these problems), the structure is grammatically incorrect or unacceptable; or even if the vocabulary, grammar, style, mechanics, etc. have improved when compared to the initial draft...the content is basically unclear.

3. Change made by the student in response to comment, effect positive... the student has incorporated, replaced, deleted, and/or rearranged words, phrases and/or sentences, and the effect of any of these changes is positive because in the final product, the content is clear to the reader than it was in the original (upon consultant's indication) and the structure is still grammatically correct or acceptable...

4. Avoidance of problem...the student has apparently avoided dealing with the problem because he/she deleted the word, phrase, and/or sentence that was causing the problem (pp. 275–277).

Anglada concluded that online writing center use made a positive impact on writer revisions: "Although a high percentage of the revisions involve formal or structural problems—as opposed to global or macro structural concerns—the number of modifications to students incorporated in their final drafts supports the use of online writing center responses during the revision stage" (p. x).

Williams (2004) examined the text revisions of L2 writers in response to (oral) "elements of WC sessions," first in a T-unit analysis and second in a holistic, rubric-based analysis. Two raters coded writers' drafts as T-units (a main clause and its related subordinate clauses; T-units often correspond to sentences, but compound sentences consist of two T-units):

> (i) T-units that remained unchanged from the first to second draft, that is, the same text in the same sequence; (ii) those in which the elements of the text were rearranged or slightly changed; and (iii) those in which larger chunks of text, at the level of the clause or larger, were added or changed. (p. 178)

Contrary to what she expected, Williams found that positive T-unit analyses did not always correspond to positive holistic assessment of revision quality. "Although some tutor behavior and interactional features do seem related to revision," Williams concluded, "it is also apparent that WC visits and subsequent revisions do not always immediately result in better papers" (p. 196).

Most recently, Hewett (2006) analyzed revisions of writers who interacted with professional online tutors using Faigley and Witte's (1981) textual analysis rubric. She linked micro- and macrotextual revisions with a four-category interactional unit (IU) coding taxonomy for tutor online comments:

1. Category 1 addresses four primary linguistic functions of the IU: *Inform, Direct, Illicit,* and *Suggest...*
2. Category 2 addresses one of two possible general areas of attention of the IU...either the writing itself or the instructional, or tutorial, interaction...
3. Category 3 addresses the specific focus of consciousness of the language...*content, form, process, context,* and *reference...*
4. Category 4 regards the phatic (H) nature of certain utterances as a placeholder or back channel cue that keeps open the communicative lines (e.g., "hmmm," "ok," or "thinking") (p. 27).

Although Hewett's study was not carried out in a writing center setting, we recommend it as an elegant example of textual analysis of both online tutor comments and student revisions.

The Analysis of Talk

DISCOURSE ANALYSIS. In discourse analysis, the researcher reads and analyses the discourse as a text, looking for patterns and explanations of the meanings and ways communication is taking place. Kutz (1997) defined discourse analysis as the study of

> The structure of larger units of language beyond the sentence (*discourse*) in either writing or speaking, focusing on the processes involved in producing and comprehending discourse, and the social and cultural knowledge the users of particular styles of discourse (members of a discourse community) must share in order to communicate effectively. (p. 11)

Kutz' book *Language and Literacy* gives excellent advice on studying discourse in classrooms and communities, and it can be easily adapted to writing center contexts. There are a plethora of other texts discussing discourse analysis, including those from the fields of linguistics and psychology. Two older texts that present very clear explanations of what is involved in discourse analysis are Stubbs (1983) and Brown and Yule (1983). A recent update of a classic text is the second edition of Gee's *An Introduction to Discourse Analysis* (2005).

Bloome (2004) described a microethnographic approach to discourse analysis in educational contexts. In his case, it was the classroom, but the techniques of closely studying speech can be easily transferred to the tutoring situation, which is nothing if not an intensely structured conversation. Gillespie and Lerner (2008) advocated for discourse analysis of tutoring sessions in their tutor training guide. In a discourse analytic study, tutoring sessions are typically audio- or videotaped and then transcribed. The researcher then analyzes the transcripts according to whatever criteria he or she is focusing on, sometimes using an additional or outside rater for increased validity.

Blau, Hall, and Strauss (1998) conducted a discourse analysis of writing center tutorials between English L1 tutors and both L1 and L2 tutees. They recorded several tutoring sessions and also assessed the reactions of the tutor and the tutee to the session through a written survey. They focused their analysis on the linguistic features of questioning, echoing, and the use of qualifiers, and how the use of these features enhanced or discouraged collaboration between the participants.

Another sort of discourse analysis was undertaken by Mackiewicz (1999), who analyzed the talk of tutors and tutees for politeness strategies and "discourse activity frames," which basically described the process, procedure, topic, and focus of the tutoring session. The activity frames that she investigated were talk about the message of the student's writing, the medium (form and grammar), the assignment, the procedure of the tutoring session, and "small talk." She calculated time-at-talk and also analyzed politeness strategies like compliments and the use of modals (see below for a fuller treatment of linguistic categories that can be used in analysis). She also looked at the use of jargon. Kim (2009) used discourse analysis, speech act theory, and, specifically, "frame" analysis of tutorials to analyze the sessions of both L1 and L2 tutees in the writing center. She used a combination of quantitative and qualitative analyses to look at question types and frequencies of different types of questions and also volubility, which is usually calculated as number of words per turn.

Melnick (1984) studied writing center sessions through the lens of speech act theory. She audiotaped sessions and used the concept of *membershipping* to determine the success of the sessions. Some scholars have classified this membershipping talk as "small talk," that seemingly off-topic talk that allows interlocutors in an institutional discourse to relate as people. Melnick's article details the conversations she had with three writers in the writing center, focusing on issues of authority. As discourse analysts continued to encounter evidence of power and authority in spoken interaction, a new specialization was bound to develop.

CRITICAL DISCOURSE ANALYSIS. Critical Discourse Analysis, or CDA, is both a theory and a method that explores the social and ideological nature of language, especially as it relates to power and authority (Rogers, 2004). Critical discourse analysts study the relationship between form and function in language and attempt to reveal the hidden assumptions and power relations in discourse contexts. CDA is not neutral, because it attempts to improve social relations through detailed analysis of language use. Classic treatments of CDA are Fairclough's (1989, 1995).

Ritter (2002) used Critical Discourse Analysis alongside Conversation Analysis. She used CDA to explain the social context of the writing tutorial and the various roles the participants took on. Levin (2007) used CDA among other analytical approaches in her dissertation and suggested that tutors do Critical Discourse Analyses of their own and their peers' tutorials. From her CDA analysis, Levin learned that tutors enact (and sometimes reject) writing center orthodoxy in unique, individual ways as they situate themselves in the institutional hierarchy. Courtney (2009) followed a teacher, tutors, and students involved in a first-year writing program though interview, observation, and analysis of documents. She used CDA to analyze the participants' relationships to the course, the discipline, the program, and the university. She found student writers, tutors and teachers were all subject to outside pressures and power structures, often lessening their personal agency.

The advantages of using discourse analysis and CDA methods in writing center research are the immediate applicability of findings to practice, from the actual language routines tutors use to the relationships of power among writing center participants. One disadvantage, however, of discourse analytical methods is their reliance on researcher-involved techniques of interview, observation, and recognition of patterns.

CONVERSATION ANALYSIS. Conversation analysis (CA) uses recorded speech data. The researcher does not have to be present to observe the interaction, but there must be a good quality audio or video recording available. Although CA usually focuses on spoken discourse, it is conceivable CA could be used to analyze signed or interpreted conversations. CA uses a complex transcription system devised by Gail Jefferson (2004). CA takes an extremely close look at talk, at how talk works to make moves and get things done. Some of the concepts used in CA are *turn taking* and *adjacency pairs*, which will be discussed further below. Conversation analysis attempts to look closely at specific instances of conversation to extrapolate the rules or trends at work. Ten Have (2007) is a good resource for learning about how to do CA. An early example is Labov and Fanshel's work Therapeutic Discourse (1977), a book-length study that focuses on only 15 minutes of conversation (psychotherapy) data.

Waring (2005) is the classic example of CA applied to writing center data. Waring looked at advice resisting in tutoring sessions between a graduate student peer tutor and a graduate student tutee. In this case, the writer of the paper resisted the tutor's advice in several instances. Waring pointed out the ways and types of advice resisted. First was "resist advice on general academic writing issues" (p. 147); in this case, the specific technique was "cite resource difficulty." In other words, when the tutor suggested that the writer find some more research, the writer offered excuses why she could not. The second was "resist advice on certain content-related matters," which manifested itself in "assert own agenda," "invoke authority," and "doing being irrational." So, when the tutor made a suggestion, the tutee asserted that that was not what she was doing, that the teacher didn't want her to do it that way, or she just whined and said things like, "I can't do this. I don't want to" (p. 158). The third was "resist advice on mechanics of writing," displayed by "minimize import of advice." For instance, when the tutor pointed out an error, the tutee insisted that she would fix it later and that it didn't matter.

In writing center studies, Conversation Analysis is often used in conjunction with other methods, something actually not permitted of orthodox CA researchers. The first reason why writing center researchers engage in methodological syncretism is that CA is theoretically opposed to contextualization of speech analysis, but writing center studies are by their very nature highly contextualized and written for a specific professional audience. A second reason is that CA seeks to define the parameters of mundane (or "normal") conversation (Ten Have, 2007), and writing center researchers, most notably discourse analysts, have discovered that writing center interaction is anything but mundane (e.g., Thonus, 1999a). Some writing center studies employing hybrid methodologies are Thonus (1999a, 2002, 2008), who used CA with speech acts, ethnography, and quantitative analysis; Ritter (2002), who used CA and Critical Discourse Analysis (CDA); and Zdrojkowski (2007), who used CA, ethnography, and quantitative analysis of discourse features.

Discourse features

In the rest of the chapter, we move from methodologies of analyzing talk to some of the components of talk that have been researched empirically in the writing center context. We use these to illustrate the possibilities that exist for this detailed level of research and its possible outcomes in practice and ongoing theory development.

TURN-TAKING. Turn-taking is a major focus in Conversation Analysis studies (Sacks, Schegloff, & Jefferson, 1974). Turns are usually organized into *adjacency pairs*. The most common type of adjacency pair is the question and answer sequence, although greetings and leave-takings also occur in adjacency pairs. Adjacency pairs do not have to always occur in twos, however. In educational contexts, Sinclair and Coulthard (1975) found the IRE sequence prevailed. This is the Initiation-Response-Evaluation sequence that occurs in classrooms and also often in tutorials. Adjacency pairs can be broken up, such as when a side issue intrudes. This is called an Insertion sequence:

A: Shall I wear the blue shoes?
B: You've got the black ones
A: They're not comfortable
B: Yeah, they're the best then, wear the blue ones (Pridham, 2001 p. 28)

Thonus (1999a, 1999b, 2002) investigated turn-taking in tutoring conversations and offered the following sequences: the diagnosis, directive, and report phases. The directive phase can take the following form:

1. Tutor evaluation of global or specific problems
2. Student acceptance or rejection of the evaluation (verbal or tacit)
3. Tutor suggestion (occasionally substituted or augmented by student suggestion)
4. Student acceptance (or rejection) of the suggestion (1999a, p. 233)

Thonus (2002) examined various features, but most relevant to turn-taking, she looked at *overlap*, "the initiation of a contribution by a second party before the first has finished" (p. 116), including *joint production* (when one interlocutor finishes the sentence of another), and *simultaneous speech*, "a main-channel overlap without taking the floor" (p. 117).

QUESTIONS. Since much of tutoring takes place through questions, an investigation of question asking and answering in the tutoring session is a valuable undertaking. Questions can be divided into different types. Some researchers have used *open-ended*, *closed-ended*, and *leading* questions as categories for analysis. Closed-ended questions can also be referred to as *test questions*, meaning a question that the asker already knows the answer to. In the context of the tutoring session, these types of questions have also been broken down into *real questions* (ones the tutor does not know the answer to) and *teacher questions* (ones for which the tutor already has an answer in mind). Another type of question used in tutoring is the *rhetorical question*, in which the answer is given as part of the question. Grammatically, questions can also be divided into *yes/no questions, either/or questions, tag questions,* and *wh- (content) questions. Why Do You Ask?: The Function of Questions in Institutional Discourse* (Freed & Ehrlich, 2010) provides an excellent background for researching this topic.

Questions by nature are incomplete, so they compel a response. Status and power roles influence how questions are interpreted (Goody, 1978). The form of an utterance does not always correspond with the intention. For instance, a question may not be a direct request for information but an indirect request for behavior from the hearer. This often happens in "nondirective" tutoring, in which the "questions" are actually not true questions but veiled requests by the tutor for some sort of behavior from the tutee. For example, if a tutor asks "Can you read this?," the expected response is not "yes" or "no" but for the student to begin reading. A question, as the first part of an adjacency pair, "compels, requires, may even demand, a response" (Goody, 1978, p. 23). Goody goes on to explain that "the *direct* illocutionary force of all questions is the elicitation of a response—but not necessarily a verbal response" (p. 26). Of course, rhetorical questions are or must be an exception to this. Questions also exert a function of control, related to the statement above that a question *compels* a response from the hearer. In the context of the tutoring session, since it is the tutor who typically asks the questions, the tutor, by default, controls the situation and the conversation. In a truly student-centered tutorial, the student would or should be the one asking most of the questions.

Several studies have looked at questions in the tutoring session. Thonus (1999b) observed tutors using more closed, tag, either/or, and leading questions with second-language writers and noted that these types of questions limited the tutee's options for response. Haas (1986) found tutors using two types of questions: "real questions" to which they truly did not know the answer, and "teacher questions" which "do call for a specific answer and are then evaluated by the questioner" (p. 290). Haas noted that the most successful questions and those most "useful in getting students to become engaged and active participants were those 'real questions' which allowed for a variety of answers." Haas also noticed one tutee asking a great many questions. These questions were important to the tutorial interaction and helped the tutor to discover the tutee's concerns. In a tutorial analyzed by Fletcher (1993), the tutor used only closed-ended questions, sometimes of questionable utility, and seemed to ignore the real concerns of the tutee.

SPEECH ACTS. Speech act theory was developed by Austin (1962) and refined by Searle (1969). The classic Speech Act is defined by the performative, which is an act that brings about its intended consequence and makes itself true just by being spoken, such as a bet, a judge's sentencing, a baptism, or the christening of a ship. Some other kinds of speech acts more recently proposed are meta-interactive acts that frame the conversation, such as greetings or leave takings; turn-taking acts such as asking for the floor or passing it on; and interactive acts, which are broken down into eliciting (asking for information, a decision, an agreement, clarification or repetition), informing (offering information or responding to elicitation), acknowledging (positive or negative feedback), and directing (asking for an immediate or future action) (Gramley & Pätzold, 2004, p. 171). These acts can be analyzed in the tutoring session.

Speech acts relate to the pragmatics of a conversation, sometimes described as locutionary, illocutionary, and perlocutionary acts. Locutionary acts are the actual words of the speaker. Illocutionary acts consist of the actual intent of the speaker. Perlocutionary acts are the actual effect and result on the hearer (Gramley & Pätzold, 2004, p. 171). Illocutionary acts can be broken down into the categories of *representatives* (representing a state of affairs), *directives* (getting the speaker to do something), *commissives* (promising, threatening, vowing regarding some future action), *expressives* (expressing one's mental state, especially to express approval or disapproval), and *declarations* (the classic performative acts described above) (Curzan & Adams, 2006, p. 247).

Most tutoring acts are directives (Babcock, forthcoming) because the tutor wants the tutee to provide some information, but the directive can be either directly or indirectly stated. It is important to keep in mind the difference between non-directive (or Socratic) tutoring, in which the tutor attempts to draw ideas out of the student, and indirect speech acts, which are actually requests for information or behavior couched in language that is conventionally polite. When investigating tutorials with L2 writers, the work of Gars and Neu (2006) is helpful in understanding how speech acts operate across cultures. The authors offer several studies of the acquisition of speech acts in language learning and cross-cultural comparisons of realizations of speech acts.

Since the participants in a tutoring session are purportedly engaged in a mutual goal-oriented, collaborative behavior, the concept of the Cooperative Principle (Grice, 1991) is relevant: "Make your conversational contribution such as required, at the stage at which it occurs, by the accepted purpose or direction of the talk exchange in which you are engaged" (p. 26). Grice's "Maxims," which logically derive from the Cooperative Principle, are invoked in speech act theory and analytical practice:

The Maxim of Quantity:
1. Make your contribution to the conversation as informative as necessary.
2. Do not make your contribution to the conversation more informative than necessary.

The Maxim of Quality:
1. Do not say what you believe to be false.
2. Do not say that for which you lack adequate evidence.

The Maxim of Relevance:
1. Be relevant (i.e., say things related to the current topic of the conversation).

The Maxim of Manner:
1. Avoid obscurity of expression.
2. Avoid ambiguity.
3. Be brief (avoid unnecessary wordiness).
4. Be orderly.

We have several reservations about using this framework for writing center research. First, Grice was a philosopher, and the Maxims derive from philosophical thinking rather than actual observation of naturalistic data. Second, since the writing center tutorial is an institutional rather than mundane conversation, the Maxims apply in a non-conventional way. That is, in order for the tutoring session to succeed, each party must play along with frequent, ritualized violations of normal conversational implicature. In other words, in traditional tutoring, it is up to the tutee to figure out why the tutor is being ambiguous or obscure: The procedure is usually tacit and seldom explained. Nevertheless, we see knowledge of the Maxims as important when performing a speech act analysis of tutorial conversations, and any violations of the Maxims should be noted as pivotal.

POLITENESS. Politeness, according to Brown and Levinson (1987) rests on the concept of face. This theory proposes that people have positive and negative face wants, meaning that they want to be unimpeded in their actions (negative face), and that they want their "wants to be desirable to at least some others" (positive face, p. 62). Any act that impinges on these face wants is considered a *face-threatening act* (FTA), and several linguistic devices are used to mitigate these acts. In positive politeness, the speaker pays a compliment to the hearer such as, "What a great lawnmower; can I borrow it?," and in negative politeness, the speaker attempts to lessen the imposition on the hearer, such as "If it's not too much trouble, may I borrow your lawnmower?" The tutoring session itself can be seen as an FTA, since any suggestion for revision of a paper affects the student's desire to proceed unimpeded in his or her writing of the paper. If the tutor finds anything in the paper that needs revision, this would indicate that something in the student's paper is viewed as undesirable by the tutor. For these and other reasons, a study of politeness in the tutoring session is warranted.

Politeness is often achieved through speech acts, and these acts can be analyzed in the tutoring session. To mitigate a face-threatening act, the act is sometimes done "off-record." Off-record acts are those that can have more than one interpretation and hence can be either taken as a request, or whatever the illocutionary force was, or ignored or responded to otherwise. For example,

> TUTOR: OK. Here you have "and" here and someplace else. How would those sound if, if you took those "ands" out and made two independent sentences?
> TUTEE: I don't know.

The tutor's intent is to get the student to revise the sentence accordingly, but the tutee answers as if it were a genuine request for information and she does not know the answer.

These types of off-record acts violate Gricean Maxims. Brown & Levinson (1978) offer an explanation of how the Maxims can be violated when performing FTAs:

- The Maxim of Manner can be violated by being vague or ambiguous, in-cluding overgeneralization and ellipsis, and a strategy called "Displace H" where someone other than the addressee is addressed.
- The Maxim of Relevance can be violated by giving hints, giving associa-tion clues, and presupposing.
- The Maxim of Quantity can be violated by understating, overstating, and use of tautologies.
- The Maxim of Quality can be violated by using contradictions, irony, metaphors, and rhetorical questions. (p. 219)

Some of what speakers of Standard American English consider indirect requests have actually become conventionalized and are no longer perceived as indirect. For example, "Can you pass the salt?" which is referring to a felicity condition, can be modified with "please," so that "Can you please pass the salt?" has become conven-tionalized. The tutor's question, "How would it sound if…?" cannot add "please," showing its true indirectness and off-record nature.

Watts (2003) offered an alternative to the Brown and Levinson analysis of po-liteness. He defined *politic* behavior as that which can reasonably be expected in a given situation, and *polite* or *impolite* behavior as that which would exceed or differ from what was expected. Watts also insisted that the reaction or under-standing of the hearer is crucial to determining whether an act is seen as polite or impolite. He claimed that there are no inherently polite utterances, because an utterance that is "too polite" in context might actually be interpreted negatively by the hearer.

Tutors, as functioning members of society, already know how to converse, how to make polite requests, etc. It seems that these are the factors that need to be ne-gotiated, and in the tutoring relationship the identity of these factors may be un-clear. Once the participants' relationships and the work at hand are clarified, conversation should continue naturally. For instance, in Watts' model, interlocu-tors must be familiar with what is expected in a given social situation to be able to judge if an utterance is polite or not.

As might be expected, politeness strategies and conventions vary across cultures and languages (Brown and Levinson, 1978, 1987). Conflicting strategies may cause confusion in the tutoring session if for one person indirectness is a conventional-ized strategy, while for the other it is not so obvious. Scholars such as Delpit (1988) and Michaels (1986) have noted classroom clashes in communication between groups who understood indirectness differently. Often Americans view themselves as quite direct and judge those who are more direct than they are as rude. In fact, Americans are more direct than some cultures, but Germans, Israelis and Deaf people are all more direct than Americans (Mindess, 2006, p. 83-84).

The extensive literature on directness and indirectness in tutoring writing (Chapter 1) suggests to us that traditional tutoring practice is heavily based on American White middle-class norms: Direct (positive politeness) is bad; indirect (negative politeness) is good. But only a few writing center researchers have chosen to look at politeness as a category for exploration within writing consultations. Wolff-Murphy (2001) found negative politeness much more prevalent than positive politeness in tutoring sessions. This might have stemmed from the common writing center practice of discouraging tutors from evaluating student papers, so compliments would be rarer than off-record suggestions for revision or requests for behavior. An example of negative politeness (mitigating the infringement or imposition on the hearer) from Wolff-Murphy is, "So if you don't mind, could you read it out loud for me?" (p. 99). An example of positive politeness is when a tutor asked, "What's most helpful for you?" (p. 122), allowing the tutee's wants to guide the session. Young (1992) studied tutoring sessions between L1 tutors and L2 tutees and discovered that the expectations of the two groups clashed with the L2 tutees preferring "impolite" suggestions because they lined up with their cultural preference for perceiving the tutor as an authority figure.

Thonus (1999b) also used politeness as an analytical category. Investigating consultations between L1 tutors and L2 tutees, she found that bald on-record directives (FTAs) such as "Write that down" (p. 259) were extremely comprehensible while possibly impolite. L2 tutees were likely to misinterpret indirect polite speech acts "that do not map directly between linguistic form and function" (p. 259), including questions that are actually directives. Thonus also noticed that tutors used Illocutionary Force Indicating Devices (IFIDs) to reduce possible ambiguity, such as the statement, "That's just a suggestion" (p. 274) after several indirect speech acts intended to offer ideas for revision.

DISCOURSE FEATURES. Discourse analysts find it interesting to look at features beyond the obvious words of talk. Kutz (1997), for example, suggested analysts take into account the *topic* of a discourse. Is it always the subject of the sentence? How does the topic shift as new information is brought in? What information is treated as new, and what is treated as given? Second, Kutz suggested scrutinizing the *structure* of sentences. What is the word order? Is it always subject + verb + object, or something else? How can one account for discrepancies? Third, Kutz suggested analyzing *cohesive elements* such as pronouns, conjunctions, and "patterned substitutions of one lexical item for another" (p. 284). Fourth, she suggested attending to *meanings*, specifically which word meanings are contrasted or opposed in the transcript or text. Finally, Kutz suggested the researcher examine *shifts*, changes in tense, person, point of view, and formality of register. Gee (2005) showed how these features work together to produce 112 different possible meanings for a single sentence!

Several studies have looked at discourse features in writing center talk. Blau, Hall and Strauss (1998) looked at discourse features of *echoing* and *qualifying* in the tutoring session. Echoing of the interlocutor's use of discourse markers, syntactic patterns, and playful use of language created an affirmation of understanding and rapport in the session. Other studies have looked at the use of *pronouns*. pronouns. Moser (2002), for example, discussed the use of pronouns in online tutors' responses as being inclusive (*we*), more distant (*I*), very distant (no pronoun) or intimate, where names and other intimacy markers were used. Ritter (2002) and Thonus (1998) looked at *modals* and attempted to categorize them on a scale of direct to indirect and mitigated ("Maybe the thesis doesn't have to say everything") to imperative ("Think about that") (Thonus, 1998, p. 90).

Conclusion

Our overview of writing center scholarship suggests some promising directions: a continued interest in the conceptual and historical roots of our field; the valuing of both theory and knowledge production; openness to self-reflective, qualitative, and quantitative methodologies as data sources; and growing acceptance and significance of *research* as a term in the writing center professional literature.

In Chapter 1, we discussed key differences between writing center *research* and *assessment*, the usually quantitative evaluation of practice in comparison to a set of institutional standards. Often, assessment is all writing center professionals have time for; because it is our bread and butter, we must "report the numbers." Our listserv WCenter is an invaluable resource as we inform and support one another in our day-to-day work as writing center administrators. Once our funding and institutional mandates are secure, however, we turn to writing center scholarship, a vibrant, expanding *agora* of intellectual discussion and argument. Here is where our conferences and institutes and publications have proliferated. Trends thus far have been putting *theory* to the test in *practice* or noting what in our practice should better inform our theorizing.

Our argument throughout has been that writing center theory has often bypassed empirical research in its urgency to immediately inform practice. Our theories have rarely been recognized for what they are: ontological and epistemological constructs that privilege anecdote and experience while overlooking empirical evidence. Because of roots in the humanities, English, and composition studies, writing center studies have typically reasoned directly from theory to practice. We have made writing center scholarship *artistic*, not *scientific*, in a field where both perspectives can and must inform our practice. Here, again, our field has co-opted an intense debate in composition studies (Massey, 2006).

If our field had sprung from education or a social science, in which the theory-practice link is most often mediated by empirical inquiry, the history of writing center scholarship might have been very different. Today, those pursuing writing center scholarship must critically evaluate *evidence*, its role in our practice, and the theorizing that arises from it. To define *evidence*, we turn again to the *Oxford English Dictionary*: "ground for belief; testimony or facts tending to prove or disprove any conclusion" [c1380].

Our argument in this book has been that writing center scholarship, while continuing to value lore and anecdotal evidence, must begin to collect, analyze, and theorize from empirical research evidence to mediate between theory and practice. It is our contention that writing center theory is best nourished by effective practices rooted in the results of data-driven and methodologically sophisticated research studies. As writing centers become, increasingly, sites for writing across the disciplines, this scholarship is poised to enter into that "big, cross-disciplinary tent" of writing center research (Lerner, 2007, p. 56) and take a seat at the "head table" with our academic colleagues (Harris, 2000).

CHAPTER THREE

The Contexts of Tutoring

To understand writing centers is to understand the dynamic, interactive relationship that exists between a specific center and the environment in which it exists. (Kinkead & Harris, 1993, p. xvi)

What should a writing center look like? Where should it be located administratively, and to whom should its administrator(s) report? Where should funds come from to support staff salaries, tutor wages, and outreach efforts? What are the impacts of funding source(s), departmental structure, service modes, and expectations of faculty, students, and staff, both cultural and cross-cultural? How do these impact writing center tutors? How many tutors should a writing center employ, and how should they be trained? In this chapter, we explore the institutional contexts of academic writing centers as investigated in the empirical research literature. The sources cited in this chapter display the development of writing center RAD research: individual writing center assessments expanded to regional or even nationwide surveys, descriptions of writing center organization yielding questions for research studies, and recommendations for practice reframed as research results.

The major issue we discuss is that much that has been written about the contexts of tutoring has described individual writing centers, without recourse to comparison with other writing centers or, better still, a set of standards for writing centers. For example, Wright (1994) of Oklahoma State University surveyed that university's "peer institutions" for information about institutional positioning, reporting lines, salaries, budget, staff, and operational details. The reason? "We need accurate information to set benchmarks for professional standards, facilities, and appropriate working conditions" (p. 4). If the "we" here is collective rather than singular, this type of survey has the potential for becoming RAD research, as findings become the property of the entire writing center community (see Chapters 1 and 2). Discourse about writing centers is by its very nature inclusive and supportive of diversity, not critical. "Let a thousand flowers bloom" could be our motto. We do not question our belief that writing centers are good and that every high school, college, university, and community should have one. What is difficult for writing center scholars is turning assessment of their specific contexts into research questions and RAD inquiry that can benefit the entire field.

The work of Muriel Harris provides an excellent example of the shift from assessment in specific contexts to research across a number of contexts. "Diverse Research Methodologies at Work for Diverse Audiences: Shaping the Writing Center to the Institution" (1999b) illustrated a back-and-forth look between assessment and research, between the particular and the generalizable, and between diversity and commonality. At the same time that Harris cited Healy's (1995) pronouncement that "most discussions of writing centers eventually descend to the particular—or at least they should" (p. 13), she encouraged reflective practitioners to employ "interviews, ethnographies, questionnaires, data and textual analyses, case studies, participant observation, and so on" in amassing a "research archive" for their centers (pp. 9–10) that could then be shared with "other writing center directors and professional contexts" (p. 14). Eight years later, in "Work in Progress: Publishing Writing Center Scholarship," Harris' emphasis landed fully on research, the generalizable, and commonality:

> Write for others beyond your local context. Because many of us start by reflecting on our own centers, some essays stay too locally focused....Those hundreds of readers who work in different contexts are not likely to be interested in a list of statistics about a particular writing center unless the statistics are relevant to some larger point being made....Articles written to prove to the larger writing center world the glories and success of that particular center generally don't have much content beyond "hey, aren't we great." This too is not a useful contribution to the literature of writing centers, even though the author may be justifiably proud of what's been accomplished. However, a study of how that center achieved its success, in terms of how that might help other struggling centers, can be useful (DeCiccio, Ede, Lerner, Boquet, & Harris, 2007, p. 1).

One of the major ways writing center scholars have attempted to look beyond the particular to the general is to survey writing center administrators, the topic of the next section.

Surveys of Writing Centers

Early in the history of writing centers, administrators sought to create community and comparability through the use of surveys more geared to administrative and institutional issues rather than teaching methods. Some of these were Thornton's 1938 thesis "A Limited Survey of the Laboratory Method in Teaching English Composition," Moore's 1950 article in *College English*, "The Writing Clinic and the Writing Laboratory," and Shouse's 1953 dissertation "The Writing Laboratory in Colleges and Universities" (all qtd in Lerner, 2006). Broder's (1981) is the earliest study we uncovered on institutional relationships. In the early days of writing centers as "lab" adjuncts to English courses, her observation could not have been truer: "Administrators of writing labs face a delicate problem: the students we work with have, in effect, two teachers for their English courses: one in the classroom, and the other in the lab" (p. 7). Broder sent questionnaires to twenty-five writing center directors, trying to ascertain steps they had taken to deal with "problems" that had occurred in the writing center-classroom relationship. Answers to questionnaires revealed a lack of understanding on the part of English teachers as to the ability and role of writing center tutors (i.e., no, they don't edit and proofread papers); also common were "faculty members who refuse to refer students to the lab, or who delay referring them until it is impossible to give them adequate help in the time remaining" (p. 7). Solutions proposed included having the lab director secure from the English faculty consensus about guidelines for tutoring students, making sure that tutors did not critique instructors or their assignments and adhered to instructor policies about tutoring their students, and inviting English faculty to participate in tutor training. Others, such as Hayward (1983), Davis (1993), and Wright (1994), are later examples of writing center directors using survey methods to answer questions about institutional positioning and attitudes toward their centers. Theses and dissertations describing writing centers at individual institutions are many and some are of excellent quality (e.g., Dettman, 2006; Staben, 2005).

Descriptive studies based on small or large surveys of existing writing centers provided the burgeoning community some notion of the variety of institutional positioning and funding sources, and they paved the way for more in-depth, empirically rigorous research on these topics. One example is Jordan-Henley (1995), who surveyed 13 community college writing centers, asking questions about funding, staffing, tutoring issues, computer use, and effectiveness surveys. She found (at that time) trends toward incorporating writing centers into larger learning centers and a growing incorporation of computer technology. Norris (2010) wrote a comparative case study of two writing centers ("East" and "West") for his doctoral dissertation. As an education researcher, he used Wenger's communities of practice framework (1998) to understand how multiple participants contributed to the teaching of writing to "differently prepared" college-level students (p. 93). While Norris correctly stated that the intent of his research as an "impartial researcher" was to "supplement the mountains of data on writing centers collected by practitioner inquirers," we judged the study disappointing in that it was more descriptive than persuasive. Our view is that one of the functions of empirical research is to argue for changes in practice, something that a mere reframing and renaming of current practices cannot accomplish. Nonetheless, if Norris' dissertation is viewed as an argument for the communities of practice framework as a superior methodology for the study of writing centers, the study will be of interest to writing center researchers.

An exemplary RAD study for its time is Johnson (1997). To get at the "current status of writing centers" (p. 79), the author surveyed 146 writing center directors from secondary schools, two-year colleges, four-year colleges, and universities for information on physical plant, staff, clientele, services, funding, networking and outreach, and evaluation. With a 49% response rate (50% is the average for academic studies according to Baruch, 1999), Johnson interviewed ten of the directors via telephone and e-mail. Regarding the physical plant, Johnson found it interesting that few directors knew the square footage of their centers, only how many "stations" they could hold. Tutor counts averaged 14 for the ten centers, including faculty, staff, and students, and average user count per week was 370. All of the directors knew the source(s) of their funding, but only two knew the current status of their budgets. Most reported that they did not have enough funding to pursue their centers' missions, when "funding equals status" in their institutions (p. 84). Some networking with library staff was reported, and 6 of the 10 directors relied on client, tutor, and faculty reports to evaluate the effectiveness of their writing centers (p. 41) because directors were not sure "what to evaluate" and "how to evaluate" (p. 84). Overall, Johnson learned that secondary school writing centers were more "wired" than their college/university counterparts, that writing centers inhabited "private, secure spaces" (p. 80) that were not always accessible to people with disabilities, and that writing center directors were overworked and had little time for professional development. Secondary school writing centers were more likely to work with writers based on teacher referral, while writing centers in higher education worked with writers who were also self-referred or referred by friends. Johnson concluded that "the status of writing centers is far from secure in the academy—they are still the Cinderellas sitting in the ashes of other marginalized programs in academia" (p. 89). What writing centers needed, Johnson opined, was "a fairy godmother," which she identified as the National Writing Centers Association (now the IWCA) and its affiliates. We will investigate the influence of the NWCA/IWCA on writing centers later in this chapter.

Comparable or benchmark data are useful to writing center administrators in their work. Enter the Writing Center Research Project, founded by Carol Mattingly (personal communication, November 23, 2011) and colleagues at the University of Louisville in 2001. The latest results posted are from the 2003–2004 online survey of over 1,000 writing centers for information on "operations, tutor/consultant information, student usage, and administrative information" (p. 1). Data from 191 respondents revealed that a third of centers had been open less than 10 years, a third between 10–20 years, and a third between 20–54 years. The authors asked these research questions:

- What do writing centers look like?
- Whom do writing centers serve?
- Who are the consultants?
- Who are the directors?

Respondents (n = 219) reported the majority of writing centers were funded by or their directors reported to English or Writing departments (41%) or were "independent" (27%), while most of the rest were funded by or their directors reported to university-wide entities such as student services or specific colleges. Despite their institutional affiliations and funding sources, writing centers were usually expected to serve all students at their institutions.

In terms of location, only 2% of centers reported having their own buildings, and 2% reported multiple locations. Fifty-two percent were located in classroom buildings, 16% in libraries, 10% in learning centers, and 5% in academic departments. Median square footage was 1000, and increased space usually correlated with increased usage, regardless of increases or decreases in the institution's total enrollment.

Most writing centers reported being the only writing support service on their campuses. The majority of centers were open 40–84 hours per week and available to students, faculty, and staff, though undergraduates represented the majority of clients. Respondents had difficulty answering survey questions about number of second-language or multilingual writers served. Average session length (for face-to-face consultations?) was 30–40 minutes. The median number of online consultations reported was 74.

Regarding consultants, most centers reported they hired more than one "category" of consultant, and 28% reported they hired from three or more "categories." The median number of consultants on writing center payrolls was 13. Wages for undergraduate tutors averaged $7.00, with graduate and professional tutors receiving more (~$10.50 and ~$16.00 per hour, respectively). Tutors worked a mean of 13 hours per week.

Writing center directors, full-time and part-time, reported that they had received graduate degrees (49% PhDs and 47% MAs). (Most assistant directors held MA degrees.) The majority of directors were female and held faculty positions, most in nontenurable lines, who held appointments in the writing center varying from 10–100%, with 50% and 100% being the most frequent. Ten-month appointment contracts were most common, with 12-month and academic-year appointments being less common. Mean time on the job was 6.3 years, and the standard salary range was between $34,000 and $55,000. Number of years' experience correlated significantly with higher pay.

The Writing Center Research Project (WCRP) also maintains an archive, currently with 185 records, "a research repository of historical, empirical, and scholarly materials related to Writing Center Studies," including a good many oral history interviews. We await the results of the 2007-2008 survey, and we hope the WCRP will continue to survey writing centers, eventually creating a detailed history of their characteristics and development. One research project that someone should take on is a comparison among the 2000–2001 (Ervin, 2002), 2003–2004, and 2007–2008 surveys. Any takers?

Writing Center Location and Space Design

If little empirical research has been published on writing centers in general, then even less has been published on writing center location and design. As Levin (2007) noted, "Accounting for writing center space is a current pursuit not only for administrators seeking to practice intentionality in their centers, but for anyone involved in writing center scholarship" (p. 267). Oliver (2009) made the astute observation that writing center scholars had yet to reach a consensus about the optimum "physical configurations" of a writing center and how these would best foster collaboration and student writing development. In addition, Oliver noted that most scholarship on writing center "space" gave voice to administrators' views, so she wrote her master's thesis on tutor and tutee perceptions of writing center location to "understand if and how the institutional location and/or physical environment within a writing center affects the tutors' and tutees' perception of the writing center and/or affects the dynamic of a peer tutoring session" (p. ii). As institutional players, writing centers can function either as "safe houses" (Severino, 1992) or as "gatekeepers" (Grimm, 1999).

Studying three writing center locations at Southern Illinois University (one in an academic building and two in residence halls), Oliver sought to understand "if and how the institutional location and/or physical environment within a writing center affects the tutors' and tutees' perception of the writing center and/or affects the dynamic of a peer tutoring session" (p. ii). In this case study, tutors and tutees answered quantitative and qualitative survey questions, and some volunteered for follow-up interviews. Tutors rated the academic building location as superior to residence hall locations because it was "more convenient," "less chaotic," and sessions were therefore "more productive" (p. 72). Tutees did not voice a clear preference. While the majority of tutors rated the residence hall locations as noisy, tutees (especially second-language writers) were more likely to say that the academic building location was noisy and negatively affected tutorial outcomes. Both tutors and tutees liked "closed" tutoring spaces (cubicles/dividers) better than "open" tutoring spaces. Tutees favored adding writing center locations in the campus library or student center, while tutors were less likely to do so. Neither tutors nor tutees in any way connected physical locations of the writing center with the institutional placement of the writing center, a clear distinction made here between their and administrators' interpretations of writing center location as "marginalized" equals "remediation" (p. 109). Rather than offering an "ideal" writing center location/configuration, Oliver hoped that future research on this topic would discover "how individual writing centers might consider ways to work with their given physical environment configurations to, for example, offset any disadvantages that campus location and/or building location might have on the tutors' and tutees' as well as faculty and administrators' perception of the writing center" (p. 120).

Perhaps because so few writing centers have a choice of what spaces they could occupy, the discussion of physical space has often turned to metaphor, providing writing center administrators with at least some control. This emphasis on what we term the *metaphorical* space of writing centers is rife in the literature. In his dissertation, Hobson (1992), for example, rapidly moved from physical descriptions of writing centers to the "epistemological space within which the writing center can exist." And Boquet (2002) examined the metaphors of *writing lab/clinic/center* with regard both to space and to community.

Owens (2008) described the evolution of the St. John's University writing center from the *closet* (an eight-by-ten cubicle in a basement), to a *family room* (a second-floor office suite on a "pedestrian avenue," to *center stage* in "more high-traffic, publicly visible locale[s]" on two campuses (p. 82). McKinney (2005) argued that the dominant metaphor of writing center spaces, based on characterizations she gathered from writing center marketing, was that of *home* (see also McInerney, 1998). She showed how this metaphor was associated with upper-and middle-class White ideas of comfort, the feminine and feminism, and a refuge from the institution. McKinney did not place a value judgment on these characterizations; rather, she urged writing center administrators to "continue to create spaces and write about them. We ought to do both in a more critical fashion, questioning how we create an identity, if we create the identity we desire, and why we desire that identity in the first place" (p. 19).

Other researchers have looked at the connection between metaphorical and physical writing center spaces. Bell and Hübler (2001), for instance, performed a rhetorical analysis of 287 postings to an asynchronous listserv for writing consultants at the University of Alabama, Huntsville Writing Center. The purpose of the listserv was to create an *ethos*, a virtual writing center community. Results were somewhat sketchy, and it is no wonder that the authors urge further study of "whether participation in the virtual center impacts the effectiveness and work time of consultants in the physical center" (p. 74). They also wondered how the use of virtual spaces interacted with "physical and symbolic spaces occupied by the writing center within the University community" (p. 74).

In the same vein, Bemer (2010) studied "the [visual] rhetoric of space in academic computer writing spaces" (p. 1), including computer labs, computer classrooms, and writing centers. Of writing centers, Bemer asked: "What are the main points of interaction for students with writing centers?" and "How can we rhetorically design the sites of these interactions to encourage and facilitate student use of these centers?" (p. 7). She was particularly interested in how writers interacted with computers in these spaces. Using surveys, interviews, and observation, Bemer first examined forty writing center websites as spaces, followed by visits to and analysis of numerous writing center spaces, concluding with an analysis of "the way...computers influence student perception of text ownership" (p. 14). "Zoning" a large space into five identifiable, visually separate work areas (individual work, group work, private work, printing, spaces without computers for reading or conversation) fulfilled all three principles. Bemer wrote, "Creating a space that explicitly and clearly shows students their work options (and having a space that actually offers these options) is perhaps more important than having one computer per student" (p. 81).

Historically, Bemer (2010) noted, writing center space was conceived as the antithesis of classroom space in order to differentiate collaboration with peers as opposed to instruction by an authority. "The physical design of the writing center can rhetorically enhance or diminish this desired interpretation of equality" (p. 114). Bemer suggested that those designing writing center spaces adhere to three principles: *identification* ("students need to see that writing centers meet their needs and will help them succeed"); *pathos* ("students feel comfortable and wanted"); and *ethos* (students are provided with a sense of authority in order to "retain ownership" of their texts) (p. 121). Bemer discovered that students are more likely to identify with writing centers that offer multiple means of scheduling appointments, including online appointments. Designing for *pathos*, according to Bemer, involved creating a sense of ease for students and tutors at the beginning, during, and at the end of writing consultations. Physical space design could include both open and partitioned yet accessible space depending on participants' tolerance for distraction. Use of desktop computers, center laptops, or student laptops was optional; writers could work from a screen or from hard copy. Again, offering choices within the writing center space seemed to produce the most satisfaction. Designing for *ethos* was "about the writing center having credibility" (p. 152) as a site for both collaboration and sharing of expertise. Bemer illustrated ethos spatially by analyzing whether writers felt ownership of furniture and computers in the writing center space, specifically whether they had permission and encouragement to move them as needed during consultations. She found that by bringing their own laptops, students could retain ownership of their texts, physically and metaphorically.

We look forward to more empirical studies of physical and metaphorical writing center spaces. In particular, we are curious to know how writing centers in the enviable position of being able to design and build their own spaces have done so, and how these planned spaces have met or failed to meet their desired intentions.

Institutional Positioning

In mining the history of writing centers, Boquet (1995) noted the pervasiveness of the terms *marginal* and *central* in descriptions of their institutional positioning. Mauriello, Macauley, and Koch (2007) summarized the connection between writing centers and their institutional hosts in these questions: "What are writing centers responsible for? And who are they responsible to?" (p. 1). Their edited volume, *Before and after the Tutorial: Writing Centers and Institutional Relationships*, reminds us of Kinkead and Harris' earlier collection, Twelve Case Studies (1993), with a narrower focus but the same weakness: excellent descriptions of specific writing centers but no generalization to best practices. The one possible exception is Pemberton's chapter, "Revisiting 'Tales Too Terrible to Tell': A Survey of Graduate Coursework in Writing Program and Writing Center Administration." Pemberton lamented the fact that "newly minted" rhetoric and composition scholars went into university jobs without the requisite training to become writing program or writing center administrators. By searching out websites and posting requests on professional listservs, Pemberton unearthed only 16 courses on writing center administration taught at the graduate level nationwide. He listed the topics taught in each course, compared writing program administration courses with writing center administration courses, and lamented (again) the dearth of such courses. We were somewhat disappointed that Pemberton omitted discussion of the informal administrative apprenticeships many graduate student tutors engage in while working in writing centers, which, though they do not appear on university transcripts, may serve the purpose just as well (see Babcock, Carter-Tod, & Thonus, forthcoming).

Lerner (2005) argued that the absorption of writing centers into the "internal outsourcing" of learning centers would have a negative impact on the teaching of writing. Citing data from the Writing Centers Research Project (2004), Lerner noted that

[Writing centers and writing programs] often represent a model for situating administrative and pedagogical expertise fully within the academic heart of our institutions. In contrast, learning centers are often aligned with student services or student affairs, and their directors often have no faculty status and consequently lack direct access to the committee and governance structures that faculty control, particularly in terms of curriculum. (pp. 81–82)

If writing programs and writing centers had to be "internally outsourced" as a cost-cutting measure, Lerner advocated a move to university-wide centers for teaching and learning, where "several functions could be situated within the teaching and research roles of the faculty" (p. 92). Future research of this sort should involve tutor and student writer voices as well as administrators'.

Writing Center Administration

The position of writing center director is further complicated by the institutional definition of "writing program" and "writing program administrator" (Haviland & Stephenson, 2002). Is the writing center autonomous, or is it institutionally positioned as a support service for writing program students?

Johnson-Shull and Wyche (2001), for example, examined the effects of the addition of an assessment office to the Washington State University Writing Center. The authors hoped for a "butterfly effect" (drawn from chaos theory), believing that a small change in the system could produce a large and positive impact. The assessment office in the writing center offered the writing placement examination for new and transfer students, maintained student records, trained faculty in portfolio evaluation, and referred writers to tutorial support. As a result, "the writing center was finally emerging from the underfunded fringes to a place of higher visibility and increased institutional respect" (p. 29). Unfortunately, just as the writing center was receiving more institutional notice, the writing center director and the writing program administrator reached an impasse about budget and responsibility for evaluating student portfolios. The authors concluded, "Unless the power relationships within a system are clearly defined, misunderstandings regarding who is responsible for doing what will be common ... the writing center had a sophisticated sense of mentoring students into positions of responsibility but no system for inviting faculty peers who had other more complex agendas" (p. 33). As a result, the writing center and the assessment office now operate separately.

In *More Things Than Dreamt of in Our Philosophy*, Levin (2007) studied how writing center administrators and tutors were "deeply informed by forces other than published writing center theory" (p. vii). Using a grounded theory approach, Levin employed critical discourse analysis in searching tutorial observations, transcripts, and interviews for emerging themes. She contextualized her research in "a close reading of a particular location" (p. 54) as one way to "ground" her findings. The culture of the writing center, Levin found, was one of "adherence to a code of professionalism" (p. 77), which amounted to "assumed knowledge of how to succeed at higher levels of the university" more than "inculcated and demonstrated knowledge of writing-center specific theory of tutoring strategies" (p. 80). This resulted, Levin explained, because the writing center employed both undergraduate tutors who had received a semester of formal training and graduate tutors who were hired by virtue of their discipline-specific expertise and in many cases functioned as teaching assistants in their respective departments. A pay differential was also in place, demonstrating that "academic professionalism trumps tutoring professionalism" (p. 85). Levin critiqued the "smoothed-over idealism" of much writing center theory and commented on its creation of "a reductive us-them binary" between writing center and university aims (p. 89). Writing centers were no longer "professional spaces in isolation from the larger institution in which they were housed," if they ever had been (p. 89). Based on her findings, Levin recommended that administrators "develop intentionality" by scrutinizing their own writing center philosophies; by keeping local conditions (such as funding, space, reporting lines) central to decision-making; by conducting assessment and research; and by engaging tutors in inquiry so that they, too, can articulate their pedagogical beliefs and practices.

Larrance and Brady (1995) investigated writing center staff reports/narratives that documented details about completed writing tutorials. Their survey was ambitious: 484 were mailed to public and private two- and four-year colleges and universities, and 161 were returned (a 33% response rate, not bad for a pre-electronic attempt). The authors learned that 35% of respondents did not document tutorials either because of poor staffing or to protect students' privacy. Centers that did document tutorials generally presented these as short narratives or letters to faculty members written by tutors, although 71% did not send these if writers requested confidentiality. Reports or narratives were used by directors as references for follow-up tutoring sessions, for "public relations" purposes, to evaluate effectiveness, and to inform planning for future semesters. The authors found it ironic that writers were not included in the "feedback loop" and questioned whether there was "a writing center discourse that can communicate with multiple audiences" (p. 6).

Baxter Magolda and Rogers (1987) investigated the effects of frequency of interaction (more or less than four hours of tutoring per week) on the intellectual development of college peer tutors of various subjects. Fifty-six tutors completed the Measure of Epistemological Reflection twice, at the beginning of the fall semester and at the end of the spring semester. The authors could find no significant relationship between interaction frequency and intellectual development, but they did find a relationship in the opposite direction: "Tutors at different levels of intellectual development define and subsequently participate in collaboration differently" (p. 288). Tutors at lower levels of intellectual development were likely to "view their role as one of explaining the truth to the tutee" (p. 293)—in other words, a one-way lecture. Tutors at slightly higher levels of intellectual development viewed tutoring as "a method through which the tutor shows the tutee the right processes for finding the answers and the two would work together in an attempt to find the truth" (p. 293)—that is, a conversation among equals. Interestingly, Baxter Magolda and Rogers also realized that *tutees'* levels of intellectual development tended to match their tutors': "In the tutors' attempts to meet the tutees' expectations, they were prone to tutor as they viewed appropriate rather than as their training emphasized" (p. 294). Those who have tutored writing and trained writing tutors will recognize how powerful tutor-tutee accommodation can be.

Writing Center Collaborations

The most obvious collaboration writing centers engage in is with course faculty. Bruffee (1999) documented one of the best-attested outcomes of peer tutoring is

> Professors changing their course structure and teaching practices. That change goes to the heart of college and university education. It challenges traditional prerogatives and assumptions about the authority of teachers and the authority of knowledge. Peer tutors can help change the interests, values, assumptions, and practices of teachers and students alike. (p. 95)

In "Leading a Horse to Water," Clark (1985) asked whether instructors' requiring writing center visits of their students was really as counterproductive as North (1984a) had posited. Intrinsic motivation, Clark argued, was not necessary to student improvement in writing: "It seems equally sensible that if the horse has not at least been led to the water that he will be even less likely to drink" (p. 31). Clark surveyed a systematically selected random sample of 329 writing center users from 26 composition sections at the University of Southern California. The majority of those surveyed cited *both* teacher requirement and intrinsic motivation as reasons for seeking writing center assistance. (See Morrison & Nadeau, 2003 and Van Dam, 1985 for additional studies of required writing center attendance.) Young and Fritzsche (2002) turned the question around: Should writing centers forbid course faculty from requiring writing center use?

> On one hand, insofar as required visits reinforce the perception that writing center use is an unpleasant bureaucratic task, teacher requirements

could deter students from using the writing center. On the other hand, if a requirement adds the necessary extra motivation for procrastinators to drag themselves into the writing center, required writing center visits would help writing centers achieve their missions. (p. 54)

Gordon (2008) found that first year students required to visit the writing center reported positive attitudes toward the writing center and a likelihood that they would return. All students surveyed reported either gains in the quality of their papers or that they had thought about writing "more deeply" (p. 156). Finally, 81% of students surveyed agreed with the requirement that first year students should visit the writing center "at least once" (p. 157).

Barnett and Blumner (1999) produced an excellent volume on writing centers and WAC programs. Chapters in the volume investigate every sort of possible relationship between writing centers and WAC programs, from writing centers without WAC (Harris, 1999a), to writing centers as WAC centers (Kuriloff, 1999), to writing centers as faculty development sites (Childers). The only chapter, however, to move beyond the descriptive to the generalizable is Hobson and Lerner's "Writing Centers/WAC in Pharmacy Education: A Changing Prescription." The authors described a two-year process of embedding writing center work into the pharmacy curriculum. During the first phase, faculty were surveyed about their purposes for assigning writing, the types of writing tasks assigned, and ranking of writing assessment criteria. During the second phase, faculty and student workshops were held and one-on-one instruction emphasized. Hobson and Lerner's assessment of this endeavor resulted in four "important guidelines for other WAC programs and writing centers":

1. WAC must be a grassroots effort.
2. The writing center can lead this grassroots effort by helping faculty examine the current role that writing plays in their intellectual and professional lives.
3. Once faculty are aware of the importance of writing in the intellectual life of their disciplines, we can begin to talk about the ways they can use writing in their courses to inculcate students into this disciplinary conversation.
4. WAC's attractiveness to a professional curriculum lies in its efficiency. (pp. 167–168)

These guidelines, as principles for practice, should be replicable and assessable in other settings, whereas the practice reported in other chapters in the volume can only be replicable or assessable by analogy.

Elmborg and Hook's edited volume, *Centers for Learning: Writing Centers and Libraries in Collaboration* (2005), reads much like Mauriello et al.'s volume: A com-

THE CONTEXTS OF TUTORING | 71

pendium of "studies in collaboration" from individual universities prefaced by chapters on theory and practice written by the editors. We appreciated Elmborg's statement that "both writing centers and information literacy instruction have grown to a point where formal collaborative partnerships might be the best way to open development" (p. 1). However, Elmborg also noted that the path towards institutional collaboration going beyond shared location would be fraught with difficulty despite writing centers' and libraries' common goals of supporting research-based writing. As director of the KU Writing Center, Thonus found Currie and Eodice's description of writing center-library collaboration at the University of Kansas highly informative. Nonetheless, authors in the collection inaccurately used the term *case study* to label their contributions, which were actually detailed descriptions. These are, in principle, unreplicable outside of individual contexts.

Tutors: Background, Training, and Effectiveness

Peer Tutors

Writing centers should recognize that they, like learning centers, sprang from the "supervised study" model adopted by American universities in the 1920s and 30s (Lerner, 2005). The link between subject-area tutoring and writing tutoring is rooted in history. It is therefore surprising if not shocking that the writing center literature pays so little attention to research studies investigating models of peer tutoring across the disciplines, especially since, as Bruffee (1999) noted, peer writing tutoring preceded peer subject-matter tutoring by decades (p. 93). When all writing labs and writing centers were the province of English departments, Broder (1981) wrote that English-major tutors cemented relationships between faculty members and peer tutors, since they were, concurrently, students of the same instructors. This is one of the benefits peer tutors bring to writing center work, but it is not the only one by a long shot.

One of the most complete investigations of peer tutors in a writing center setting is by Fallon (2010). He defined peer tutors as "undergraduate writing tutors who meet with writers one-to-one" (p. 15), who first appeared on the writing center scene in the 1970s. Without peer tutors, there would have been no peer tutoring model; they are "instrumental in making an epistemology for the writing centers possible" (p. 16). Like Dinitz and Kiedaisch (2003), Fallon contended that "tutors are often absent from theory building discussions" (p. 53), with writing center theorizing and praxis suffering as a result. We would contend that Fallon's argument is even more convincing since it is bolstered by empirical research findings, despite his assertion that his dissertation is a "theoretical exercise" (p. 75). His research approach was qualitative, and data included writing center director and tutor interviews, tutorial and staff meeting observations, and staff education materials. Fallon also interviewed Kenneth Bruffee ("Peer Tutoring and 'the Conversation of Mankind'") and Harvey Kail (Peer Writing Tutor Alumni Research Project), arguably the theoretical "prime mover" and "documenter," respectively, of peerness in writing tutoring. Fallon coded the data for "critical events" and structures of relationships, themes, and productivity. Emergent themes were

- Listening: "an awareness of the concerns that arise during a session."
- Presence: "an assertion of one's intellectual energy during a session and akin to the collaborative process in tutoring and writing because both parties need to be engaged for a successful experience of working and learning together."
- Frame: "the ways tutors structure and focus their sessions and deal with issues of focus and structure in writing."
- Confidence: "how tutors help and support writers in negotiating various writing tasks and in making decisions with conviction." (p. 123)

Tutors connected these themes with the relationships they built with writers. Fallon concluded:

> What we know about peer tutors from this study is that they have clear ideas about how they help writers write and learn about writing. They are aware of the kinds of relationships that they are able to have with student writers that differ from other teaching and learning relationships. They employ techniques for helping writers that develop out of their personal experiences, their experiences in school, and their past experiences with other writers. They have ways of approaching and understanding their sessions that certainly drive them in their practice and in their philosophy of tutoring. (p. 185)

He argued that the *lived* (as opposed to *perceived* or *conceived*) experiences of writing center peer tutors have been largely ignored in the writing center literature. Fallon's attempt to "renegotiate the idyllic nature" of previous characterizations of peer tutors' experiences (p. 31) successfully bridges the theory-practice divide. From his interviews with Bruffee and Kail, Fallon learned that "we still have the ability to redirect the theoretical flow currently used in writing centers and to help position peer tutors in institutional spaces that draw on their ability to alter the relationships we think are possible in the academy" (p. 231).

The Peer Tutor Alumni Research Project (Gillespie, Hughes, & Kail, 1997) has been instrumental in showing how writing center tutors develop academically, socially, and professionally during their undergraduate and graduate experiences at U.S. colleges and universities. Its research approach is qualitative; its data collection methods are surveys (80%+ response rate!), interviews, and focus groups across institutions; and its products are written and video narratives:

> Our research into the value of collaborative learning for former peer tutors demonstrates convincingly that while these peer tutor alumni are smart and appropriately critical about higher education, they are also unfailingly enthusiastic, insightful, specific, and articulate about the benefits of their training and work. (p. 35)

Tutor alumni reported that their work as writing tutors or writing fellows had helped them to

- Boost their confidence
- Feel intellectually engaged in the educational mission and thus closer to the "center" of their institutions
- Understand and value collaborative learning
- Become better cross-cultural communicators
- Improve writing and critical thinking skills
- Learn new research and presentation skills
- Acquire job application, interview, and people skills

Gillespie, Hughes, and Kail argued that peer tutor alumni not only contributed to the writers they served but also became effective communicators and received a broad, cross-disciplinary education in the process. A powerful argument for the centrality (rather than marginalization) of the writing center in the academy can be made, the authors argue, because "we can't imagine better educators and advocates for our centers than our peer-tutor alumni" (p. 40). The PTARP has expanded from its initial centers at the University of Maine, the University of Wisconsin-Madison, and Marquette University to include "colleague contributions." Regional and international writing center conferences have showcased projects from small and large, public and private institutions, documenting the positive educational and affective outcomes of peer tutoring "downstream" (e.g., Ozias et al., 2008).

Not all investigations of peer tutors have reached such positive conclusions. Peguesse (2000), who studied the writing centers at Arizona State University and at the University of Arizona, stands out. The author examined peer tutors' concepts of professionalism. At the ASU writing center, professionalism was defined as *organization*; one tutor noted, "We have good hierarchy here" (p. 102). Tutors referenced a clear "chain of command" in the writing center structure that defined their roles *vis* à vis administrators and writers. Although administrators believed that they had so-cialized tutors into "the professional conversation" through their actions and words, tutors revealed they had not been. To the tutors, confidence, expertise, and "doing what is necessary to assist student writers" (p. 106) were what constituted profes-sionalism. At the University of Arizona, peer writing tutors cited *good conduct* as key; one tutor noted, "It looks better if you have a secretary" (p. 85). Collegiality, stan-dardized review, and evaluations were all considered part of what made the writing centers work from the tutor point of view. Peguesse observed that peer writing cen-ter tutors at both institutions were not always aware of how their work comple-mented other academic support services. They experienced a huge divide between their writing center work and the rest of their academic activities. This was partic-ularly true of non-English majors, Peguesse discovered, who "joined the writing center community as club members rather than initiates into a discipline" (p. 76).

Graduate-Student Tutors

Ianetta, McCamley, and Quick (2007) examined the role of the writing center in the training of graduate students as composition instructors (TAs). Their data came from a nationwide survey of writing program administrators of programs in which graduate students' participation as writing tutors was obligatory and those in which participation was optional. The survey asked administrators to compare "an inventory of claims concerning the writing center's role in TA training" (p. 105) gleaned from previous scholarship with their own analyses of first-year TAs with and without writing center experience. Based on 28 survey responses, the authors found that administrators largely supported previous research findings (e.g., Clark, 1988; Cogie, 1997): "While the results of this study suggests that writing center tu-toring is an extremely valuable experience for TAs in writing programs, the results of such programs for the writing center are less clear" (p. 119). While this study made an important contribution by aligning opinion-on-the-ground with earlier scholarship, we see the need for inclusion of TA and writer voices in response to this question. Does writing center tutoring before teaching "prevent wrecks" in later teaching (Manguson, 1986), or does it denigrate writing center tutoring as mere "training wheels" (Nicolas, 2005)?

Mick (1999) investigated the "cognitive dissonance" of the relationship between graduate-student tutors and writing center tutees by surveying the writers. She learned that about half of the writers characterized graduate-student tutors as peers since they were "more relaxed than their professors in demeanor and language" (p. 41). The other half of the writers characterized their graduate-student tutors as "lit-tle professors." Mick's findings correspond well to Severino's (1992) distinction be-tween "hierarchical" and "dialogic" collaboration (p. 85). Mick argued that writers had "reached this conclusion based on the graduate students' demonstration of expertise, not their aura of authority" (p. 41). We question Mick's separation of expertise and authority, especially because they have been conflated in student feedback in other studies based on surveys (e.g., Thonus, 2001).

What is it that we seek in such research? Why do we need it? Vandenberg (1999) summed it up this way:

> Tutors need *theory* in the sense that Hey and Nahrwold [1994] use the term, as a way of explaining and predicting; but to assume an informed, critical stance to their location in the disciplinary and institutional web that defines writing centers, tutors need theory as Ede [1996] implicitly defines it, as a privileged discourse we sometimes call *Theory*, the ownership of which defines teachers' and tutors' expertise in institutional terms. (p. 66)

Vandenberg cited Fulkerson's (1990) taxonomy of theories, all of which writing tutors need to "know": Theories of value, knowledge, procedure, and of practice. Tutors' understanding of all of these is essential so that they can advance beyond their construction as "a compliant, multipurpose workforce" of "token" professionals (p. 78). This is what it means to introduce tutors to "the professional discourse," which Vandenberg put in motion by requiring tutors in his training course to contribute to a listserv, *WriteOn*, as well as to participate in group workshops focused on their own writing. Although students were not required to submit conference proposals based on these discussions, eleven did so and presented at professional venues. Through this process, Vandenberg claimed that tutors were invited to "consciously explore their implication in an intensely competitive economy of literacy that both distributes rewards and exacts costs" (p. 79).

Tutor Dissonances

Plummer and Thonus (1999) analyzed tutorial transcripts for evidence of tutoring *mythology* "based on 'what not to do,' or, more precisely, 'how to be up here and not to be a teacher when in the role of writing tutor.'" By operationalizing this mythology, tutoring methodology constrains the tutor's role, limiting it to issues of personality and strategies of interpersonal interaction" (Thonus, 2001, p. 61). Plummer and Thonus found these features in tutorial transcripts:

- Tutors evaluate student work and suggest (almost) as often as they ask "Socratic" questions.
- Tutors teach academic writing and disciplinary conventions.
- Tutors teach content, often indirectly.

- Tutors think and comment critically about others' pedagogy, including the pedagogical practices of course instructors.

Plummer and Thonus questioned the "peership" (Bruffee, 1999) of writing center tutors and the role constructions of tutors by the writing center literature as compared with tutors' enactment of their roles during writing tutorials. Thonus' ethnographic study (2001) took the investigation further by including the perceptions of writers and their instructors in the definition of the tutor role. Data were collected through recordings and transcriptions of writing consultations; tutors' records of consultations; recordings and transcriptions of interviews with tutors, tutees, and course instructors; and tutees' assignment sheets and drafts. Thonus used the qualitative data method of *triangulation* (seven tutor-tutee-instructor "triangles") to arrive at a multilayered "thick description" of writing tutor roles (see Chapter 2). Results showed that "little unanimity exists in perceptions of the tutor role by the members of the tutor triangle" (p. 77). Thonus suggested that tutors' divergence from the peer role had less to do with poor training and learning or insufficient experience and more to do with tutors' assimilation of "teacherly" tutor role perceptions held by tutees and instructors. She argued that tutor training should (a) base itself more on evidence than anecdote and (b) normalize tutors' *de facto* practice while moving to modify it.

In her doctoral dissertation, Courtney (2009) noted the "casualness of the labor for teaching and tutoring writing and the standardization of the writing curriculum" as casualties of "the corporatized university" (p. 2). She cited the results of the Conference on College Composition and Communication's study of part-time/adjunct issues, which noted that composition instructors and writing center tutors are treated as outsiders by the academy: "How ironic that the writing teacher and tutor who is supposedly providing students with the skills and knowledge (or *capital*, to use Bourdieu's representation) to succeed in the academic world is actually being marginalized by this environment" (p. 3). Using a qualitative research approach including ethnographic case study and critical discourse analysis, Courtney argued that "the corporatized university's practices work to decrease agency amongst its workers" (p. 129). Partly because of this, she also concluded that "the corporatized university's labor practices managed to restrict the teaching and learning of student writers" (p. 124). Courtney argued that one way out of this miasma was for "casual" workers "to demand professionalization of these communities of practice" (p. 130). Tenured positions may be out of reach, but "the professional community within a writing center (directors, tutors, work-study students) can be fostered through much discussion and immersion into writing center research combined with the agency of lived experience of tutoring" (p. 131). While writing centers support student writing, Courtney contended that writing center *professionals* be labeled as exactly that, rather than as "repair agents" (p. 131).

Corbett (2011) studied course-based tutors in both writing fellows and class-room-based tutoring programs. Tutors in these programs experienced different roles than those in writing centers. In the model he examined, the classroom-based tutor had more of a role in the classroom and was more familiar with course assignments and materials than writing center tutors, while the writing advisor tutor met with students outside of class and did not attend class sessions beyond the first. The classroom-based tutor exhibited more directive behaviors in the tutoring sessions she conducted, but Corbett could not make a definitive connection here, because this tutor also had not been trained in non-directive techniques, and because the tutor was an African American, directness in communication could have been a cultural preference. The writing advisor tutor was more non-directive, and this was the model that she had been trained in.

The "casualness" of contingent labor and the search for professional identity in the writing center context bear further empirical study. An excellent theoretical framework for such research is Scott's *Dangerous Writing: Understanding the Political Economy of Composition* (2009).

Service Mode

Individual vs. Group

When we think of writing center work, what most often comes to mind is the dyad of tutor and student. But writing centers need not be defined solely by one-to-one interactions. Montgomery (1994) studied the "writing workshops" of three writing center peer tutors to investigate how they facilitated talk about student texts over the course of the semester. (This study is not well known in the writing center literature because it was published in *Focuses*.) Montgomery began with the premise that "helping students acquire useful metalanguage for talking about their emerging texts may be the tutors' most important role in facilitating an effective writing workshop" (p. 80). Her data sources were group session transcripts framed by interviews with tutors. One weakness of this study is that the connection between the results of Montgomery's data analysis and her interpretation of them was not adequately explained. She concluded that tutors needed "extensive training" in creating a "trusting environment," in sharing with writers "power and authority" over texts and learning processes, in facilitating "critical peer feedback," and in supporting "definite plans for change"—which we take to mean revision (p. 86).

Hess (2008) also explored writing center-based collaborative group tutorials, which she argued could permit greater student learning when compared to both classroom-based writing groups and individual writing center tutorials: "Writing center group tutorials foster students' roles as readers and responders through intense engagement with texts, the guidance of a trained tutor, and with the help of response techniques that gradually build rhetorical abilities" (p. 1). Building on the work of Gilewicz (2004) and Gilewicz and Thonus (2000, 2004), Hess examined transcripts of stable, semester-long writing center groups of two–four students (from different classes) meeting with the same tutors for 50 minutes twice per week. Students registered for the groups and received credit/no credit "grades" from their writing tutors. Tutors were trained in and trained writers in the type of response recommended by Elbow and Belanoff (2003). Hess argued that such writing group tutorials foregrounded the role of the *reader* (as opposed to the *writer*) "which overlooks the role of readers and the interconnected nature of the ability to read rhetorically and the ability to write rhetorically" (p. 7). Characterizing the relationship between tutor as learner and writer as reader in Vygotskyan terms, Hess argued that these tutorials evidenced actual collaboration since, as Bruffee (1999) noted, writing tutors functioned as group members, not as authority figures. For student writers, group tutorials resulted in "a highly valuable learning experience that enables them to make meaning not only of the larger function of reading and writing, but also of their own learning process as readers and writers" (p. 43).

Gilewicz and Thonus (2001) and Thonus (2003) studied outcomes for L2 writers in writing center peer writing groups. The research approach was interactional sociolinguistics (Schiffrin, 1996), which admits contextual data such as characteristics of the setting, information about the participants, student writing, and interpretations of both researchers and participants. Transcripts of group tutorials were analyzed for strategies in the negotiation of meaning, patterns of student solicitation for feedback, and the pragmatics of language in utterances related to the evaluation of student writing and to suggestions for revision. While group tutorials should have offered L2 writers increased access to interaction and negotiation (Gilewicz, 2004), they were barred from this access through marginalization by tutors and other group members. Even worse, L2 writers failed to receive negotiated comprehensible input necessary both to language acquisition and effective writing improvement. Specifically, Gilewicz and Thonus found that L1 writers in the groups were given priority in negotiations and in commenting on their own and others' writing. Tutors and L1 writers in their groups often discussed L2 writers' papers as if the writers were not present. L2 writers generally entered the conversation only when invited. Their feedback was often ignored or rejected by tutor and students, so they were not as likely to grow into the role and language of active readers and responders. In fact, other group members actively questioned L2 writers' language use and content expertise. More research on L2 writers in writing center groups is needed, but the research thus far does not bode well for this model as facilitative for L2 writing development.

Face-to-face vs. Online

Like individual writing consultations, face-to-face tutoring continues to be the "default" when thinking about writing center work. Coogan (1999) described his book, *Electronic Writing Centers: Computing the Field of Composition*, as "a call for the entire composition community to coordinate a new mandate for the electronic writing center; to imagine an alternate future for peer tutors and the students that they serve, not by abandoning traditional writing centers but by enhancing them with electronic counterparts" (p. xvi). Based on a three-year pilot study at SUNY-Albany, the book reports on the "dialogic literacy" effected through face-work online. (Of course, at that time electronic tutoring referred to e-mail tutoring without the accoutrements of live chat, whiteboard workspace, or an in-text comments feature.) Coogan's data sources were writers' papers and tutors' e-mail comments to writers and their replies. Tutoring in this medium was fundamentally different than face to face, Coogan argued, because it created actual collaborative texts. It "encouraged a creative fissure between the self who wrote the paper and the self who wrote the e-mail messages, allowing the student and, in some cases, the tutor, to explore alternative subject-positions in writing" (p. 99).

Synchronous vs. Asynchronous

Hewett (2000, 2004–2005, 2006, 2010) is one of the few scholars to have created a RAD research program investigating synchronous and asynchronous writing consultations. Much of Hewett's work is quantitative, and her use of statistical techniques is no doubt unfamiliar to many in the writing center audience. Some may also critique the object of her studies as instruction rather than tutoring. Nevertheless, we find the results of her studies compelling and suggestive of further research directions for online writing tutoring. Unfortunately, even from her research we cannot draw any conclusions regarding which type of online interaction yields "best results" for writing center tutoring.

Hewett (2000) compared oral and computer-mediated talk in peer revision tasks in two sections of the same upper-division composition course: One section accomplished peer revision face to face, while the other section held peer revision sessions online using Norton CONNECT, a synchronous platform. The results showed differences both in the peer interactions and in the revisions students made as a result. Oral interactions focused on global idea development and resulted in "frequent intertextual (imitative and indirect) and self-generated idea use" in revisions (p. 265). Computer-mediated interactions dealt with group management and focused on specific writing tasks. Revisions students made were the direct result of peers' suggestions. Hewett concluded that "medium shapes revision" (p. 265).

Hewett (2004–2005) investigated the communication intentions of online in-structors in asynchronous one-on-one tutoring. She used a *linguistic function tax-onomy* to describe how instructors "spoke" to secondary and post-secondary writers online. Hewett discovered that the dominant communication intention was reader response to *inform*, as well as speech acts of *direction, suggestion*, and *elicitation*. These findings could easily be compared with face-to-face instruction and tutor-ing if researchers used the same linguistic function taxonomy.

In Chapter 2, we reviewed Hewett's (2006) methodology as an example of textual analysis of both online tutor comments and student revisions. Hewett studied 52 synchronous online tutorials between students at Pennsylvania State University and Smarthinking tutors. Results showed that nearly half of the "whiteboard conversa-tions" were "oriented toward achieving interpersonal connections, facilitating the in-teraction, and communicating about the whiteboard's workspace" (p. 4). Hewett then looked at the type of revisions students made (using the typology of Faigley and Witte, 1981), finding that very few revisions affected changes in meaning.

We find Hewett's research compelling for three reasons. First, she recognizes online consulting, whether between a tutor and writer or a teacher and writer, as an instructional event. Second, Hewett is aware of both the inherent difficulties and drawbacks of online consulting and of the potential benefits it affords writers as they consult through and in writing. Third, Hewett employs the same measures of tutor-tutee interaction (Gere & Abbott, 1985) and writer revision (Faigley & Witte, 1981) across studies, creating comparability. We recognize that some writing center professionals have been uncomfortable with Hewett's collapsing of teaching and tutoring online since it challenges writing center lore, but for now hers is the only RAD research we know of that has methodically investigated revision outcomes of asynchronous and synchronous online writing conferences. Hewett (2010) takes these research findings and applies them to practice. We recommend this book for writing center tutor training.

Expectations

Cultural and Cross-cultural

Most of what we know about student expectations of writing center consulta-tions comes from anecdotal reports. Lerner (1996) and DePiero (2007) are excep-tions. DePiero (2007) surveyed 500 first-year composition students at the University of Rhode Island about their expectations of the writing center. The stu-dents were surveyed during the first week of classes, before they had learned any-thing about the writing center or set foot in the writing center. DePiero wrote,

"Most students will encounter a writing center for the first time in college. Many students have some opinion of what a writing center is and how they and their texts will be treated, but these expectations are not usually based on actual experience" (p. 4). (The author later discovered that 21% of the students had previously visited a writing center.) Survey results showed that while students lacked the metalinguistic vocabulary to express their expectations, they hoped to become better writers, write better papers, and receive better grades. Less than half of the students expressed anxiety about visiting the writing center. Sixty-three percent thought they needed to take completed assignments to the writing center, which DePiero considered a major deterrent. And only a third expected tutors to correct all of the errors in their papers. While only 1% of those surveyed said they would never attend the writing center, in fact 20% of those surveyed did not. DePiero concluded that if asked to describe in their own words what they expected of tutors, writers would probably say, "constructive criticism" (p. 80).

Lerner's dissertation (1996) was a longitudinal (academic year-long) study of interactions between four tutors and writers. He asked:

1. What are the goals and expectations that tutors and students bring to their writing center conferences and the responsibilities each should assume in order to achieve those goals?
2. What are the influences that inform these goals and expectations?
3. How do tutor and student goals and expectations guide the structure and content of writing conferences?
4. What is the dominant focus of writing center tutorials: students' writing processes and development (as the larger writing center community would hope) or students' products and fixing "sick" texts? (p. 8)

The author studied a writing center staffed entirely by graduate students "chosen for their experience in writing and teaching and their adherence to North's (1984a) 'ideal' that the focus of a tutorial should be on developing students' writing processes and not just correcting their texts" (p. 4). Lerner used a qualitative research approach, seeking data from interviews, transcriptions of writing consultations, written artifacts such as "entry cards" (on which writers wrote their goals), evaluation forms (that writers filled out at the end of each session), session notes (that tutors wrote at the end of each session), e-mail discussions (among tutors and with the researcher), and his own "field notes." Results were written up as four case studies. Lerner realized that with one exception, writers "came to the Writing Center for primarily product-oriented needs" (p. 240). The four tutors' expectations, Lerner found, were more diverse. He summarized their self-characterizations this way: tutor as *shopkeeper*, tutor as *obliger*, tutor as *proxy*, and tutor as *pastor*.

Lerner's findings demonstrated that tutor and writer expectations (or goals) were essential to the outcome of a consultation but were often incongruent. Metacommentary on student texts or the writing process nearly absent. This was especially troubling when writers visited the writing center, on average, only twice per semester. In his conclusion, Lerner reframed tutor and writer "expectations" as "responsibilities." For tutors, Lerner advised moving beyond their "folk theories" about what good tutoring was (p. 247) and embracing training that critically examined their practice through transcript analysis and reflective writing. For tutees, Lerner advised several changes in writing center administration that would foster something more than "stamping out 'corrected' students' texts" (p. 277): lengthening consulting times past 30 minutes; facilitating ongoing work with the same tutor; providing tutors versed in the subject matter of students' papers; and integrating writing center tutoring into classroom instruction. In these ways, he argued, tutor and writer expectations of writing consultations would begin to line up.

Tutor and Tutee

Babcock and colleagues (in press) synthesized the research on expectations tutors have of tutees and expectations tutees have of tutors. Thonus (2001) learned that instructor, tutor, and tutee expectations of tutor and tutee roles were as varied as the individuals who enacted them. These expectations influenced session content and outcomes. Lerner (1996) argued that role conflicts were inevitable between tutor and tutee if (and when) they expected different outcomes from the writing consultation. Hunter (1993) reported an example of this: A tutee arrived at the writing center expecting to have her paper edited, but instead the tutor asked the writer questions about "matters of punctuation and syntax," which annoyed her (p. 133). Ritter (2002) found that L2 writers were even more likely than L1 writers to expect directive instruction from tutors. Vallejo's dissertation (2004) also documented that international students expected their tutors to be authoritative and knowledgeable.

Tutors also have expectations of tutees, of what they have written and of what they will say and do during writing consultations. These expectations can strongly influence session content and outcomes. Ritter (2002) exemplified what could happen when tutors (partly due to time pressure?) failed to properly "meet" their tutees. For example, without knowledge of their tutees' academic level (freshman, sophomore, graduate student) and reasons for writing, expectations of neither tutor nor student were fulfilled. Even with a small time frame within which to work, tutors should dedicate time to the opening phase or "preliminaries" of writing consultations.

Certification and Accreditation of Writing Centers

Johnson's (1997) invocation of a national association of writing centers as a "fairy godmother" (p. 61) has partly come to fruition. Established in 1982, the National Writing Centers Association (NWCA) "saw itself in an advocacy role, offering the authority of a professional organization" (Kinkead, 1996, p. 137). Smitherman (2007) wrote her dissertation about the association using oral history methods. To include multiple points of view, she collected oral histories from four of the founding board members—Jeanette Harris, Jay Jacoby, Joyce Kinkead, and Jeanne Simpson—supplemented by members' publications and association documents. She analyzed these through the lens of symbolic convergence theory (Bormann, 1985). By creating their own symbols, the founding members moved together to form a "group fantasy," which, when shared by the entire group, created a "rhetorical community" and "a rhetorical vision" (p. 81). Symbolic connections were created over the marginalization of writing center work, the urgent need for secure funding, and the push towards professionalization of that work. This resulted in actions such as the creation of a "start-up kit" for new writing center directors and the recasting of the *Writing Center Journal* as a refereed publication. Through her work, Smitherman claimed to have provided readers "a better sense of the writing center personality" (p. 87) and "the back stories to the lore shared in professional articles" (p. 88).

Regional, national, and now international conferences, listservs, websites, job boards, grants, and research networks have proliferated under the renamed *International* Writing Centers Association (IWCA) umbrella, and the National Conference on Peer Tutoring in Writing (NCPTW) has held annual meetings since 1984. Yet neither association has supported certification, focusing instead on "the need to create quality, highly accessible development resources" and piloting a "Mentor Matching" program (IWCA Year in Review, 2011).

Certification of centers and/or individual tutors is available through the College Reading and Learning Association, the National Tutoring Association, the National College Learning Center Association, or the Association for the Tutoring Profession (Devet & Gaetke, 2007), and some writing centers solicit (and pay the price) for this official recognition. At one point, NWCA considered a certification/accreditation program, and IWCA currently provides consultant-evaluators through the Council of Writing Program Administrators program. In a personal communication to Johnson (1997), Joan Mullin, one of the founders of the association, explained:

> NWCA has wrestled with accreditation for years now. My summary: we don't think much of the certification programs for writing center tutors. Mostly, while they give tutoring basics, people have found their methodology uninformed by theory except for, perhaps, counseling theories. We

train our tutors in ways far beyond that, and demand far more of our tutors so such a certification would seem somewhat bogus (my opinion.) We are now drawing up an accreditation plan that will account for the diversity and situatedness of writing centers—for the variety within different contexts and missions. Several of us have had need of such teams when we undergo program review, and I've gone to other campuses in that capacity. We think we're at a point of being able to do this. (pp. 90–91)

Mullin's dream was not realized. We do not anticipate that IWCA will develop certification or program review standards in the near future, but we predict that they will (and should) eventually.

Comparing IWCA's path with another association's may be instructive. Teachers of English for Speakers of Other Languages (TESOL), the largest association for English as a second/foreign language teachers and administrators, resorted to the development of standards (and thus certification/program review) as a response to state and federal policies and legislation. In 1995, the association began to develop standards for college/university ESL programs in the United States, "encouraged" by requirements of the U.S. Department of Education. Not long after, the Commission on English Language Program Accreditation (CEA) was formed to recognize programs that were compliant—and this program review is now legally mandated. TESOL developed its PreK-12 Language Proficiency Standards in 1997 to enable second-language educators to incorporate language learning into ever more restrictive federal and state content standards. The TESOL Standards for ESL/EFL Teachers of Adults (for adult education and migrant programs) were established in 2003.

TESOL viewed the implementation of its standards as a means of advocating for L2 learners' needs, as a means of marketing excellent programs, and as a means of raising the professional profile of its members, many of whom had come to the profession through other disciplines (TESOL Standards Committee, 2002). We believe that as writing center work becomes ever more prevalent and internationalized, IWCA "Standards," possibly coupled with accreditation, will raise the professional profile of the field. Members of the South Central Writing Centers Association are developing outcomes statements that will be presented to IWCA.

In the meantime, writing center administrators in high-school, college, and university contexts will continue to do their best with the hands they have been dealt: worse than we've hoped for institutional positioning, physical location, budgets, staffing, and relationships with instructors and their students. For a small number of centers, generous donations will permit planning and forethought as opposed to "landing" and afterthought. We hope for more of these. However, as Kinkead (1996) noted, there is a danger that focusing on the negatives creates a "celebration of marginality": "Messages that focus on what is being done to us (e.g., limited space and funding), rather than what we do well, place writing centers in a reactive rather than proactive stance." She called for writing center administrators to demonstrate "strength and resilience," continually fighting to "place our writing centers at the core of academe" (p. 139).

In Chapters 4–6, we present research-based studies that offer some answers to a host of practical questions asked by writing center administrators and tutors on a daily basis: How can tutors best collaborate with distinct student populations, such as basic writers, students with disabilities, English language learners, and graduate students? How can writing centers effectively use service modes such as face-to-face, online, and group consultation? How should tutoring activities, whether reading, writing, talking, or revision, be pursued most constructively? What effects do details of format, interaction, and negotiation have on session outcomes?

Recommendations for Practice

- Consider providing "private" tutoring space through the use of dividers or cubicles in addition to open tutoring spaces (Bemer, 2010; Oliver, 2009).
- Provide computers as well as work space for students to bring their own laptops or to work with hard copies (Bemer, 2010).
- Rethink the stricture against required visits (Gordon, 2008).
- Recruit potential tutors by educating them about the personal and professional benefits of writing center work (Fallon, 2010; Gillespie, Hughes, & Kail, 2011).
- Encourage tutors to present at conferences (Vandenberg, 1999).
- Work to professionalize peer tutors (Courtney, 2009).
- Consider scheduling group tutorials in addition to individual ones (Hess, 2008; Montgomery, 1994) while being cautious about scheduling mixed groups with both L1 and L2 writers (Thonus & Gilewicz; 2001; Thonus, 2003b).
- Lengthen consulting times past 30 minutes; facilitate ongoing work with the same tutor; provide tutors versed in the subject matter of students' papers; and integrate writing center tutoring into classroom instruction (Lerner, 1996).
- The IWCA should develop outcomes standards and accreditation procedures.

CHAPTER FOUR

Tutoring "Different" Populations[1]

> Writing centers should attempt to help all students in ways they can best be helped. For some students, this will consist of help with editing and proofreading, contrary to many writing centers' policies....Tutors may feel uncomfortable if they have been trained to use an extreme hands-off, minimal tutoring style. (Babcock, 2008b, pp. 63–64)

One of the most thought-provoking essays we have read in the *Writing Center Journal* is "Pedagogies of Belonging: Listening to Students and Peers" (Bokser, 2005). While not an empirical study, Bokser's article lays out the challenge writing center administrators and tutors experience when faced with difference, "those whose socioeconomic, racial, ethnic, linguistic, and/or educational worlds differ markedly from the academic world they encounter in college" (p. 43). Bokser asked, "How can we better train tutors to tutor imaginatively and effectively?" (p. 44).

Basic writers, writers with disabilities, second-language writers, and graduate student writers have been treated as "different" populations in the writing center literature. Tutoring practice with these writers diverges somewhat from that peer-centered, collaborative "orthodoxy of current practice" in the writing center (Lockett, 2008). In this chapter, we examine empirical research studies done on tutoring of each group in the writing center setting, and, based on this evidence, make recommendations for practice.

Basic Writers

The characterization and the characteristics of some college writers as *basic writers* (Shaugnessy, 1977; Bizzell, 1986; Lu, 1992; Horner & Lu, 2000) has proven problematic among some compositionists. The same is true for writing center scholars and administrators. Carino (2002), among others, noted that in order to distance themselves from the imposed "fix-it" shop characterization, writing centers have tended to "play down work done with under-prepared students. Indeed, it has become less prestigious to claim affinity with basic writers than to tout services for the more accomplished" (p. 102). Lerner (2007) called this distancing "rejecting the remedial brand."

But perhaps rejecting the brand places more student writers at risk (Cook-Gumperz, 1993). Gardner and Ramsey (2005), like Lunsford (1979) before them, argued that early college writers "lack the epistemic maturity to perform advanced cognitive operations"(p. 35). If moving beyond "basic" means developing skills in active discussion and problem solving, the writing center is essential to the mission of the university. They argued that writing centers could have a direct impact on student retention and graduation if institutions recognize that all beginning students can profit from using them.

Mandatory Consultations

Clark (1985) reported that students were more likely to attend the writing center if encouraged to do so by their course instructors. There is some research evidence that basic writers can benefit from mandatory consultations. If part or all of their remedial writing courses are substituted with writing center tutoring, students have little say in the matter. In studying just such a situation, Soliday and Gleason (1997) reported positive results for such students, who felt more authoritative as writers and less marginalized from their peers. Unfortunately, Soliday and Gleason's methodology lacked a control group, so it is not clear what the comparisons for "more authoritative" and "less marginalized" were.

Stonerock (2005) examined a tutoring program that paired writers in need of "remediation" with tutors in the writing center for a tutorial course component. This writing center component was a three-credit course attached to the freshman composition requirement. The credits did not count toward graduation, but writing tutorials were mandatory. The population in her study was mostly white and middle class. Stonerock's analysis focused more on the tutors than on the basic writers themselves. In one case, she discussed Sean, a basic writer and his tutor, Calvin, who implemented the non-directive practices advocated in his tutor training. At first, Sean seemed very enthusiastic about the tutoring sessions, but as the semester progressed, his attitude fluctuated. Calvin, as well, seemed to change from helpful and involved to uninterested. This finding was contradicted by Robinson (2009), who examined writer post-consultation surveys and discovered that the more writing center visits a student attended, the more the locus of control moved from extrinsic (grammar, punctuation, organization) to intrinsic (reading interpretation, idea generation). Could it be that the basic writers in Stonerock's study were so demoralized as to reject greater control of their own writing?

When faced with such results, it is important to recall that the term "basic writer" means different things in different institutional contexts (Bell, 1999; Gardner & Ramsay, 2005). This is illustrated by Osman's (2007) quantitative study of basic writers at a historically Black university. She found that "students' perceptions of tutoring efficacy were significantly associated with academic success" (p. iii) in both freshman and sophomore level writing courses. In fact, "the higher the level of agreement, the better students performed on their initial attempts to pass freshman composition" (p. 147). However, it is not clear whether effective tutoring caused these results, or whether students with better attitudes in general were more likely to "actively participate in the learning process" (p. 198).

Smith (2010) studied basic writers enrolled in a remedial college writing class in mandatory writing center consultations. Although Smith began her dissertation with an anecdote, the study methodology combined quasi-experimental with ethnographic methodologies to discover how mandatory writing center attendance affected academic achievement. In offering justification for her study, Smith wrote: "Certainly, the lack of connection between the basic writing student and the writing center as a borderland is plainly a result of writing center and composition scholarship's gradual shift away from the basic writer" (p. 19). Smith compared two sections of a basic writing course taught by one private-college instructor. One of her research questions was, "Do mandatory writing center visits in developmental college writing classes improve retention rates?" (p. 26). Data collection included quantitative measures (pass/fail rates, one-semester and one-year retention rates) and qualitative measures (surveys, questionnaires, classroom interaction, and student writing submitted in class and in portfolios). Study results showed that retention rates for the experimental basic writing section were higher than those for the control section. In addition, writers in the experimental section submitted more portfolios with more drafts in those portfolios, and they received higher scores on their portfolios than those in the control section. While not all of the mandatory writing center sessions featured motivated writers, the majority of students in the experimental group (and the control group) reported that they had benefited from those sessions.

One-on-One Tutoring

Haas (1986) realized that when basic writers took drafts with teacher comments to the writing center, tutor-tutee talk focused on error correction and surface features rather than on the students' ideas. Tutors lost their focus on the students and their writing and became "mini-teachers" (p. 3). Simultaneously, because they focused on instructor comments, the developmental writers themselves were more concerned with grammatical features than with the ideas in their own texts—even if their instructors had commented on content as well. Overall, when writers and tutors worked with texts that had been marked by an instructor, their interaction followed "a linear pattern"; when they worked with unmarked drafts, their interaction became "a recursive discourse" (p. 287). Summarizing her findings, Haas argued that "students are engaged when they have a choice about *how a* subject is discussed, as well as a choice of subject matter" (p. 290). In our view, this study demonstrates how effective writing center tutoring parallel (as opposed to adjunct) to a writing course can be for basic writers—and perhaps all writers.

Research results are almost unanimous that through attendance at the writing center, basic writers develop more confidence as academic writers. However, there is less of a consensus that basic writers' writing improves or that their writing apprehension declines as a result of tutoring. For example, Fischer (1989) surveyed and interviewed basic writers receiving tutoring in a writing center. The writers "indicated that they advanced in their efforts to become independent college writers" (p. iii), had "a favorable experience as a result of working in the writing center" (p. 109), and thought the writing center was "worthwhile" (p. 110). But experimental results showed no significant difference on test results between basic writers who used the writing center and those in a control group who did not.

Basic writers who received one-on-one writing center tutoring and PLATO (computer software) tutoring in Grinnell's (2003) quantitative study did not show a statistically significant reduction in writing apprehension. Weaver (1978), in another quantitative study, found that over the course of a semester, basic writers reduced their apprehension whether tutored or not. Fischer (1989) also discovered that writing apprehension decreased for both tutored and non-tutored groups, but with no statistically significant difference between the two groups. Therefore, tutoring does not appear to have an effect on writing apprehension.

Fischer (1989) conducted a quasi-experimental study in which one group of basic writers received tutoring in editing skills in addition to classroom instruction, and the other group received classroom instruction only. Students were tested before and after the tutoring, and no statistical difference was found between the scores of the two groups. The weakness of this study was its short duration (ten weeks), perhaps not enough time to show improvement in editing skills. As a result, Fischer recommended a longer-term longitudinal study be done since the development of these skills is a "slow and arduous process" (p. 127) that "takes years of reinforced practice" (p. 138). Fischer also commented on writers being frustrated "over the lack of qualified tutors and sufficient lab facilities" (p. 123). Students also commented that the writing center often "tax[ed] the frustration level" (p. 133) of basic writers. This was unfortunate because it certainly discouraged the very writers who most needed it from seeking writing center support. Perhaps interacting with non-human tutors can be less frustrating for basic writers. Grinnell (2003) saw a significant increase in writing skill, measured through essays and grammar tests, in basic writers tutored *both* through PLATO software and one-on-one writing center tutoring.

Group Tutoring

In the research literature on basic writers and writing centers, we found a number of studies of adjunct group tutoring. Beaumont (1978), for example, looked at a program called "Muir 10," a developmental program for students who scored "under 600 on the English Achievement portion of their college entrance exams" (p. 2). (We believe she was referring to the SAT.) Students met twice a week for two-hour blocks to work on writing with a graduate teaching assistant (full group) and several undergraduate tutors (small groups or individuals). Tutoring and conferencing all took place as part of the class work.

Beaumont's data consisted of interviews, observations of tutorials, and writing samples discussed in tutorials. Structured interviews were conducted with both students and tutors, with either individuals or in small groups. For her qualitative analysis, she collected the rough drafts and the final drafts of the papers and also compared them to observations of the consultations in which each was discussed. Draft quality was measured by the researcher and assistant, each writing a half-page description; unfortunately, this analysis of the writers' "improvement" lacked objectivity and thus calls into question the validity of this part of the study.

Beaumont was more systematic in her analysis of tutor roles gleaned from observation data. She posited nine possible tutor roles: Evaluator, Expert, Initiator, Interested Reader, Learner/Student, Listener, Partner in Writing, Peer, and Rule-Giver (pp. 89–90). She discovered that the roles which resulted in the most student improvement were Interested Reader/Listener, Supportive Evaluator, and Partner in Writing: "Tutors who gave their students on-target criticisms, appropriate praise, and suggestions and questions rather than demands, enabled students to control their own revisions" (p. 75). Beaumont concluded that the effective tutor was "variable in his approach, according to the needs of the student and his paper. The tutor should concentrate on playing the role ... that will most benefit his student, and he should be free to assume more than one role in a conference" (p. 17).

The most thorough study done to date on basic writers in the writing center is *At the Point of Need* (Nelson, 1991), a multi-year teacher-research study using symbolic interactionism, grounded theory, and microethnographic methods. Students in a basic writing course met with graduate tutors in small groups to work on their writing outside of class. The tutoring resembled an Elbowian teacherless writing class, in that students could write whatever they wanted. Students read their drafts aloud to each other, receiving feedback and revising their writing while in the group setting. The graduate students (as research confederates) kept logs of events in their writing groups, and each year's team analyzed these and attempted to improve the subsequent year's program based on their findings. The study results showed that basic writers actually cared a lot about their writing, and that this produced anxiety for them.

The most surprising finding, to Nelson, was that working in groups was motivating to the basic writers, perhaps more motivating than working one on one: "I was wrong to assume that a one-to-one ratio would be ideal. Almost immediately... tutors began complaining that single students were harder to motivate than groups of two or three. Enthusiasm grew fastest in groups of four" (p. 38). According to one tutor, who preferred working in groups to one on one, "There was just more interaction and it helped them," and "It's harder to work singly with students. It's almost like it's overpowering for them. It's a more real-world situation for them to work among their peers."Tutors reported positive results in groups of five, but effectiveness declined in groups of six. (This is interesting because Elbow suggested working in groups of six–twelve.) They also found that diverse groups were more successful. The groups also featured laughter that created and reinforced bonding, and friendships developed that enhanced the group's work.

Nelson realized that as time went by, tutees became more and more independent. Tutors went from being proactive to reactive, but this took several weeks. In many contexts, *proactive* is a positive term and *reactive* a negative term, but in this study proactive meant that tutors were more directive, took charge more, and reactive meant that they just sat back and watched the group unfold, only contributing when asked to. As the book title implies, students became more likely to remember and use information learned when they were ready, when they most wanted or needed to know it. Nelson also found that the most actively resistant students had the most potential for a dramatic turn-around, because, in fact, the resistance "showed how much students cared" (p. 115).

Since neither Beaumont's nor Nelson's study focused on one-on-one tutoring, we may ask of what relevance they are to writing center research. Perhaps the success of group tutoring indicates that this model be seriously considered for serving basic writers. Studies by Gilewicz and colleagues of tutoring at the California State University Fresno Writing Center, which by any conceivable measure serves students classified as basic writers, have shown the validity of tutoring groups as an effective, and even superior, means of supporting basic writers in the writing center (Gilewicz, 2004; Gilewicz & Thonus, 2000; Hess, 2008).

Recommendations for Practice

- Writing center administrators should consider recommending mandatory consultations for students in developmental writing classes (Clark, 1985; Osman, 2007; Smith, 2010; Stonerock, 2005).
- Center directors should pay special attention to the availability of adequate facilities and qualified tutors for basic writers (Fischer, 1989).
- With basic writers, tutors should assume the roles of Interested Reader/Listener, Supportive Evaluator, and Partner in Writing (Beaumont, 1978).
- If possible, tutors should work with writers on drafts free of instructor comments (Haas, 1986).
- Writing centers can combine human tutoring with computer tutoring for basic writers (Grinnell, 2003).
- Tutors, basic writers, and their instructors should expect variable outcomes in terms of student buy-in, writing apprehension, and writing skill improvement as a result of tutoring (Fischer, 1989; Grinnell, 2003; Robinson, 2009; Smith, 2010; Soliday & Gleason, 1997; Weaver, 1978).
- Writing centers can implement group tutoring with diverse groups of 2–5 basic writers (Beaumont, 1978; Nelson, 1991) and try to keep these groups intact during the duration of students' developmental writing courses (Gilewicz, 2004; Gilewicz & Thonus, 2000; Hess, 2008).

Writers with Disabilities

The International Writing Centers Association (IWCA) *Position Statement on Disability and Writing Centers* reads:

> IWCA encourages *scholarship* that explores the ways disability intersects with writing center work…IWCA will include disability as a category for special consideration in IWCA training materials and will encourage publishers and authors to include disability as a category in their tutor train-

ing materials...IWCA will request that the Outstanding Research
Awards Committee encourage and recognize *research* into the ways disability intersects with writing center work. (italics ours)

Unfortunately, with few exceptions, the writing center literature contains no formal
research studies focusing specifically on students with disabilities. Most scholarship
about tutoring students with disabilities consists of informal anecdotes about tutoring students who are "different." Faerm (1992), Marron (1993), Wood (1995), and
Weaver (1996) all narrated tutoring sessions with deaf students; however, these are
extended anecdotal accounts rather than formal case studies, in which data are systematically gathered to answer a specific research question. The work of Hawkes
(2006), an overview of legal and accessibility issues, is an exception:

> Writing centers are an important resource that, unfortunately, may be ill
> equipped to deal with the increasing demands of disabled students. In
> truth, the writing center should be the focal point of a concerned cam-
> puswide effort to know and understand the needs of the growing popula-
> tion of disabled students, who know they are entitled to extra help. (p. 377)

Under the Americans with Disabilities Act, accommodation for students with special needs does not end in the classroom but extends to all educational contexts, including the writing center.

Learning Disabilities

Huot's "Working with Charlotte: A Close Look at Tutoring the Special Learner"
(1988), Marek's "Right Brain Processing and Learning Disabilities: Conclusions Not to
Reach in the Writing Center" (1991/1992), and Cosgrove's "Conferencing for the
'Learning Disabled': How We Might Really Help" (1993) introduced the topic to the
writing center literature. Mullin (1994, 2002), Neff (1994/2008), Pemberton (1998), and
Konstant (1992) are perhaps the most widely read sources on this topic in writing center literature, although these authors' advice is not based on original research studies in
the writing center. Kiedaisch and Dinitz (1991) discovered that students with learning
disabilities (LD) rated their writing center consultations lower than any other group.
The writers wished that they had more time for each session; the tutors reported feeling frustrated about how to proceed, while the writers reported the need for more precise assistance. From this study, we learn how important it is for students with learning
disabilities to disclose their conditions in order to be successfully accommodated in
the writing center. Kiedaish and Dinitz invited a panel of LD writers to speak to their
tutor-training classes and recommended that other writing centers do the same.

Dyslexia

"Guides" for working with dyslexic students have appeared in the writing center literature (see, for example, Corrigan, 1997; Lauby, 1985); however, the recommendations of these authors were not based on empirical research studies in the writing center context. Wewers (1999) surveyed writing tutors and a focus group of dyslexic students. She asked the tutors what they knew about dyslexia and asked the students how tutors could best help them. She found that tutors knew little about dyslexia except for folk knowledge gleaned from the media, most of it stereotypical and unscientific. Based on these findings, she suggested that tutors be flexible: "Certain assumptions about how we expect a tutoring session to be conducted may need to be revised" (p. 233). The dyslexic writers suggested that tutors meet their problems head on—but with tact. For instance, tutors may need to deal with dyslexic students' procrastination and disorganization, understanding that these are not signs of laziness. If writers are comfortable talking about ideas, tutors could take notes for them as ideas emerged. Tutors could also analyze a model paper along with the tutee. And tutors' reading writers' texts aloud may not have the desired consciousness-raising effect. These writers may need more time to process tutor questions and should ask the tutor to rephrase when necessary. Tutors could also point out specific places where the paper seemed disorganized or incoherent. As for grammar, spelling and mechanics, dyslexic students wanted specific help. They needed tutors to point out specific errors and tell them how to correct them. In general, writing center administrators should rethink rigid rules that preclude tutors from offering this kind of help (Babcock, 2008b).

With so little research on assisting those with learning disabilities in the writing center, we suggest readers consult sources dealing with college writing instruction and assistive technology in general. Highly useful are Li and Hamel's (2003) meta-synthesis of writing difficulties and supports for college students with learning and writing disabilities, and Engstrom's (2005) curriculum for teaching reading and writing at Landmark College, the only educational institution in the United States specifically founded for students with learning disabilities.

Deafness

Babcock (2005, 2011a) studied deaf[2] students in a college writing center context. She performed a grounded theory study using data observations of tutoring sessions of deaf students, their tutors, and interpreters. None of the tutoring sessions with deaf students in the corpus was conducted without an interpreter, and this is a finding in itself. The study was conducted at two colleges, a private open-admissions institution that focused on communications and the arts in a major Midwestern city, and a community college in the suburbs of the same city. In addition to observing tutoring sessions, the researcher collected relevant documents and interviewed stakeholders (tutors, tutees, interpreters, relevant administrators). Babcock found that deaf students needed more help with reading than their hearing counterparts as well as help summarizing and paraphrasing what they read. Another finding was that sometimes tutors forgot that they were working with deaf students; for example, one tutor said to a deaf tutee, "I'm gonna read [aloud]. You tell me how it sounds. OK?" The interpreter stopped her, and they negotiated that they would both read the text silently together. Another aspect that emerged from the study was directness. Sometimes deaf tutees were frustrated with non-directive tutoring techniques and appreciated directness (Babcock, 2008a, 2009). One deaf tutee said she valued "clear feedback, honest opinions, pointing out 'weak areas,' encouragement, and even ideas of what to write about" (2011a, p. 105). None of these, save perhaps encouragement, are considered correct practice in a "hands-off" tutoring session. Some visual tutoring practices were effective, such as putting the text in view of both the tutor and the tutee and reading it together, and using a computer to compose and facilitate direct communication. Problems may occur around cultural themes and issues, such as the deaf tutee who had trouble with the concept of Janet Jackson as a singer (she saw her as a dancer and a hard worker) and with the concept of top-five singles.

Pragmatic Impairment

Babcock (2011b) explored the concept of pragmatic impairment and compensation in the writing tutorial. People with pragmatic impairment have trouble understanding indirect aspects of language communication such as indirect requests, sarcasm, irony, and jokes. The condition can be associated with such diagnoses as autism, learning disability, and ADHD. Writers with pragmatic impairment have difficulty decoding inferences, an ability required by such common tutoring practices as Socratic questioning. In one case Babcock analyzed, the tutee understood the tutor's questions about the book she was writing about as genuine interest in what happened in the book, when the tutor's intention was to provide a scaffolding activity to help the writer brainstorm ideas for her paper. In another case, the tutee misunderstood a hint that a sentence needed to be revised as an actual request for information. Tutor question: "How would those sound if you....?" Tutee answer: "I don't know" (p. 8). Babcock suggested that tutors make the reasons for their questions and indirect hints explicit to accommodate tutees with this type of impairment. Returning to the example above, the tutor could have explained, "I'm trying to give you ideas on how to revise this sentence," when it was obvious the tutee didn't understand the reason behind her question.

The following recommendations are based on the results of these studies. To our knowledge, only deaf students, students with learning disabilities, and students with pragmatic impairment have been researched in the writing center setting, so we are limited in our recommendations. In no way do we imply that deafness, learning disabilities, and pragmatic impairment are related, nor do we suggest that students with other disabilities should not be important in writing center practice. They are. They have just not been researched.

Recommendations for Practice

- Administrators and tutors can encourage self-identification by learning disabled and dyslexic tutees (Kiedaisch & Dinitz, 1991).
- Writing centers can invite learning-disabled tutees to speak at tutor-training meetings (Kiedaisch & Dinitz, 1991).
- Although it may seem obvious, tutors can use visual methods with deaf writers, including provision of an ASL interpreter if requested (Babcock, 2011a).
- Tutors should be aware of cultural issues when tutoring deaf tutees (Babcock, 2011a).
- Tutors must pay special attention to understanding readings, summarizing, and paraphrasing with deaf students (Babcock, 2008a, 2009, 2011a), as these activities can be a challenge for these writers.
- Tutors can find alternatives to reading aloud when working with deaf and dyslexic tutees (Babcock, 2011a; Wewers, 1999).
- Tutors can point out specific errors to dyslexic students and explicitly teach how to correct them (Wewers, 1999).
- Tutors can explain the reasons behind the activities of the tutoring session; for instance, questions about the student's readings are to generate material for the paper, not because the tutor is curious (Babcock, 2011b).

Second-Language Writers

We believe Bokser's (2005) question ("How can we better train tutors to tutor imaginatively and effectively?") is particularly nontrivial when tutees are second-language (L2) learners. Thonus (1998) discovered that tutors and tutees rarely referred to the linguistic status of L2 tutees. This covert denial is akin to the proverbial elephant in the room—understood by all but rarely acknowledged. The notion that "all tutoring is good tutoring" falls particularly flat with L2 writers, and tutors prepared to work only with monolingual English speakers (hereafter termed *L1 writers*) will find that many conventional practices do not work well with multilingual writers.

Linguistic Status

In most writing center research studies of L2 writers, the tutor assumes the linguistic status of native speaker while the tutee assumes that of nonnative speaker (an exception is Kim, 2007). Because the constructs of *native speaker*, and therefore, that of *nonnative speaker*, are problematic (Davies, 1991, 2003; Han, 2004), we prefer to classify both participants in the writing consultation as English users and to focus on participants' common status as academic writers. We label those who learned to write in English before any other language *L1 writers* and those who learned to write in English after acquiring one or more languages *L2 writers*. We subsume under the *L2 writer* label so-called Generation 1.5 writers (Harklau, Losey, & Siegal, 1999; Roberge, Siegal, & Harklau, 2009), since it is quite common for these students to be literate only in English, their L2 (or L3 or L4). The *L1* and *L2 writer* labels also leave room for simultaneous bilinguals/multilinguals, who may be L1 (or L2) writers in several languages.

The literature on L2 writing research and pedagogy is voluminous (e.g., Leki, Cumming, & Silva, 2008; Silva & Matsuda, 2010; Williams, 2005), but the literature, particularly the empirical research literature, on tutoring L2 writers in the writing center is miniscule by comparison. We summarize those we could uncover here.

According to Hyland (2003), L2 writers can considerately be viewed as different from monolingual L1 writers in these important ways:

- Linguistic proficiencies and intuitions about language
- Learning experiences and classroom expectations
- Sense of audience and writer
- Preferences for ways of organizing texts
- Writing processes
- Understandings of text uses and the social value of different text types (p. 31)

These characteristics, taken as a whole, affect ways that tutors (usually L1 writers) and L2 writers interact and work on student texts in the writing center.

Contextual Factors in L2 Tutoring

Can L2 writing instruction be delivered one-on-one as well as or better than in the classroom? One of the earliest studies to advocate for locating and instructing beginning L2 writers in the writing center was Watkins-Goffman's (1986) case study of a 6th-grade writing group. The author argued that the one-on-one interaction afforded in the writing center featured a quality and quantity of input and immediate feedback superior to that which students would have received in a classroom setting.

More recently, Chiu (2011), in research employing multiple case study and discourse analysis, found that writing center consultations provided a unique and important opportunity for L2 writers to resolve "the ESL writer's sense of linguistic uncertainty" (p. 145). He reviewed the research on written and oral feedback and their impact on L2 writer revisions. Based on his study, Chiu, like Watkins-Goffman, proposed that writing center interactions provided an equivalent, and perhaps even superior, context for writing development as compared with classroom instruction.

For many writing center users, online consultations are imagined as a poor substitute for face-to-face interaction. However, L2 writers may actually benefit more from written than from oral feedback. To work with L2 writers successfully online, however, writing centers may need to investigate changing certain procedures. Newton (1990), for example, reported on a study of an e-tutor used with L2 writers. Students e-mailed their papers and received comments on grammar, mechanics, content, logic, and organization. The drafts with comments were then compared to the students' final drafts. Newton indicated that writers were more likely to attempt the mechanical rather than the substantive changes recommended, but for the changes the students attempted, they were successful 68–70% of the time for all types of comments.

Jones, Garralda, Li, and Lock (2006) compared face-to-face and synchronous online tutorials with L2 writers, looking at dominance, control, and content focus of the tutoring session. In the face-to-face tutorials, tutors talked on the average twice as much as students did. But in the online environment, students talked (typed) more, and initiated more topics. Their results showed that online conference relationships were more egalitarian and participants more likely to focus on global issues.

Some of the successes of tutoring L2 writers online can be transferred to face-to-face consultations. Weigle and Nelson (2004) compared L1 and L2 tutors consulting with L2 tutees. Tutees e-mailed written drafts to their tutors in advance of their sessions. During their sessions, both pairs found it beneficial to write things down, because sometimes the L2 tutees had trouble understanding their tutors' oral comments. In addition, the written comments served as a "take-home" reminder of revisions to be made.

Linguistic Proficiencies

What do L2 writers really *know* about English? Typically, only the most advanced L2 learner possesses the same linguistic intuitions as a monolingual English speaker, who has a tacit knowledge of what is "grammatical" or "sounds right" but may be unable to explain why. Unfortunately, this observation often leads (L1) tutors to believe that their role is to *teach language*, to provide information about "grammar" so that L2 writers can "fix" their papers. While being a linguistic informant may be one the tutor's roles, it is not the only one.

In fact, Williams (2008) claimed that writing center tutors need not have acquired explicit knowledge of "the rules" of English (in most cases, their L1) in order to create positive outcomes in L2 writers' oral and written language acquisition. To test that hypothesis, Thonus (in press), in a naturalistic study of corrective feedback in language-related episodes (LREs), uncovered two contrasting theory-practice orientations held by writing tutors: (a) Because they are native speakers of English, tutors can explain rules and teach language deductively; and (b) because both tutors and writers are *users* of English, through negotiation of meaning language can be learned inductively. While preferring the second orientation as more realistic and more effective, Thonus saw that each correlated with specific interactional moves and associated pedagogical outcomes:

> Inevitably, negotiation and scaffolded metalinguistic explanations take more time than explicit instruction and recasts—but, as the research suggests, taking more time results in more durable and transferable language and writing skills. Tutors' ability to provide immediate, explicit corrections and rule statements appears less important than their ability to prompt L2 writers, validate their contributions, and follow through to revision of grammar, lexis, and discourse features. While it may be a laudable goal for writing tutors to "know all the rules," this study suggests that it is far less important than interactional competence.

To overcome the perceived language barrier in L2 consultations, several writing centers have hired L2 writers as tutors. Outside of the U.S., this is quite common: Several writing centers at Japanese and Korean universities (e.g., Waseda University, Tokyo; Hanyang University, Seoul and Seoul National University, Korea) offer tutoring in the language(s) of instruction as well as allow students to choose which consultant they want to work with depending on the language of the specific writing assignment and the consultant's linguistic abilities (Sadoshima & Turner, 2008). Youngs and Green (2001) developed a writing assistant program (outside of the United States) in which many of the writing assistants were L2 writers. Unfortunately, the authors did not detail which languages were used during consulting.

Taylor (2007) recruited L2 writers-as-tutors for her research study. She found that the "NNS [nonnative-speaking] tutors' grammatical explanations were consistently more accurate" than the native-speaking tutors' (p. 51). Some research studies suggest that tutoring L2 writers in their dominant language can have positive and even superior results when compared with tutoring in English. But Cumming and So (1996) created an experiment in which tutors interacted with L2 writers both in English and in the students' dominant languages, and found they noticed no significant differences in the outcomes of the tutorials related to language medium.

L2 Writer Learning Experiences and Expectations

Many L2 writers, particularly international students, have experienced educational systems in which teachers are unquestioned authorities or at least of higher status than students in the academic institution. L2 writers may have learned subject matter primarily through rote memorization and been evaluated quantitatively (through multiple-choice exams) rather than qualitatively (through essay exams and research papers). Because of their learning experiences, L2 writers may treat their writing center tutors as "a type of teacher" (Thonus, 1998, 2001), ascribing to them institutionally superior rather than peer status (see also Vallejo, 2004 and Carter-Tod, 1995). For example, in her discourse-analytic study, Kim (2009) found that L2 tutees were more likely to ask questions of their tutors than L1 writers. Another example is an L2 tutee in Thonus' dissertation study (1998), who demanded "honest" feedback, even if it meant the tutor telling him his paper was "terrible" (p. 357). The same tutee was surprised to learn that he could (or was allowed to) disagree with his tutor. Study after study has discovered that L2 writers tend to view tutors as more authoritative than do L1 writers (e.g., Ritter, 2002; Thonus, 1999a, b; Williams, 2004). This has definite consequences in tutor and writer attitudes and behaviors during writing consultations (see below).

Not surprisingly, L2 writers' expectations (and often, their demands) that tutors act as authorities rather than peers have a direct impact on both tutor and tutee satisfaction with consulting sessions (Blalock, 1997). Through post-consultation surveys, Kiedaisch and Dinitz (1991) learned that L2 writers were less satisfied with their tutoring sessions than their L1 peers. Specifically, they requested more time and reported feeling uncomfortable during their consultations. Tutors reported being unsure of how to help them. Administrators tried to overcome this problem by inviting an "ESL expert" and L2 students to talk to the tutors. They also hired an L2 writer as a writing tutor.

Moser (1993) noticed that ESL students visited the writing center once or twice and then did not return. To find out why, so she conducted a two-semester long study, videotaping tutoring sessions between Haitian undergraduates and American peer tutors, and interviewing the participants about their assessment of the tutoring sessions and their ideas and suggestions for improvement. Tutors reported that the L2 writers were too silent and passive; as a result, tutors ended up answering their own questions and offering "fixes." They also reported that tutees' spoken English was difficult to understand. For their part, the L2 writers reported they had nothing against their tutors other than the fact that they weren't as "knowledgeable" as their teachers. Their reaction was to seek help from their instructors or from study groups of same-culture friends. In situations that have reached this point, Moser suggested that the writing center create programs where study groups could meet independently, with support from a tutor if desired. Tutoring in this setting may more closely resemble "desk-side coaching" than a concerted focus on student texts; nevertheless, it may be the best way to support writers in this context.

Tutors as Cultural Informants

"Playing audience" is one way in which tutors can be authoritative without completely abandoning their goal of interacting as peers. Blau, Hall, Davis, and Gravitz (2001) found that L1 tutors, in sessions with L2 writers, acted as "cultural informants" (p. 2). In another study both an L1 and an L2 tutor acted as "language informants" to an L2 writer (Weigle & Nelson, 2004). Blau, Hall, and Sparks (2002) demonstrated how the cultural informant concept built rapport between tutor and writer, so that the tutee could share information about his or her home culture and how learning experiences and expectations differed, affecting his or her academic writing.

Hinds (1987) proposed the notion of *reader-* vs. *writer-responsible languages/cultures.* He contrasted English texts (writer-responsible), for example, with Japanese texts (reader-responsible). In reader-responsible cultures (from the writer-responsible view!), it is the reader's job to derive arguments, to impose sequencing, and to "read between the lines" to intuit the writer's intent. In writer-responsible cultures, it is incumbent on the writer, for example, to announce the topic of the text and the "point" of the argument early on, to support every argument with detailed examples, and to sequence the text either chronologically or logically with clear transitions. While Hinds' dichotomy is now viewed as more of a continuum, tutors might find the concepts useful in opening a discussion of audience expectations across cultures.

Severino (1993b) applied this idea to writing center practice, inviting L2 writers to write about their rhetorical training in their native language, and tutors used this information to better help their tutees to write for an American audience. Fox (1989) wrote a case study of her work with a Chinese writer and the attention they paid to differing audience expectations. Fox employed specific tutoring strategies, using guided questions to prompt the student, giving grammar explanations, listening to students' concerns, and having both tutor and tutee read aloud. In fact, more than just analyzing the strategies that were effective for one immigrant student in the writing center, Fox underscored the importance of talk—the negotiating type that takes place in the writing center—to all L2 writers in composition courses.

As cultural informants, tutors should also be aware of contrastive rhetoric, cultural and linguistic patterns in text organization and development. By the mid-1980s, sentence-level comparisons of languages (contrastive analysis) had largely given way to analyses of textual organization itself (contrastive rhetoric, a type of discourse analysis) as a more useful tool in teaching L2 writing (e.g., Connor, 1996; Hirose, 2003; Purves, 1988; but see also Swan & Smith, 2001). Matsuda (1997) and others have shown that the influence of L2 rhetorical patterns on L1 writing cannot be overlooked; this bi-directional model of transfer means that writing consultants can talk openly with their L2 tutees about textual patterns in English and other languages, tying these in with audience expectations for particular academic writing genres.

Tutorial Topics

L2 writers may insist that consultations be about "grammar" even when significant rhetorical and content issues (so-called "higher-order concerns") present themselves. Bell and Elledge (2008) learned that many times the L2 writer negotiated work on grammar and diction contrary to the tutor's wishes. Wolcott (1989) noted that many of the L2 tutorials in her study focused on diction, particularly idiomatic usage. And Carter-Tod (1995) described a case study in which an upper-level L2 student came to the writing center with finished drafts, concerned only with making her English more idiomatic. Ultimately, tutors typically give in to L2 writers' wishes, often gladly: Ritter (2002) found that tutors with less experience reverted to "grammar" because they sensed (often correctly) that they lacked the expertise to assist writers, especially those who were writing upper-level papers in unfamiliar disciplines. In one study, proofreading (attention to surface-level errors) was the most common concern tutors addressed with L2 tutees (Bell & Elledge, 2008).

Yet some researchers have learned that working on "grammar" (a.k.a. lower- or later-order concerns) is not only what L2 writers want but exactly what they need. Blau, Hall, and Sparks (2002) argued that it might be useful for a tutor to go over an L2 writer's paper for mechanics. From their data, they showed how a tutoring session could weave together work on both global and local concerns. They also demonstrated how beneficial it could be for the tutee when the tutor worked line-by-line through a portion of the paper, illustrating editing and proofreading strategies. Cogie (2006) found that L2 writers could much more easily understand and negotiate interaction focused on local concerns than they could on global concerns: Discussion of the organization and level of detail of the assignment was unsuccessful, seemingly because the tutees did not understand what the tutors were getting at (see also Cogie, Strain, & Lorinskas, 1999).

Taylor's (2007) data showed that tutors' rhetorical feedback to L2 writers outweighed linguistic feedback almost two to one. Taylor noticed that content and grammar were actually intimately connected, as often a grammatical error was "clarified and corrected through a discussion of the content" or "when an idea was unclear, it was often easily clarified through an examination of the grammatical structure used to convey the idea" (p. 77).

Sometimes when L2 writers ask for assistance with *grammar*, they really mean *vocabulary* (word choice, word form, word use in correct grammatical context). The more advanced the language proficiency of the L2 writer, the more likely it is that their concerns revolve around lexical issues. Thonus (1998) observed international tutees working with tutors primarily on lexical meanings and choices. (Recall that even monolingual English speakers continue to expand their vocabularies throughout their lives.)

We know of only two studies that have investigated L2 writers' acquisition of English vocabulary in the writing center context. Nakamaru (2010) studied both foreign-educated and American-educated L2 writers (Generation 1.5 students) in their writing center tutorials. The international students worked more on lexical issues in their writing than the American-educated students, while the American-educated students focused more on grammatical correctness. Another interesting finding from this study is that even when tutors worked on vocabulary with writers, they characterized it as assistance with "content" or "grammar" (of which lexis is neither).

Severino and Deifell (2011) wrote a tutor-research case study of the vocabulary development of an L2 writer, Fan, through his writing center tutorials. Research questions asked how an advanced L2 writer learns vocabulary, what types of errors are made along the way, and what kind of feedback results in better learning. Data included Fan's drafts with comments from both the tutor and instructor, his final drafts, interviews, the researcher's notes on the tutoring sessions, and quantitative data about the numbers and types of errors in Fan's papers. These fell into four types: word-meaning or wrong word, word form, pattern or word behavior problems, and collocation errors. Severino and Deifell learned that Fan knew a lot of words from reading, especially advanced books and fiction, and he had many words in his written vocabulary that he did not know how to pronounce. Error feedback was given in both face-to-face and online sessions. The researchers found little difference in error correction between the two formats, and Fan demonstrated excellent uptake of the corrections the tutor made. This research is promising not only for writing center researchers and tutors, but also for L2 acquisition researchers who tend to investigate language development either in naturalistic settings or in classrooms.

Tutor-Tutee Interaction

Indirectness is highly prized in a Socratic tutoring approach. For L2 writers, however, tutor indirectness often succeeds only in generating frustration. The research literature we consulted suggests that L2 writers desire or even require more directive feedback than L1 tutees. Thonus (1998) observed that tutors used fewer mitigated directives with L2 tutees. In another study, tutors who were determined to take a non-directive stance frustrated their tutees, while creating guilty feelings for tutors if they abandoned the non-directive practices advocated in training (Blau, Hall, & Sparks, 2002). Williams (2004) studied Generation 1.5 writers and noted that they were more likely to enact revisions based on explicit (directive) suggestions made by their tutors, as opposed to those made implicitly. When tutees outwardly resisted or ignored tutor advice, revisions were unlikely to be made. However, when tutor suggestions were explicit and the tutees wrote them down or were actively involved in the conversation, they were more likely to revise their drafts, although the revisions may not have been exactly what the tutor had suggested (Williams, 2005).

If trained primarily in "current-traditional" writing center lore, tutors are likely to resist being "directive," with certain rather predictable outcomes: Williams (2005), for example, found that tutors deflected tutees' concerns or ignored them altogether (see also Thonus, 2009). Thonus (2004) noticed that tutors took time to "teach the tutorial" to L2 writers, something that they did not do with L1 writers. Tutors also frequently referred L2 writers to their instructors rather than trying to answer questions if they believed that L2 writers would not understand them. And Fox (1989) found that tutors explicitly invited L1 tutees, but not L2 tutees, to return to the writing center.

As tutors resist the authoritative role, however, L2 tutees are likely to become more insistent that they accept it—and usually get their way (Fox, 1989). As a result, tutors often dominate interactions, at least until they have discovered an "adequate frame" for writing consultations with L2 writers (Thonus, 2004). Tutors' interactional dominance takes a variety of forms: using institutional discourse (Ritter, 2002; Thonus, 1998); talking approximately twice as much as tutees (Bell & Elledge, 2008); controlling the topic of talk (Williams, 2005); asking fewer open-ended questions and, when doing so, answering these questions themselves (Fox, 1989); covering fewer topics with L2 writers than with L1 writers (Fox, 1989; Thonus, 1998); and taking longer turns and interrupting more frequently (Williams, 2005). The only study of L2 tutors and dominance we are aware of is Kim (2007); his findings from L2-L2 tutorials confirmed the notions of tutor authority and dominance.

But findings (and certainly interpretations) of tutor dominance in L2 consultations are somewhat inconsistent in the literature. When she noticed that tutors talked between twice and three times as much as L2 tutees, Taylor (2007) equated volubility with dominance. On second thought, however, she argued that tutors' extra talk could be interpreted as collaborative, since it included such moves as recasts of students' ideas. In the same way, Coelho (2011) argued that volubility (time at talk) had been too closely and even erroneously linked with concepts of tutor *appropriation*, not only of the conversational floor but of writers' drafts as well.

Implicated in directness (or directiveness) are tutors' and tutees' interpretations of politeness. Bell and Youmans (2006) observed that L2 writers misunderstood tutors' politeness strategies and took them at face value, misunderstanding the tutors' intent. Previous studies on politeness in L2 writing consultations yielded similar results (Thonus, 1999b; Young, 1992; Wolff-Murphy, 2001). Thonus (1999b) found that tutors' use of IFIDs (Illocutionary Force Indicating Devices) more often with L2 tutees than with L1 tutees facilitated L2 writers' understanding. For example, after uttering a suggestion, the tutor said, "That's just a suggestion," so the L2 tutee could realize the intended illocutionary force (politeness) of the utterance, which, due to their pragmatic competence, L1 speakers would be expected to comprehend immediately.[3]

Recommendations for Practice

- Writing centers may do well to hire L2 writers as tutors, and tutoring in the tutee's native language is acceptable if the tutor is fluent (Cumming & So, 1996; Sadoshima & Turner, 2008).
- Writing centers can allow L2 writers to e-mail their papers in advance (Weigle & Nelson, 2004) or to conduct L2 tutoring entirely online (Jones, Garralda, Li, & Lock, 2006).
- Group tutoring or "desk-side consultations" may prove more effective than one-on-one tutoring for students from some cultures (Moser, 2002).
- Tutors should make sure they understand as much about their L2 tutees as possible, including the student's language proficiency level, rhetorical understanding, and the type of feedback they desire (Ritter, 2002; Severino, 1993b; Taylor, 2007).
- In addition to acting as "cultural informants" in matters of academic discourse and contrastive rhetoric, tutors can ask tutees to apprise them of the academic writing practices of their home countries (Blau, Hall, Davis, & Gravitz, 2001; Blau, Hall, & Sparks, 2002; Severino, 1993b).
- For tutors, grammatical competence is not nearly as important as interactional competence (Williams, 2008; Thonus, in press).
- Tutors should move away from the "content" versus "grammar" divide and realize that L2 tutees may ask for help with "grammar" when they really want or need something else. Sometimes, issues of content and grammar are intertwined (Taylor, 2007). Often, L2 writers need more help with vocabulary (word choice, form, and appropriate use in grammatical context) than with anything else (Nakamaru, 2010).
- Tutors can use more directive tutoring approaches with L2 writers (Thonus, 1998), especially those who are less proficient (Weigle & Nelson, 2004), or if error correction/revision is the goal (Williams, 2004). Tutors can also use Illocutionary Force Indicating Devices with L2 writers to make their intentions clear (Thonus, 1999b).
- Encourage tutees to take notes of revisions to be made later (Williams, 2005).
- Tutors should explicitly invite L2 writers to return to the writing center (Fox, 1989).

Graduate Students

Graduate students are a "different" group at least as far as writing center research is concerned, because in their early history college writing centers focused almost exclusively on undergraduate writers. In recent years, it has become evident that graduate student writers are no less likely to seek assistance with their writing than undergraduates, and, in fact, at some university writing centers they are the majority of users. At some institutions, graduate students frequent the writing center alongside undergraduates, while at other places, separate graduate writing centers have been founded (Snivley, Freeman, & Prentice, 2006).

Writer Identity and Competence

Farrell (1994) indicated that little research on graduate students as a group existed. Since then, however, significant research on graduate students in the writing center has been done. These studies focus on the identity and competence of graduate writers, and how these come into play during writing consultations.

Welch (1995) wrote of graduate students positioning themselves in between the authority of academic discourse and the actual content of what they wanted to say. She realized that in the writing center, graduate students could "stretch" what they were doing in order to finally achieve a balance between academic conventions of their fields and their own words and ideas. Graduate writers more familiar with disciplinary conventions or those who had already mastered them had more success when questioning and engaging with the authority of academic discourse. Welch argued that for less academically acculturated writers, the writing center could serve as a place for them to achieve that balance and to forge their own paths.

Leverenz (2001) conducted a year-long study of graduate writers at the writing center where she worked. By observing sessions and conducting surveys and interviews, she found that graduate writers were interacting with complex concepts of expertise. These writers were seldom provided explicit instruction in disciplinary conventions and academic writing by professors. In the writing center, they could address these concerns and even vent their frustrations. Tutors could assist writers in articulating their resistance to academic conventions while assisting them in appropriating those very conventions that they needed to succeed as writers. Leverenz suggested specifically that tutors "attempt to address graduate students' need for rhetorical knowledge by analyzing with them examples of published articles and completed theses in the field" (p. 56). Finally, Leverenz saw that developing relationships was perhaps the most important and fruitful aspect of writing center work with graduate students. Graduate tutees could take on the role of experts in explaining their work to tutors, and tutors could offer intelligent, honest responses to graduate students who would otherwise feel alone and isolated.

Sniveley (2008) conducted a qualitative study of graduate students working in a graduate writing center at Harvard. Through interviews with ten graduate writers, she developed codes and reported on them in a qualitative narrative structure. She found that graduate students appreciated the safety of the writing center to be able to brainstorm, share drafts, and ask "dumb" questions. In this way, they did not have to display their ignorance to a faculty member, but they could ask their questions in the safe space of the writing center with tutors who were also graduate students. Graduate writers also appreciated the validation they got from readers when their ideas made sense. The safe space was enhanced by the professional factor: Students felt more comfortable seeking help from tutors than from classmates with whom they might compete or to whom they might then "owe a favor" (p. 92). A difference between graduate and undergraduate tutoring was that the graduate tutors had expertise that they shared with other graduate students about research methods and disciplinary knowledge, and, while remaining novices with respect to content, lend an air of objectivity to the reading. Another difference between the undergraduate and graduate writing center was the possibility of working on editing with graduate students, especially those from other countries. The graduate writing center also kept an archive of successful proposals for students to consult. In this particular graduate writing center, students appreciated the continuity of working with the same tutors over time.

Graduate students seeking writing center assistance are often international students or resident bilinguals. Powers and Nelson (1995) reported that for the 1993–1994 academic year, 82% of the consultations at the University of Wyoming Writing Center were with L2 writers. The authors decided to survey writing centers across the country to ascertain if they were experiencing similar trends. Overall, 83% of the institutions surveyed indicated that they consulted with L2 writers who were also graduate students. The master's thesis was the most common type of writing (73%) that L2 graduate writers took to consultations. The type of help that these writers most requested was with correctness and style (3.70 and 3.43 on a 4-point scale, with 4 being "almost always" and 1 being "almost never"). Writing centers surveyed expressed as their greatest challenges writers' unfamiliar technical content and their ambivalent attitudes toward writing.

Because of their language proficiency, graduate L2 writers have been mistaken for younger, inexperienced, or inexpert students (Ritter, 2002). Tutors working with these writers need to remind themselves frequently that English language proficiency does not correlate with intelligence or subject-matter expertise.

Advice and Accounts

Waring (2005; 2007a; 2007b) examined tutoring events at a graduate writing center and analyzed her data using conversation-analytic methods. All tutees were graduate students, and tutors were either graduate students or alumni of the institution. Waring's focus was tutor advice coupled with *accounts*, explanations or justifications for the advice offered. Tutors typically offered accounts in the pre-advice stage, immediately after advice was given, just after a "problematic uptake from the client [the graduate student writer]" (p. 380), or, least commonly, after the tutee accepted the advice. They omitted accounts when recommending changes in "grammar, mechanics, conventions, wording and style" (2007b, p. 373), or when tutors responded to tutee elicitation or questions. Waring noticed that tutor accounts served to minimize face-threat, to minimize resistance, and to expedite acceptance of the advice: "The tutee's perspective needs to be elicited fully prior to the delivery of advice to preempt some of the potential resistance" (2005, p. 163). In sum, Waring proposed that tutor use of accounts helped to socialize graduate students into the discursive practices of academic writing.

Waring also investigated how graduate student writers accepted or rejected tutor advice, and she encouraged tutors to pay attention to these responses. Simple advice acceptance consisted of tutee tokens such as "okay," which served to acknowledge and accept the tutor's advice. In complex advice acceptance, tutees "accept[ed] with claims of comparable thinking" and "accept[ed] with accounts" (2007a, p. 117). Graduate students' use of complex advice acceptance showed their desire to assert their competence and to attain greater symmetry with their writing consultants. For their part, by accepting their tutees' desire to display their competence "in content-related matters or mechanics of writing" (2005, p. 164), tutors moved beyond offering quick fixes to suggesting substantive changes to students' academic writing.

The Need for Graduate Tutors

In Powers and Nelson's survey (1995), many writing centers reported that their staff required more tutor training and that they needed more professional staff to adequately support graduate L2 writers. Considering graduate student writers' needs as a whole, the brief accumulated research suggests that they be paired with graduate student or professional staff tutors. If collaboration among peers is a crucial hallmark of writing center work, pairing a graduate student who is writing original research with another graduate student or staff member with at least a master's degree makes sense. This does not mean that undergraduate peer tutors have *nothing* to offer graduate writers; we are simply making an observation that they may have less to offer than well-trained readers and writers who are walking or have walked a similar academic path, regardless of their disciplinary affiliation.

Recommendations for Practice

- Administrators can encourage graduate writers to attend the writing center and either have graduate-level tutors available or establish a separate graduate writing center (Snively, 2008).
- Administrators can consider hiring tutors with L2 writing expertise to work with international and other multilingual graduate students (Powers & Nelson, 1995).
- Tutors can let graduate students vent about their writing difficulties but at the same time, they can offer support for their acquisition of academic discourse (Welch, 1995; Leverenz, 2001).
- Tutors can offer accounts along with their suggestions and permit graduate writers to display their competence, especially in subject matter (Waring, 2007a, 2007b).
- Tutors can listen for and encourage complex advice acceptance from their graduate tutees. (Waring, 2005)

Conclusion

In concluding this chapter on writers who are "different," we underscore the need of writing centers and writing center researchers not only to consider specific practices likely to better support such writers but at the same time to avoid "othering" them. Kiedaisch and Dinitz's "Changing Notions of Difference in the Writing Center: The Possibilities of Universal Design" (2007) challenged us to examine "current/traditional approaches to issues of difference in tutor preparation" (p. 42). Such practices, they argued, pre-empted the need to recreate all difference as identity (both of tutor and tutee) and to create a "Universal Design and tutoring praxis" (p. 51). Writing instruction offered by tutors, they suggested, should be (1) simple and intuitive; (2) flexible in use; (3) tolerant of error; and create a community of learners. Universal Design in "writing center spaces, resources, and services" (p. 54) would result in (1) equitable use; (2) perceptible information; (3) low physical effort; (4) a size and space for approach and use; and (5) an instructional climate "designed to be welcoming and inclusive" (p. 56).

Implementing Universal Design is not as daunting as it may seem. For example, one of us (Thonus) collaborated with an instructional designer to create a writing center website accessible to screen-readers used by the visually impaired and with video clips close-captioned for the hearing impaired. Making writing center services more inclusive, we believe, will benefit all writers and their tutors.

Notes

1. Funding for research on parts of this chapter was provided to Rebecca Babcock by the International Writing Centers Association and the Rock Valley Foundation. She would like to thank Kellye Manning, Brian Fallon, and the members of her University of Texas, Permian Basin Fall 2006 Advanced Composition course for their feedback on an earlier draft of portions of this chapter. Thanks to Julie McCown for research assistance.
2. In the literature on disability, *deaf* (lower case) refers to the inability to hear; *Deaf* (upper case) refers to cultural deafness.
3. An exception may be L1 writers with certain disabilities or impairments. For more on this, see Babcock (2011a).

CHAPTER FIVE

Tutoring Activities

Talk is everything. If the writing center is ever to prove its worth in other than quantitative terms—number of students seen, for example, or hours of tutorials provided—it will have to do so by describing its talk: What characterizes it, what effects it has, how it can be enhanced.…The variations on the kind of talk are endless. We can question, praise, cajole, criticize, acknowledge, badger, plead—even cry. We can read: silently, aloud, together, separately. We can play with options. We can both write.…We can ask writers to compose aloud while we listen, or we can compose aloud, and the writer can watch and listen. (North, 1984a, pp. 75–76)

In this chapter, we categorize tutoring activities according to the four language skills of speaking, listening, reading, and writing. Finally, we review studies on revision talk, meta-discourse, and reflection, since these activities figure prominently in the tutoring sessions that researchers have investigated.

Speaking

Two main types of talk appear in tutoring sessions: the actual discourse of tutoring itself (instructional talk) and other talk (small talk), which serves a more interpersonal or *phatic* purpose.

Instructional Talk

Citing Thonus (1998), Ritter (2002) divided the tutoring session into the *diagnosis phase* (discussed in the next chapter under *agenda-setting*), the *directive phase*, in which most of the actual tutoring happens, and the *closing phase*. Within suggestion sequences, which are part of the directive phase, students have the opportunity to "speak through" tutor moves, including:

1. Indirect suggestions with rising intonation
2. Indirect suggestions repeated twice
3. Interrogative suggestions
4. *Either/or* suggestions that invite the student to choose a suggestion (p. 193)

Vallejo (2004) categorized the discourse in the tutoring sessions he observed as either *grammar-checking discourse*, in which tutors corrected tutees' mistakes while tutees looked on and made minimal contributions, or *grammar-checking dialogues*, in which tutors explained to tutees how to make the corrections, and it was the tutee who actually made them. The latter discourse was termed *dialogue* because tutees made suggestions and asked questions for clarification. He observed several non-directive approaches, including *collaborative dialogue*, which involved tutors asking questions and making suggestions for discussion and consideration rather than corrections, as well as *collaborative-oriented assumption*, in which tutors aided tutees with global rhetorical issues. Finally, Vallejo observed what he called *a directive stance in transition*, containing features of both a directive and a collaborative approach through which tutors dealt with issues other than grammar.

MacDonald (1991) based his coding scheme for tutorial conversation on IRE (Initiation-Response-Evaluation) moves, adapted to the tutoring context. He called this framework the Macdonald Tutoring Interaction Codes, adding *marker* and *addition* to IRE moves since those categories only accounted for half of the moves he found in his analysis of tutorials. MacDonald concluded that the classic image of tutoring, in which the tutor asks questions and the tutee responds, was not always accurate. In fact, just as common as that sequence was what MacDonald termed an *informational pattern* in which tutor or tutee supplied information that was not asked for, and the other person responded with what MacDonald called a *marker*, more commonly known to linguists as a *backchannel cue*. Wilder (2009) looked at talk that brought about student agency. She based her categories on MacDonald's and adapted them through coding work.

Stachera (2003) analyzed tutor talk between five consultants and five writers. She specifically focused on the type of questions tutors asked (open = non-directive; closed = directive), and found that tutors asked closed, directive questions. Stachera concluded that non-directive questions are "hard to define, hard to practice, and infrequently used" (p. 192) because they are potentially dishonest: Tutors "rarely provided honest reader-response feedback, fearing this would contradict the 'hands-off' element to the non-directive method" (p. viii). Like MacDonald's, Stachera's test of tutoring lore in practice yielded conflicting results.

Brown (2008) discussed "reader response" as one move that tutors often used. This technique is somewhat self-explanatory, as the tutor thinks through his or her reaction to some aspect of the paper without necessarily offering a specific suggestion for revision. Brown realized that reader response strategies were not as effective for later-order concerns, which were more likely to be rule bound.

Kane (2011) investigated the talk between generalist writing tutors who were unfamiliar with the genre-specific language of the business world and business-student writers. She assigned the tutors to different training methods: the first, to class observation and microethnographic field notes; the second, to business writing handouts from the Purdue Online Writing Lab (OWL). Kane made her own observations, collected audio recordings and transcriptions of tutoring sessions, conducted follow-up interviews with tutors and writers, and examined writer drafts. She found that during consultations, the second generalist tutor focused on "how" the writer had written his document rather than "why," a question that would have led the tutor to increased genre knowledge. This tutor had "embraced a [higher-order concerns] before [lower-order concerns] writing center pedagogy" (p. 62), offering "feedback about content...predominantly unrelated to form" (p. 67). Unfortunately, business writing demands greater attention to form than do many other genres. Although the first generalist tutor had observed business class sessions and had extensive contact with the course instructor, her feedback to the writer was just as focused on content and just as lacking in discipline-specific guidance. One weakness of the study is that writers' contributions to talk did not receive the same level of detailed analysis that tutors' did. Kane concluded that interdiscursivity ("the connections between the conventions of their own discourse community and those of the business discourse community," p. 156) was difficult to attain if tutors were trained as generalists and writing centers construed as locations for assistance with "academic writing" as a monolithic whole.

Small Talk

Small talk (*phatic* talk) is an important part of the tutoring session but is sometimes overlooked or belittled by researchers. For instance, Block (2010) termed it "chit-chat" (p. 26) and did not transcribe it or use it in her coding or analysis. Others recognized its importance, such as Frank (1983), who mentioned that a whole session might be spent talking about the tutee's "interests, family, or life experiences" (p. 77).

Haas (1986) observed that small talk assisted in relationship building. Similarly, Cardenas (2000) described a successful tutorial in which participants spoke of personal topics, adding to the session's "friendly, interactive environment" (p. 113). Hunter (1993) called this kind of interaction "talk-off-task," and noticed that one tutee, Yvonne, and her tutors did not hesitate to engage in it:

> Talk-off-task has the obvious advantage of interspersing the difficult work of writing and revising with pleasant, human exchanges. It also has the less obvious advantages of making the writer feel more comfortable in college and helping her navigate in her academic and personal lives as she gains confidence in her abilities. (pp. 207–208)

When Yvonne was done with her paper, she engaged in "talk-off-task" to gain information about college life. This was probably not the main goal of her tutors but no doubt was of use to Yvonne.

When studying graduate student tutors who were also teachers, Wolcott (1989) found no small talk at the beginning of tutoring sessions. She and the tutors used the terms "business-like" (p. 19) and "task-oriented" (p. 25) to describe these small-talk-free sessions, which Wolcott did not evaluate as either better or worse than sessions with small talk. Ritter (2002) observed that L1 tutors were reluctant to engage in small talk with L2 tutees, perhaps due to the discomfort they felt working with these writers. Thonus (1998) did not record small talk in every tutorial she observed, no doubt because of her institutional characterization of tutorial discourse. When small talk did occur, it most often came at the end of the tutorial, serving, according to one study participant, as a means of relaxing at the end of the session. Consultations that included small talk were more highly rated by both tutors and writers. However, participant status and the content of small talk had to be symmetrical to result in high ratings.

Williams (2005) also studied small talk. She noticed that tutors used it to lessen status differences, in one case by asserting common status as students, and in another, common status as Asians. However, in one case Williams observed, the tutee was not really interested in the topic of small talk that the tutor wanted to pursue. In studying online consultations, Hewett (2004–2005, 2006) underscored the amount of phatic talk she uncovered and argued that it provided important context for instructional interactions.

Frank (1983) showed that phatic talk could develop into topic generation, as with a student he helped to "develop prewriting strategies by getting him to talk about his interests and life" (p. 78). Montgomery (1994) also researched how phatic talk could lead to topic generation, though she did not use those terms. By studying writing workshops that met in the writing center with a tutor as facilitator, Montgomery discovered the importance tutors placed on creating a comfortable atmosphere and facilitating discourse that enabled revision and analysis of writing. This type of talk featured

1. Posing probing questions designed to elicit thoughtful responses from writers
2. Reinforcing writer remarks through paraphrasing
3. Asking for repetition of an observation
4. Calling attention to a comment with a phrase such as "What an interesting idea!"
5. Making connecting statements indicating that everyone needs to listen on a "global" level
6. Summarizing by either the tutor or the writers (p. 81)

Tutors also attempted to involve student writers in the discussion of their own material. This was done by encouraging peers to give feedback or to model proper responses.

Listening

Although it would seem that tutors and tutees both need to listen in a tutoring session, the focus of most research studies is on the listening behavior of the tutor—obviously easier for writing administrators to address. McClure (1990), for example, described tutors in her study as listeners, as did the tutors themselves and the students they tutored. One tutor in McClure's study used listening to help students find ideas of what to write about. On the other hand, Seckendorf (1986) noticed that when a consultant failed to listen to her tutee and was insensitive to what she wanted from the consultation, the consultant chose her own focus, unaware of the messages that the tutee was sending about what she wanted from the session. Brown (2008) observed a tutoring session in which the tutor did not appear to listen as the tutee expressed that she was tired, overwhelmed, and could not answer any more questions. The tutor continued to ask the same type of open-ended questions over and over—doing as she had been trained to do—with no positive results. Fallon (2010) noted of two of the tutors he researched: "Matthew and Tom show that it is possible that all the tips and tools that tutors find in guides and in training courses, the techniques that frame a session, mean nothing if a tutor is not listening carefully enough to the tutorial situation" (p. 109).

Cardenas (2000) studied several tutoring sessions, the majority judged as unsuccessful, in which consultants also failed to listen to their tutees. In fact, one tutor did not listen to her tutee's answers to her questions, causing her to have to ask the same questions over again. In another consultation, the tutor apparently didn't listen to what the student wanted to work on (brainstorming) but instead steered her into organization. The tutee tried to express his goals, but the tutor didn't pick up on them. The tutee did not return for tutoring with this consultant but chose to see another consultant to work on the paper. When reflecting on the session, the consultant admitted that she needed to "listen better" (Cardenas, 2000, p. 70).

Not all examples of listening in Cardenas' study were negative. In one case, a tutor listened effectively, which helped the tutor to understand the tutee's "commitment to her subject" and to understand the tutee's needs, which elicited strategies to help the tutee "move toward her goals" (p. 98). This tutor employed what Cardenas called "active listening," allowing the tutee to "express herself," including "paraphrasing; referring to ideas expressed previously by [the tutee] ... and [asking] questions" (p. 98).

Boudreaux (1998) found that tutorial participants used different "response types," exhibiting behavior that could be misinterpreted as listening or not listening when the opposite might have been the case. For instance, in one session in Boudreaux's data set, a writer wrote while the tutor talked. Although the tutor interpreted this behavior as "not listening," the writer was actually listening very closely, taking notes on what the tutor was saying. However, the writer looked at the tutor and gave backchannel cues only infrequently, so his actions were misinterpreted. The writer ended up asking for a different tutor.

After noticing that most tutor training manuals offered little instruction on listening (or reading), Edgington (2008) surveyed a small group of peer tutors at the University of Toledo to "better understand how tutors read and listen to student texts" (p. 9). Tutors explained that their listening was compromised when the writing center was noisy or when they were listening to topics "for which they had little background knowledge or that bored them" (p. 10). To increase their listening effectiveness, tutors reported engaging in conversation, taking notes, and rereading (or listening again).

Reading

Weigle & Nelson (2004) examined untrained consultants as they worked one-on-one with graduate students who were L2 writers. One of the pairs decided to read aloud although they were not trained specifically to do so. They decided to this so that the writer could catch her own mistakes. Thonus (2008) described a session in which a tutor and L2 writer spent time reading aloud from the tutee's source materials as well as from her draft. While she encouraged tutors to act "as a reader" (p. 251), Stachera (2003) noted that tutor dominance was guaranteed if *tutors* read writers' papers aloud during consultations, since once tutors gained the floor, they rarely relinquished it. This research supports the guidance of writing center lore that tutees' work be read aloud, preferably by the tutees themselves (see, for example, Gillespie & Lerner, 2008).

Recent research, however, suggests that reading can be multifaceted. Ritter (2002), for example, observed that reading occurred three different ways during writing center consultations. In the first format, the tutor or tutee read aloud or the tutor read silently. In the second format, when a tutee read the paper aloud, he or she paused after each paragraph, and the tutor made comments. In the third format, when the tutor read silently or aloud, the tutor stopped whenever he or she desired to give feedback, usually every few sentences. In all of these models, the tutor gave positive feedback and suggestions about the writing after the whole paper was read. Among these formats, Ritter found no difference among these three formats that she could relate to greater or lesser access to learning opportunities for tutees.

Research by Block (2010) was more conclusive. She uncovered three reading aloud methods that were used in tutoring sessions: *tutor-read, client-read,* and *tutor-read with point-predict.* In the point-predict method, the tutor paused to describe what the paper had accomplished thus far, and what he or she predicted would come next. Block noticed that tutor-read sessions led to a focus more on lower-level (sentence-level and formatting) concerns, and the tutor-read point-predict sessions led to more of a focus on global issues like content and organization. Block used a quasi-experimental approach in which she asked the tutors in the study to use each of the three methods in turn with the client participants. In interviews, tutors reflected on the efficacy of the method and decided that the point-predict method would not work as well for clients who just wanted help with sentence-level issues, and it also would not be productive to use with writers whose paper is "going nowhere" or literally all over the place because the method might bring a writer "to tears" (p. 65). One of Block's tutors commented that the point-predict method would work best for those interested in true "revision," and Block noted that "there will always be some who are not willing to do the work required for 'true revision,' and for those who fall in that category, point-predict may simply be an exercise in frustration or a waste of time" (p. 66).

Writing

Anecdotally, we found few writing centers that, on their websites, promote writing *during* consultations. One exception is "Be prepared to participate actively: to think, *write,* and talk about the writing that is on the page and the *words that aren't yet written*" (emphasis ours). This dictum appears on the websites of the New York University Writing Center and the Georgetown University Writing Center. In terms of tutor training, Gillespie and Lerner (2008) urged this activity only at the end of a writing center session, when writers could jot down their plans of what to do next (p. 43). Hewett (2010) also advocated tutee writing after a tutorial, "independently of the instructor" (p. 136). *Tutor* writing about a session is accomplished after the writer leaves or logs off, during the *report phase* (Thonus, 1998).

Hunter (1993) was the only study we found that looked at writing as a tutorial activity. Hunter observed that sometimes students wrote in response to a tutor question or comment. While we find it disappointing that few, if any, other studies of writing as a tutorial activity exist, it does not surprise us: Writing consultations have typically been construed as talk about writing, not writing itself. Writing during a session conjures up visions of tutors writing for tutees, of tutors writing on tutees' papers, of tutors appropriating student drafts as their own. Brown (2008) made an observation that upholds this admonishment against tutors writing on tutees' papers: In one tutorial, a tutor wrote corrections on a tutee's paper while mumbling to himself, failing to give any suggestions or explanations as he read. In an interview afterward, the tutee voiced his disappointment with this tutoring technique. Yet there are so many other ways writing can support the work of the tutorial: Writers can take notes or draft sentences and paragraphs; tutors can "take dictation" as writers brainstorm and make helpful marginal notes on writers' drafts that do not "give it all away."

Revision Talk and Meta-Discourse

An early study of talk about revision during writing center tutorials is Stay (1983). He emphasized the importance of tutors' talking through ideas in the tutoring session rather than just making corrections on paper. Stay wrote that writers came to realize through discussions with their tutors that "they had more to contribute than was evidenced in the original drafts" and that the instructor "helped keep the student's attention fixed on larger questions of organization, especially in early drafts" (p. 23). We noticed that Stay focused more on textual changes writers made than the relationship between what happened in revision talk during the sessions and the textual changes. In fact, there is no evidence that Stay actually observed, recorded, or transcribed tutorial sessions. In addition, we should point out, as did Bell (2002), that the tutors in this particular writing center were faculty (assistant professors). This reduces the generalizability of Stay's findings to a narrow selection of writing centers staffed entirely by faculty tutors.

Bell (2002) investigated writing center tutoring sessions with both peer and professional tutors to see if writers would improve as revisers. He measured improvement by analyzing which revisions discussed in the tutoring session were implemented by writers. Bell determined the objective of each consultation by listening to the recording of the session. Then, he and a coder analyzed the drafts that writers took to their writing center consultations and the final drafts they submitted to their instructors. When writers met with peer tutors, most of the revisions were made *during* the tutoring sessions, so Bell surmised that there was no evidence that the tutees had become better writers or even that they had learned anything (although they could have). He then examined the sessions writers had with professional tutors, whom he directed not to make the revisions during sessions but instead to ask writers to make them afterwards. Although fewer revisions were made during consultations with professional tutors, those that were made were 98% positive. Bell also observed that the peer tutors acted more as editors in the tutoring sessions while the professional tutors taught rules and strategies to be used later. Rather than surmising from these results that professional tutors should be employed instead of peer tutors, we comprehend that peer tutors can be trained in the moves that result in student learning and enhanced revision.

In the sessions that Bell and Elledge (2008) observed, they were surprised to find just how much of revision talk focused on proofreading concerns (64–71%). Talk about global issues accounted for 0–10% of talk, and talk about local concerns, which in their definition included "clarification within paragraphs, sentence organization, transitions between ideas, introductions, and conclusions" (p. 23), accounted for a mere 20–33% of the talk in the sessions they analyzed. These sessions were held with L2 writers, so that fact may have contributed to the study outcomes.

Williams (2004) also studied revisions made by undergraduate L2 writers. She found, not surprisingly, that the focus of writing center sessions influenced the subsequent revisions that writers made. Surface-level errors that were discussed during the tutoring sessions were more likely to be corrected by the writers than larger, global problems; writers were more likely to make broad textual revisions after extended negotiation. Also, issues directly addressed by the tutor were more likely to be corrected than those that were implicitly addressed, and a tutee's reaction to a tutor's suggestion predicted whether or not a change would be made. For instance, if a writer resisted a suggestion or gave a minimal response rather than agreeing with the tutor's suggestion and writing it down, he or she was less likely to implement it, and, not surprisingly, tutees were more likely to write down tutors' direct suggestions. Williams also noticed that strategies such as scaffolding and reminding the writer of the goals of the session were effective in sponsoring revision. Although writers in her study made substantial revisions, by applying a holistic rating scale Williams found that these did not always achieve the goal of improving the paper. In fact, the first and second drafts were evaluated the same by the raters, with only two drafts showing any improvement in the ratings; interestingly, these were the ones with the fewest overall revisions.

Camps and Milian (2000) defined *metalanguage* as "communicative talk about language as well as referring to systematic relations among linguistic elements" (p. 14). Metalinguistic talk can be referred to more generally as *meta-discourse*. Montgomery's (1994) analysis of group tutoring sessions (writing workshop groups) led her to conclude that the tutor's most important role in the writers' workshop was helping students to develop a metalanguage with which to talk about their texts. We see this as an important role for tutors in individual sessions as well and caution that acquiring a metalanguage takes time and much practice.

Ritter (2002) categorized revision as different from language concerns. In her data, tutors often turned to revision after reading through the entire student paper, beginning with a reader-response comment followed by a suggestion for revision. She observed tutors making broad, general comments about a student's paper in the closing phase: "That is a really interesting paper" (p. 165). For purposes of analyzing revision talk in future studies, we recommend that researchers not code content and language feedback offered by tutors into separate categories; both types of feedback are essential to revision and to writing development (Thonus, in press).

Recommendations for Practice

- Small talk—otherwise known as talk-off-task, phatic talk, or "chit-chat"—appears to have value, so it should be neither discounted nor avoided unless the writer shows a clear preference otherwise (Frank, 1983; Hewett, 2006; Montgomery, 1994).
- For consultations in which content, organization, and other global issues are a priority, try the *point-predict* reading method (Block, 2010). For sessions in which spelling, grammar, and other editing concerns are a focus, the tutor or tutee may choose to read the paper aloud.
- Encourage writers to take notes (Williams, 2004), and, if writers resist tutor suggestions, attempt to negotiate a more acceptable solution; encourage active participation.
- It cannot be stressed enough that tutors must listen carefully to tutees (Cardenas, 2000; Brown, 2008; Fallon, 2010).
- Tutors should directly address items for revision in tutorials with L2 writers (Williams, 2004).
- Encourage tutees to make revisions after the session rather than during it (Bell, 2002).

CHAPTER SIX

The Details? They Matter

As a concept, instructional conversation contains a paradox: "Instruction" and "conversation" appear contrary, the one implying authority and planning, the other equality and responsiveness....To enable the transformation of experience into knowledge to be organized most effectively...we need to understand why conversational discourse has this powerful epistemic potential (Wells & Haneda, 2009).

The contents of this chapter are based on the concerns of studies that have been done on writing center interaction. These involve the content and format of tutoring sessions (*session focus and format*), the interpersonal dimension (*interpersonal interactions, negotiation*), and linguistic concerns (*politeness and directiveness, paralinguistic features*).

Session Focus and Format

The focus of writing center tutorials depends on the negotiation of concerns between the tutor and tutee. Sometimes the session focus is contested between the desires of the tutor, tutee, and course instructor (Haas, 1986).

Writer-Centered

Truly writer-centered tutorials, ones in which the tutee takes charge and sets the agenda for the session and asks questions of the tutor, are rare in study data. When a student does get to set the agenda, sometimes the consultation can become directive, especially when grammar is involved. In his study, Vallejo (2004) noticed that when tutors asked L2 tutees what they wanted to work on, most of the time the answer was "grammar," and a directive stance was the most common way to deal with this topic. Therefore, a paradox can occur between writer-centeredness (the tutee chooses the topic) and the way the topic is dealt with (directive grammar help).

Cardenas (2000) observed thirty consultations, and of these, only three were student centered. In the student-centered consultations tutees took on an expert role and were assertive about their goals for the session. Cardenas called these consultations examples of "minimalist tutoring." In Ritter's data, (2002) an experienced tutee, a business student from France, found a way to guide the tutor to give up her usual practice of taking control of the session and led the session toward her own (the tutee's) concerns by asking the tutor specific questions about lexical items that she was unsure about.

Tutor-Centered

In tutor-centered consultations, the tutor takes the lead and controls the conversation and direction of the session. Roswell (1992) noticed that tutors sometimes had an "ideal" text in mind that they attempted to impose on the tutee. Tutors in Stachera's (2003) study were so comfortable talking about writing that they talked more, and sometimes they did not even notice that the tutee didn't want to participate. At one point, Stachera observed a tutee raising her hand to speak, which would seem odd in a tutoring session anyway, but to top things off the tutor was so busy talking he didn't even see her and just kept talking. A tutor in Bell's study (1989) knew that he "ran the conference," but he also "seemed quite happy to let [the tutee] take the initiative, and he was careful about his role as an authority" (p. 158). Zdrojkowski (2007) noted that tutors offered 69–96% of directives, questions, and topic initiations.

Another tutor in Bell's study took over the session and was very direct, which disarmed the tutee to the point where she stopped participating. In this case, the tutor may have actually lowered the tutee's confidence. In one tutor-centered consultation that Bell observed, the tutor steered the direction of the session but did not attempt to interfere with the content or substance of the writer's paper. Most of the tutorials Wolcott (1989) researched appeared to be teacher centered, which she attributed to the fact that the tutors were older graduate students. Vallejo (2004) found that when discussing grammar a tutor-centered session would result. Ritter (2002) called this type of consultation *being the teacher*.

Text-Centered

Most consultations Roswell (1992) observed were text centered, meaning "the text is objectified; the text's integrity is acknowledged, and the text is the occasion of all response." In this type of session, as Roswell explained, the text was "not just an artifact present in the setting, but is a voice in the conversation, in many cases, in fact, the primary voice and the one to which both the student and tutor respond" (pp. 182–183). The text-centered consultation usually has grammar as a focus, for several reasons. Nicolas (2002) observed that tutors and tutees fell back on grammar as a neutral default territory when they could not make a connection. As a negative case, Bell (1989) saw a tutoring session between two women who were relaxed and friendly with each other and who mostly focused on editing for style. These participants were pleased with the session and the tutor said it was "fun" (p. 105).

In some cases the tutee preferred a text-centered consultation, but the tutor resisted this because of training. Callaway (1993) described a dyad in which the tutee wanted to talk about the text while the tutor preferred to talk about writing in general. Finally, in the sixth tutoring session of the semester, the tutor gave the tutee suggestions to improve her paper. This made the tutor feel like the session was a failure, but the student was pleased to receive directive comments on her draft and ended up being very happy with the session. McClure (1990) studied tutorials in which the consultation became so text centered that the consultant became "engrossed in the draft," while the tutee "signaled growing inattention as well as dissatisfaction" with body language, such as pushing the chair away from the table (p. 155). In this case, the text actually took over the attention of the tutor from the writer! However, McClure also described a face-to-face consultation focused on grammar that showed reciprocity and balance. It should be noted here that according to Robertson (2005), online tutorials are entirely text based, though Hewett (2006, 2010) conceived of them as just as dialogic as face-to-face sessions.

Furthermore, in Vallejo (2004), when tutors engaged in grammar-checking discourse, they became very text-centered, basically just correcting the text while the student (who in this case was an L2 writer) watched and listened. The writers in Vallejo's study wanted tutors to offer them very directive grammar correction, but tutors did not know enough about grammar to be able to explain their corrections of the students' mistakes.

Interpersonal Interactions

Several studies have investigated interpersonal factors such as who has the *author-ity* in the tutoring session, how *gender* affects the tutoring session, and the role of feelings (*affect*) on the process and results of tutoring.

Authority

Either tutor or tutee (or both) can demonstrate authority in the tutoring session. In a conversation-analytic study, Mackiewicz (1999) showed how tutor and tutee "co-constructed" their relationship as asymmetrical, with the tutor taking on the authority role. Based on her observations, Roswell (1992) argued that tutors took on the role of "hunched-shouldered authority" and tutees that of "active compliance" (pp. v–vi). Thonus (2002) noted that L2 writers, in particular, were likely to invest the tutor with authority as a "type of teacher." Mackiewicz discovered that the tutor's authority was more obvious in the "procedural frame" ("the tutor explains how the session itself will be carried out") than in the "writing discussion frame" (p. 81). A similar observation was made by Cardenas (2000), who found that the authority of the tutor allowed her to take the session in a direction that was not what the tutee had in mind. However, when speaking with the tutee about her writing, Mackiewicz observed that the tutor used extensive positive and negative politeness strategies to mitigate face-threatening acts.

It is not only the tutor who can take on a role of authority; tutees can, too. Montgomery (1994) showed how tutors encouraged their tutees to take on authority: In a group setting, tutors encouraged tutees to address not them but each other. A stance of authority can be used to take on a role in which it is appropriate to give praise and advice (McClure, 1990). This role can also backfire or be used inappropriately, as tutors may take the stance of authority to evaluate a paper negatively, and they may even hurt the tutees' feelings (Cardenas, 2000). Cardenas observed instances of tutees taking on this role, such as when the tutee was the expert on the topic or was extremely prepared for the session and knew what he or she wanted to work on.

Bell (1989) contrasted tutors' "authoritative stance" with their "passive stance" (p. 212). In one tutoring session he described, the tutor "seemed quite happy to let [the tutee] take the initiative, and he was careful about his role as an authority" (p. 158). Bean (1998) noted that the topic of grammar itself created "rigid roles, with the consultant in the position of authority and the student in a position of ignorance" (p. 149). Ritter (2002), too, found that tutors were hesitant to take on an authoritative role if they were uncomfortable with the subject matter or type of student they were tutoring, in which case they directed the session toward matters they were more confident about, such as grammar.

Gender

Little empirical research has been done on the influence of gender on writing center tutorials. Thonus (2001) examined the linguistic and interactive similarities and differences between male and female tutors in writing center consultations. The focus of the paper was on the gender of the tutors and its effects on conversational dominance and suggestion type and mitigation. Thonus (1999a) found little measurable difference in the relationship of gender to tutoring.

Hunzer (1997) argued that the gender attitudes of the tutees in her survey may have been influenced by gender stereotypes they held: "Not only did the students perceive the tutors as acting in accordance with societal gender stereotypes...but the students also attached a judgment about each tutor that was dependent upon the gender of the student" (p. 9). Bean's (1998) case study of five tutees supported her hypothesis that tutees held powerful beliefs about the intersection of gender and linguistic behavior that influenced their interactions with consultants during writing center sessions.

In contrast, Rafoth and colleagues' investigation of "Sex in the Center" (1999) found that the majority of tutors and tutees they informally surveyed believed that gender did not "matter" in the tutoring session; in particular, as compared to tutees, both male and female tutors "did most of the talking" (p. 5). However, an even greater majority of the same tutors and tutees believed that tutoring sessions would have been different if the genders of tutors and tutees were also different. In her transcript study of gender and interactional dominance, Thonus (1999) found that tutor gender had no impact on the frequency and forcefulness of directives. Based on these findings, she argued that the tutor role trumped gender as the cause of "dominance behavior."

More recently, in *Gender and the Writing Center: How Students' Problems in Writing Fall into Gendered Categories of Difference*, Threatt (2009) argued that "tutors can better serve the students if they are familiar with gender patterns or issues in writing, as they will be able to point these out to the students, getting them to recognize and potentially change these issues, and improve their writing overall" (p. 139). Threatt used transcription, coding, and qualitative analysis of 25 writing tutorials as the basis for her argument, focusing on patterns of "problems" identified in student drafts, which she had already labeled as containing conventional features of gendered writing. In presenting the results of her analysis, Threatt passed over descriptions of tutor feedback and directly to evaluation of tutoring methods, belying the title of her dissertation. In other words, readers are offered "could have/should have" evaluations of particular interactions rather than a synthesis of findings applicable to writing center practice in general. This dissertation might better have been cast as a quasi-experimental study with pretest/posttest; tutors could have been provided training in gendered response and then evaluated on the application of what they had learned. Instead, the dissertation ends with a sketch of "workshops focused on training tutors to recognize gender differences" (p. 178).

Bean (1998) claimed that writing centers are a feminized space, and that this causes discomfort for people "invested in masculine views of power and language" (p. 132). From her interviews with study participants, she concluded that "the men in my study expressed more feelings of tension and dissonance in their role as a writing center consultant than did the women." Bean also found that tutoring dyads with female tutors were more likely to have balanced amounts of talk than those with male tutors.

O'Leary (2008) discussed gender roles in consultations between writing fellows and students participating in such a program. She noticed that tutors accommodated to the gender roles that students exhibited. For instance, when a male tutee took longer turns with a female tutor, the tutor took shorter turns to accommodate him. In this same case, the male tutee completed the tutor's sentences, "seize[d] the floor several times, occasionally denied [the tutor's] suggestions, and clearly defended his point of view—behaviors the female student never exhibited" (p. 65). This accommodation is influenced by the status of the tutor and the relative formality of the session. O'Leary concluded that low-status participants in consultations (usually the tutees) exhibited more stereotypically female conversational behavior, such as agreeing with suggestions, not interrupting, and listening actively through the use of backchannels (see section on *Backchannels* below). Higher-status participants, no matter what gender, talked more, asked fewer questions, and solicited agreement. In informal conversations between a female tutor and male tutee, status and gender roles conflicted, and in this case a male will exhibit both stereotypical male and female behaviors, such as being direct, assertive, task oriented, and interrupting. In this situation, the female tutor was more likely to take on the female gendered style of allowing the tutee to interrupt. In more formal conversations, the status of the tutor overrode any gender role conflicts or issues.

Zdrojkowski (2007) found that females used more politeness strategies than male tutors. Her research results also showed that male tutors used more directives, asked more questions, initiated more topics, and inserted fewer backchannels than female tutors. However, female students issued more directives, asked more questions, initiated more topics, and interrupted more than male students.

Affect

The writing center literature includes several interesting anecdotal accounts of affect in tutorials and tutor training. One such is Bisson's "A Tutee's Tears" (2007); another is Lape's "Training Tutors in Emotional Intelligence" (2008). Unfortunately, very little empirical research has been done on affect in the writing center setting. We found two studies: Montgomery (1994), who investigated writing groups, and Babcock (2011a), who studied writing center sessions with deaf tutees. Montgomery (1994) observed that personal comfort was extremely important in the tutoring context. Using audio and video recordings as data and interviews for participant interpretations, Babcock (2011a) examined displays of affect (verbal and nonverbal). Verbal displays included expressions of gratitude or disparaging remarks about one's writing. Nonverbal displays included those of frustration: A tutor took off her glasses and sighed while tutees touched their hair, fidgeted in their chairs, played with their pencils, or hid their faces. Babcock observed that females were more likely than males to verbalize (or sign) their "interior emotional states" (p. 11). In contrast, male-male tutor-tutee dyads rarely displayed any sort of affect.

The empirical investigation of affect in the writing center setting is crucial. Educational researchers have shown the positive influence of informal learning environments (a.k.a. tutoring) on motivation (positive affect) and action (Putman & Walker, 2010), as well as the superiority of collaborative one-on-one work in generating positive affect (Waite & Davis, 2006). Cognitive scientists, computer scientists, and instructional designers have done extensive research into the role of affect in computer testing (e.g., Moridis & Economides, 2009) and in "intelligent tutoring systems" (e.g., Graesser et al., 2008; McQuiggan, Robison, & Lester, 2010). We find it amazing that one-on-one interaction between humans and so-called "virtual agents" has received more attention recently than one-on-one interaction between human tutors and tutees.

Negotiation

Nakamaru (2010), in her study of international and US-educated ESL students, found that negotiation was a key aspect of their tutoring sessions. Sometimes L2 writers' goals remained unmet because of their language proficiency. In these cases, the tutors may not have understood the tutee's oral language, so a different goal may have been agreed upon. In addition, this goal may not have even been addressed in the session! Cogie (2006) noticed that negotiation differed between L1 tutors and L2 tutees. In one tutorial she observed, the dyad successfully negotiated the meanings of words, while in another the participants could not successfully negotiate the organization and level of detail of the assignment, seemingly because the tutee did not understand the tutor's intentions.

According to the conversation analysis of Ritter (2002), negotiation occurs through particular sequences: suggestion sequences, clarification request sequences, confirmation check sequences, and extended negotiation sequences. The simple suggestion sequence will be discussed below under *Suggestions*. In clarification request sequences, the tutor reads aloud, then asks the writer a question about something that is confusing. The writer responds, and then the tutor makes a suggestion. In the confirmation check sequences, the tutor reads and then asks questions that involve re-formulating what the writer has said (*Did you mean x?*). The writer then attempts to respond with what she actually meant. This sequence can go on for a few turns before ending with a tutor suggestion. Finally, in the extended negotiation sequence, the tutor or student reads, and the sequence includes both clarification requests and confirmation checks, after which the student confirms or clarifies for the tutor. As in the above sequences, this usually ends with a tutor suggestion.

Negotiation sequences are more abbreviated in tutorials with L2 writers compared to those with L1 writers (Thonus, 2004). Williams (2004) noted that in tutorials with little negotiation, especially with L2 writers who were less active conversationalists, less revision was likely to result. Kim (2009) discovered that when tutors asked information-checking questions, it opened up a line of communication for negotiation to occur.

Agenda Setting

Agenda setting usually occurs at the beginning of a tutorial. Ritter (2002) called this the *diagnosis phase*. She found that during this phase, tutors often asked tutees about their assignments and related concerns. Tutors also asked about tutoring procedures, such as who would read the paper. In some cases, they didn't ask but stated what would happen: "I'm going to read a paragraph and then stop. And we'll see if there are any problems in there" (p. 127). Using the methodology of Conversation Analysis, Ritter suggested a structure for this phase:

> TUTOR QUESTION (INITIATING DIAGNOSIS): What is it that is worrying
> you about this paper?
> STUDENT ANSWER: I'd like to know the spelling, the grammar. Because
> you know I speak no English, so maybe I not correct.
> TUTOR PROCEDURE STATEMENT: I'll give it a read through here. I'll give
> you the pen, and when I see something, you can make the changes.
> (p. 128)

As in other adjacency pairs (as described in chapter 2) there might have been some side-sequences in which the tutor asked several questions to determine the student's focus. Ritter also noted the use of *grounders*, which are explanations by the tutor. For example, a tutor asked who would read the paper and then gave an explanation of the benefits of reading aloud. One problem that Ritter noted was that tutors sometimes made wrong assumptions about tutees in this phase, such as the tutor who assumed a tutee was a freshman when the tutee was actually a graduate student.

In tutorials with L2 writers, Thompson (2009) observed that tutors mostly followed the writer's lead in deciding the focus of the tutorial during the agenda-setting phase. These results contrast with those of Thonus (2004), who found that in L2 tutorials, tutors skipped agenda-setting entirely or shortened it considerably.

Higher- vs. Lower- (or Later-) Order Concerns

Sometimes an L2 writer arrives at the writing center wanting to focus on grammar, but the tutor sees more pressing issues in the paper having to do with logic or idea development (Blau, Hall and Sparks, 2002). Bell and Elledge (2008) discovered that L2 writers pushed their agenda of sentence-level correction even when tutors had other priorities. Nakamaru (2010) realized that L2 writers, especially international students, needed help with lexical issues, although tutors steered the focus to grammar, either because they were comfortable dealing with grammar, or in their training they were told not to provide words for a tutee. Ritter (2002) discovered through her research a category called *falling back on grammar*, which occurred when the tutor was not confident about the subject matter at hand but was confident about grammar, especially because the tutee was an L2 writer Another category that Ritter discovered related to higher- and lower-order concerns was *correcting or not correcting awkward expressions*.

Perspectives, Goals, and Roles

Hynds (1989) found that sometimes the consultant and the tutee had very different perspectives about the success of a session, or their own roles. Sometimes these could be unproductive, as in the case where a writer was insecure and the consultant did not notice. Productive dissonance occurred when tutee and tutor each struggled for control of a session, and finally the tutee experienced "a light bulb moment." The consultant was comfortable with the writer's discomfort, knowing that the writer needed to work through it, and so she persisted with non-directive questions even though the writer wanted direct advice. Hynds noted that none of the dyads she studied directly negotiated their roles or goals for the session. She suggested that tutors determine where the writer is in the writing process and how they can best be helped. Although she did not mention it, it is clear from Hynds' data that a discussion of feelings would also be a great help in the tutoring session.

Thonus (2001) determined that the tutor's role is not fixed but rather passes through "a continuum...from teacher to peer, negotiated anew in each tutorial"

(p. 61). Blau, Hall, and Strauss (1998) looked at solidarity vs. hierarchy in the tutoring session, focusing on linguistic features of questioning, echoing, and the use of qualifiers.

Finally, Corbett (2011) displayed how goals, when in conflict, can cause a breakdown in communication, with tutor and tutee talking at cross-purposes and often interrupting each other.. On the other hand, when tutor and tutee goals correspond, a collaborative session can result, with the tutor asking open-ended questions and helping the writer to jot down ideas.

Politeness and Directiveness

Due to training or to preference, tutors strive for a collaborative style during sessions, but for many, collaboration is confused or conflated with non-directiveness and politeness. Evidence-based practice should rely on research into the actual effects of polite and non-direct tutor speech on interaction with tutees and their decisions about revisions to their writing.

Directives

Blau, Hall, and Strauss (1998) was an early study of tutor avoidance of directiveness. Tutors asked questions that would have been better phrased as directives. If a tutor had some bit of information that the writer needed, the researchers argued, just telling the writer the information would have been more effective than asking questions to which the writer had no answer.

Clark (2001) and Corbett (2011) both investigated tutor behaviors along the directive/non-directive continuum. Clark reported on a 2000 study at the University of Southern California Writing Center that investigated three questions, noted in brief here:

1. Do students' perceptions of a conference as either directive or non-directive correspond to the perceptions of consultants?
2. Do different types of student writers have different perceptions of directiveness in a writing center conference?
3. Does the concept of directiveness impact students' satisfaction with a writing center conference? (p. 36)

Clark learned that consultants and writers had quite different perceptions of whether their consultants had been directive or non-directive: "Although there were some exceptions, the general tendency was for students to attribute a more significant or 'directive' role to consultants than consultants attributed to themselves" (p. 44). Tutees who considered themselves "good writers" were more likely to view consultants' impact on the interaction as less influential than tutees who considered themselves "poor writers." One of the methodological difficulties in the study was defining and exemplifying "directiveness" to writers, the "outsiders" to the writing center discourse community. Corbett (2011) attempted to use a multi-modal case study approach to measure where tutorials fall along the directive/non-directive continuum. He examined course-based tutorials in which tutors worked with writers from a particular course. Corbett triangulated results by surveying tutees, interviewing tutors and instructors, and recording tutorials. He analyzed the tutorials using familiar categories such as types of questions, overlaps, etc., resulting in a rich description of the tutorial context, but the particular factors influencing directiveness vs. non-directiveness were elusive.

Thonus (1998) found that directives could be broken down into *interaction-internal directives*, which were concerned with the here-and-now of the tutoring session, and *suggestions*, which referred to what the tutee would do outside the tutoring session. She also concluded that the sheer number of directives increased as time ran out in the tutoring sessions. Zdrojkowski (2007) observed, not surprisingly, that tutors offered more directives than did students. Interestingly, she also found that long and short tutorials evidenced more directives than average-length ones. Perhaps this is because in shorter-length tutorials, participants may be pressed for time, so the tutor may be more likely to offer directives in the name of saving time. That is, the tutor might tell the student what to fix in the paper rather than working through ideas together.

An interesting small-scale survey study by Nash (2006) investigated tutor and writer reactions to the politeness and directness of tutor utterances. She offered three L1 tutors and three L2 writers a series of bald-on-record (extremely direct), positively polite, negatively polite, and off-record (extremely indirect) utterances, asking them to identify which were (a) most and least polite, (b) most and least clear, and (c) most and least likely to be uttered during a tutorial. L2 writers classified bald-on-record utterances such as "You don't have a thesis" as "neutral," while L1 tutors characterized them as "somewhat impolite." L2 writers dismissed off-record utterances such as "Prepositions are hard in a foreign language, aren't they?" as unclear and therefore least preferred, while L1 tutors admitted they viewed such utterances as most polite" and therefore "most likely" to be uttered. Politeness strategies overall were rated as "unclear" by L2 writers; their concern was "more with clarity than with politeness" (p. 4), a finding consistent with Thonus (1999b). Nash recommended that tutors "not sacrifice clarity in an effort to be 'polite'" (p. 4) and "be aware of different cultural views of saving face and being polite" (p. 5).

Suggestions

Thonus (1999b) offered a description of the suggestion moves that occurred in the tutoring sessions she observed:

1. Tutor evaluation of global or specific problems
2. Student acceptance or rejection of the evaluation (verbal or tacit)
3. Tutor suggestion (occasionally substituted or augmented by student suggestion)
4. Student acceptance or rejection of suggestion (p. 257)

The only obligatory element in the sequence was the suggestion itself. As would be expected, most often the student accepted the tutor's suggestion. Less likely but possible was for the student to reject, deflect, or question the suggestion. Finally, sometimes the student self-suggested, usually by asking the tutor if a certain plan of action was advisable: "Should I just put 'this is the opposite'?" In shorter tutoring sessions, tutors evidenced more suggestions per turn, which is in line with the common lore that tutors are more directive when pressed for time. Finally, tutors who possessed expertise in the subject matter of writers' papers offered more suggestions per turn than those who were unfamiliar with the writers' topic(s).

Often, tutors formulate suggestions as questions to meet their own politeness expectations, sometimes frustrating both themselves and their tutees (Blau, Hall, & Strauss, 1998). For instance, instead of saying "You need a transition here," a tutor in this study asked, "Can you think of a way to make a transition sentence?" (p. 26). The tutor asked many questions that would have worked better as suggestions and moved the tutorial along more smoothly. When giving suggestions, tutors have also been found to use qualifiers to lessen their impact (Blau, Hall, & Strauss, 1998; Ritter, 2002). Tutors in Brown's (2008) study felt guilty when they offered suggestions, but the tutees valued suggestions as ways to learn and to get clear direction about what they should do with their papers. When offering suggestions for later-order concerns, tutors felt less guilty than when they offered them for higher-order concerns. Writers also valued suggestions accompanied by the recitation of a rule that was understandable to them; they felt they learned more this way.

Ritter (2002) coded suggestion types according to illocutionary force, which is related to the pragmatic directiveness of the suggestion. Ritter's types were *indirect suggestion* ("It's a little confusing."), *interrogative* ("Does this paragraph kind of repeat some information?"), *first-person modal* ("I'd put an S on checklists."), *second-person modal* ("You wanna make that plural."), *repair* ("*During* these years, instead of *at* these years."), and *imperative* ("Just put a period there.") (p. 141). These categories are identical to those of Thonus (1998) except for the addition of *repair*. In

Ritter's conversation analysis, a simple suggestion sequence consisted of the tutor or tutee reading aloud and the tutor making a suggestion, sometimes with a *grounder* (explanation for the suggestion), and sometimes offering the tutee an *either/or* choice. The tutor or the tutee could also read the writer's draft, and the tutee stopped and asked a question or made a statement, eliciting a suggestion from the tutor. Sometimes the tutor even invited the tutee to ask a question. The tutor then offered a suggestion, sometimes after negotiating meaning.

Thonus (1998) created a scale with ten levels of directness with mitigated and unmitigated versions of each one. According to study participants, the most directive of these types were the second-person modal and the imperative. Williams (2005) used a similar framework, specifically looking at mitigation. Certain modals (*could, might*) can soften the directiveness of an utterance, while others (*must, should*) can heighten it. Also, an interrogative can mitigate directiveness while an imperative will strengthen it. Sometimes tutors will use both types of mitigators in their discourse. In William's study data, tutors used more mitigation with L1 writers and more direct suggestions and upgraders with L2 writers. The explanation for this is that these would enhance comprehensibility for each group. O'Leary (2008) observed a tutee that used very indirect "interrogative or specific modal suggestions, primarily to propose revision strategies, solicit information on topics related to writing and revision, and affirm the writing fellow's suggestions" (p. 66).

Zdrojkowski (2007) used the following mitigation categories: *interrogative* ("So, could you use the story as sort of an opening tease for the entire piece?"), *subjunctive* ("You might want to reword it."), *conditional* ("Actually, I would just like you to read it over and maybe suggest something."), *aspect* ("I'm thinking that's a little off."), *tense* ("I was wondering if we might do something with this."), *politeness marker* ("All right well, if you wouldn't mind...uh filling out, uh, just filling this out."), *understater* ("I mean it's kind of vague is what I'm saying."), and *hedge* ("Yeah, just if you could describe just in a sentence.") (p. 127). Thonus (1998) used a similar list with the addition of *appealer* ("Right?"), *cajoler* ("you know"), *downtoner* ("You probably want to fill this out."), *subjectivizer* ("it seems to me"), *and upgrader* ("Again, you want to, what you want to ask yourself...") (p. 94). Thonus did not include *politeness marker* in her categories, but it appears that most of these served as such politeness markers.

Harkening back to Brown and Levinson (1987), Bell, Arnold, and Haddock (2009) argued that "writing center conversation, like other kinds of conversations, is a face-threatening situation mediated through politeness" (p. 40). The authors investigated two tutor-tutee pairs' use of politeness in sessions over a six-week period. What is important to note is that all sessions featured first-year students who were first-time writing center visitors. In their initial sessions, tutors exploited the peer relationship by using positive politeness strategies such as laughter and negative politeness strategies such as hedges and minimizers ("Just change a little bit, then"). By the sixth session, tutors were using fewer negative politeness strategies and more positive ones, especially suggestions phrased as "we." Bell and colleagues concluded that negative politeness served an important purpose: "Tutors can emphasize the magnitude of the student's role...and minimize the student's dependence on the tutor" (p. 51). Their growing reliance on positive politeness strategies as the tutorial relationship developed was effective in creating and maintaining rapport. These results underscore findings by Zdrojkowski (2007) about laughter and Thonus (2008) about acquaintanceship and familiarity.

The relationship of tutor and tutee gender and suggestion type and mitigation has been investigated by several researchers. Thonus (1999a) measured frequency of suggestions and noted that female tutors made more suggestions per turn than male tutors. L1 tutees and male tutees also "received more suggestions from their tutors than did [L2] tutees and female tutees" (p. 235), and L2 writers were less likely to receive polite (mitigated) suggestions than L1 writers. She also measured suggestions by type and second person modals (*you could, you should*, etc.) accounted for 50% of suggestion types, and Thonus (2002) reported similar findings. Suggestions were the same types mentioned in Ritter (2002) and Thonus (1999a). In this study, female tutors "were more likely to offer unmitigated suggestions" (p. 241), but they "tended to mitigate their suggestions more frequently in mixed- rather than same-gender dyads" (p. 242). O'Leary (2008) established that a female tutor working with a female student rarely made interrogative suggestions but rather indirect or modal suggestions, this in contrast to the same tutor's session with a male student, in which both participants made fairly similar suggestions. The male tutee, like his female counterpart, offered mostly interrogative suggestions, while the female tutor made specific modal suggestions. At no point did the female tutor offer a male tutee an imperative suggestion, something she did do with a female tutee.

Rejections

In general, both L1 and L2 writers were more likely to accept tutor suggestions than to reject them (Thonus, 2004). Y. J. Kim (2007), however, noted that in tutorials in which both the tutor and tutee were L2 writers (L2-L2 interactions), tutee rejections of tutor advice were quite common. Thonus (2002) realized that most rejections were supported by accounts (narrative explanations) or masked by another conversational move, such as agreeing while laughing, essentially indicating the opposite of what had been said.

Sometimes tutors reject when tutees solicit advice that tutors think is too direct or too much help. For instance, Williams (2005) observed a tutor refusing to "give" a tutee "an idea" when asked to (p. 51). When the tutee asked for an idea, the tutor responded, "I can't really *give* you an idea," and suggested that the tutee think of a title. When the tutee asked for a title, the tutor answered, "I can't really give you a title." Williams also observed a tutor getting miffed when a tutee rejected one of his suggestions by answering "maybe" (a favorite answer to challenges and refusals by L2 learners of English). Interestingly, the tutor suspected that this writer came to the writing center only to "collect the payment offered for participation in the project" (p. 54).

Through conversation analytic work, Waring (2005) found evidence that "advice resisting" was an important and "integral part" of peer tutoring (p. 146). She noted the following aspects of advice resisting in a graduate tutoring session:

1. Resist advice on general academic writing issues
   - Cite resource difficulty
2. Resist advice on specific content-related matters
   - Assert own agenda
   - Invoke authority
   - Doing being irrational
3. Resist advice on mechanics of writing
   - Minimize import of advice

This advice resisting, obviously, is a "dispreferred" response. Waring wrote, "The one who produced the advice may, for example, strengthen his/her initial suggestion by providing further support/accounts, launch a counter-argument, initiate repair ... or back down" (p. 151). The only one of these that was not self-explanatory was *doing being irrational*. In this case, the tutee had no reason to resist the advice besides the fact that she didn't "want to" work any more on her literature review (p. 158).

Paralinguistic Features

Volubility

Volubility is otherwise known as time at talk, and according to some linguists, it indicates dominance, meaning the dominant interlocutor talks more. One caveat is that since tutors and tutees often read aloud during tutoring sessions, perhaps measures of volubility will be skewed if researchers measure words read aloud in addition to spoken conversation.

Y.-K. Kim (2009) suggested through interviews with tutors and writing center directors that time-at-talk was an indication of collaboration, meaning that in a truly collaborative consultation the tutee would talk just as much as the tutor. In a session in which the tutor talked more, increased time-at-talk would demonstrate an asymmetrical relationship, with the tutor having greater control. In her study, L1 tutees as a whole spoke more words per turn than L2 tutees, but this varied with the tutor; therefore, the tutor's conception of the tutoring session, whether collaborative or under the tutor's control, affected turn length. One tutor spoke more words per turn with L1 tutees and fewer with L2 tutees, indicating her focus on more global issues with L1 writers and with specific concerns like grammar with L2 writers. This same tutor had a high ratio of words per turn in a first-time visit with an L1 tutee, presumably to orient the tutee to the procedures of the writing center and of writing in general. In general, Kim discovered that both tutors spoke more than their tutees, and L2 speakers spoke fewer words per turn overall than L1 speakers.

Bell and Elledge (2008) found that tutors on average talked 62% of the time, while tutees talked 38% of the time. O'Leary (2008) discussed volubility, but she did not quantify talk as did other researchers, so it is difficult to make comparisons between her study and others. She did note that time-at-talk appeared to be related to preparedness, as a student who came to his tutorial unprepared did very little talking. Williams (2005) measured turn length as a factor of dominance and learned that tutors in general took longer turns, with one exception being a tutoring session with an L1 writer. In sessions with L2 writers, the tutors' turns were always longer, and they were proportionally longer than those with L1 writers.

Thonus (1999b) concluded that in accordance with common lore, tutors dominated the tutorial conversation in terms of time-at-talk. Thonus (2002) found that tutors spoke one and a half times more than their tutees (with one exception), and they spoke even more with L2 writers than with L1 writers. Zdrojkowski (2007) also noted that tutors took longer turns than students, averaging "slightly over three times the number of words per turn as do students" (p. 120). In this study of L2-L2 tutorials, Y. J. Kim (2007) discovered that L2 tutors were just as likely as L1 tutors to dominate both in terms of turn length and topic persistence. Stachera (2003) listened to audio recordings and looked at transcriptions, seeking to analyze the "symmetry" between tutor and tutee time at talk. She equated asymmetry—with tutor time at talk being longer than tutee time at talk—with dominance. Not surprisingly, given research outcomes of previous studies (Thonus, 1999a; Taylor, 2007; Kim, 2009), Stachera discovered that tutor talk filled up to 96% of the first 600 words of each consultation.

Interruptions and Overlaps

Williams (2005) looked at interruptions and overlaps in tutoring sessions and learned that overwhelmingly tutors interrupted writers, with writers interrupting tutors very rarely if at all. Some overlaps occurred in Williams' data when the tutee struggled for a word or idea, and after a few seconds of wait time, the tutor offered something at the same time that the tutee came up with something, producing an overlap. Williams called these *rescues*, and O'Leary noticed a similar phenomenon and called it by a longer and more colloquial name: someone finishing another's sentence for them.

Thonus (1998) identified several different types of overlaps. These were "the initiation of a contribution by a second party before the first has finished" (p. 85), which can include *latching* or *absolute adjacency*, *joint production*, which involves one party finishing the utterance of another and can also include *predictable utterance completions*; or main channel overlap, which is "simultaneous speech without taking the floor" (p. 86). Thonus (1999b) found that "tutors were far more likely to interrupt students than were students to interrupt tutors" (p. 264). In Thonus (2002), data showed tutors and tutees overlapping at the same rate, with tutee interruptions actually a bit more frequent. Participants rated these overlaps as affiliative (that is, enhancing the relationship). Disaffiliative overlaps (those with abrupt topic changes, for instance) were more likely to be viewed as interruptions by participants. Thonus (1998, 2004) noted that overlaps in general were rare in sessions with L2 writers.

Thompson (2009) noted that through overlaps and backchanneling, a tutee could indicate both interest and agreement. The overlaps that she noticed involved the tutee saying a word at the same time as the tutor, indicating involvement and, to an extent, an ability to predict what the tutor would say.

O'Leary (2008) discussed overlaps together with interruptions. In a session between a male tutee and a female writing fellow, the two interrupted and overlapped each other equally, with the student actually having more successful interruptions. With a second tutor whose conferencing style was more formal, O'Leary noticed little interruption and overlap. Indeed, one tutee who tried to interrupt was unsuccessful each time. In a tutoring session with a female tutor and a male tutee there was much interruption and overlap, these were disruptive, and the female tutor was more likely to gain the floor.

Like O'Leary, Zdrojkowski (2007) discovered few overlaps in her transcript data, so perhaps the tutorials she observed were more in the "formal" vein. She did notice that same-sex dyads tended to evidence more overlaps than mixed dyads. In her data, she observed more interruptions than overlaps, indicating a more hierarchical relationship rather than a collaborative one. Surprisingly, the tutee tended to interrupt the tutor more often than the reverse.

Backchannels and Echoing

Backchanneling involves minimal responses that verify that the interlocutor is listening but do not serve to take the floor. Common backchannels in American

English are *uh-huh, o.k., (all) right, yeah,* and *oh* (Thonus, 2007), each of which signals a slightly different level of interactivity (Stenström, 1994).

In writing center tutorials, Thonus (2002) found that "with three exceptions, students backchanneled more often than their tutors" (p. 122). Specifically, L2 writers were more likely to backchannel than their L1 writer peers. Zdrojkowski's (2007) research showed that tutees backchanneled much more than tutors, with only one exception (an older female tutor paired with an older female student). She also concluded that laughter could function as a backchannel, though it was unclear what its specific functions were. O'Leary (2008) noticed that both female tutors in her study offered few to no backchannel cues when a female tutee was talking. On the other hand, tutees offered backchannels when the tutor was talking. With a male tutee and a female tutor, few backchannels were used at all. Williams (2005) discovered that backchannel behavior was more individually varied, with the tutors using the same amount of backchanneling with different students, and she found no difference between L1 and L2 speakers of English. Overall, student writers used less backchanneling than tutors. Since this finding directly contrasts with O'Leary's, more research must be done.

Thonus (1998) uncovered evidence to suspect that ample backchanneling may not signal supportive listening but instead impatience or hurry. In some cases, backchannels served as an attempt to take the floor or "to signal displeasure" (p. 402).

Participants in a study by Blau, Hall, and Strauss (1998), especially L2 writers, mirrored or echoed their interlocutors' use of sentence structure. Tutors and tutees were also sensitive to each other's backchannel cues because they picked up on them and repeated them. This echoing could take on a playful tone, as Haas (1986) also noted. Thonus (1998) found that echoing "signals agreement with the interlocutor's previous statement and launches the listener into his/her own turn" (p. 403)

Pauses

Gilewicz and Thonus (2003), in an article about the use and importance of accurately transcribing tutoring sessions, demonstrated the meanings and use of reflection on pauses and silence in tutoring. One tutor, when reflecting on a transcription of one of his tutoring sessions, discovered that pauses—silences—could be productive, although at first it appeared that he was setting impossible tasks for his tutees to complete during those pauses. His writing center director suggested that he allow tutees to compose a thesis on paper rather than attempt to do so orally. Another tutor used pauses to write and think, although sometimes less productively. She asked several questions of the tutee, leaving long pauses, presumably to give the tutee time to answer, while not realizing that perhaps the tutee had not understood the question or felt flustered by the tutor "piling up" questions when the tutee did not answer them. Corbett (2011) witnessed a pause of 89 seconds between a tutor asking a question and a tutee giving a relevant, detailed answer.

Laughter

Laughter has its place in tutoring sessions, and several researchers have investigated it. It can be used to make criticism easier to accept, and it can serve as a sort of padding for the emotional blows of criticism of self or other. Laughter can occur in tutoring sessions for tutees who strive for a high level of achievement and those in which tutor and tutee have very different levels of subject knowledge (Thonus, 1998). Thonus also realized that laughter could signal embarrassment, "admission of error or confusion" (p. 213) as well as sometimes stand in for a conversational turn. Laughter also could signal an outcome that was acceptable to both parties after some tension or stress. Two tutorials in Thonus' data exhibited no laughter at all, while participants in L1 tutor-L2 tutee pairs were less likely to laugh overall than those when both participants were L1 speakers of English.

Boudreaux (1998) saw laughter as signaling rapport, and noted that it could also be used to diffuse awkwardness, such as when asking for a favor or for personal information. McClure (1990) found that participants in her study laughed when they felt at ease or when they were especially pleased with a solution to a problem. Thonus (2002) heard little laughter in the tutorials she observed, but in the one that did have laughter, "the participants interpreted the laughter as a move toward 'peerness'" (p. 129).

Thonus (2008) noted that most of the laughter in writing tutorials she studied (84%) was single-party laughter. Of this single-party laughter, two-thirds was student laughter. In tutorials with very little laughter, all of it was single-party and almost all was tutee laughter. Thonus explained that "students...usually engaged in single-party laughter to display nervousness or to acknowledge error." Tutors used single-party laughter to "assert authority or to underline a critique or directive. They also used laughter to mitigate directives" (p. 342). The second type of laughter Thonus examined was coordinated laughter, which could be sequenced—this is when one party laughs and the other joins in—or simultaneous—when they laugh together. Usually, in the cases of sequenced laughter, it was the tutor who laughed first. As higher-status interlocutors, tutors were not obligated to join in with tutee laughter. Both tutors and tutees felt that simultaneous laughter made for a successful tutorial. Episodes of extended laughter were more rare in the data, but in all cases the tutee was female, while the tutors were both male and female. As Thonus hypothesized, coordinated laughter was more likely in tutorials in which tutor and tutee were acquainted. One exception was a last-minute tutorial that was required by the teacher: Perhaps the stress involved caused the participants to laugh to blow off steam.

Zdrojkowski (2007) wrote the most comprehensive study of laughter in writing tutorials thus far. She found that three-quarters of all laughter was initiated by tutors, and the same amount of responses to laughter came from tutors. The most common type of laughter initiation was *mitigation for self,* laughter that stemmed from a person being anxious or tense, especially about his or her lack of knowledge. This type of laughter came much more often from students than tutors with only one exception. However, tutors initiated more *mitigation for the other person* laughter, since students did not initiate this kind of laughter at all. Finally, *affiliative* laughter was used to support a speaker's utterance or action, and while both tutors and tutees evidenced this type of laughter, tutees did so four times as often as tutors.

In line with research on institutional discourse, the most common response from tutors to tutee laughter was neutral, and second was affiliative laughter, but affiliative responses could also be verbal or nonverbal. Counter to expectation, affiliative response rates were greater than would be suspected in purely institutional discourse. This is probably because tutors are interested in lessening the hierarchy between themselves and their tutees. A neutral response, when offered after a self-mitigating laugh, was actually supportive, because to laugh meant that the hearer agreed with the "negative self-assessment" (p. 209), but sometimes this lack of laughter was actually disaffiliative if the speaker appeared to want the hearer to join in. Laughter could function as a backchannel, mostly in response to a *laughable.* But tutees were far more likely to use laughter as a backchannel. Some tutors did not do so at all, and the ones who did, did so only minimally, with only one exception in her data. Interestingly, Zdrojkowski noted less laughter in tutorials between graduate-student tutors and undergraduate tutees, while tutoring sessions between two undergraduates of approximately the same standing evidenced more laughter. Also, there was some indication that pairs who were more familiar with each other evidenced more laughter.

Nonverbal Communication

Boudreaux (1998) studied eight tutorials between two different tutors and six different writers, paying close attention to paralinguistic behaviors such as eye gaze, silence, and laughter, in addition to turn-taking behaviors such as latching (near overlap) and simultaneous speech (actual overlap). Before and after tutorials, Boudreaux interviewed participants to "ascertain their expectations beforehand and their perceptions afterwards" (p. iv). She found that when tutors and tutees shared the same paralinguistic and turn-taking behaviors, "the sessions went smoothly with few or no repairs" (p. v). When tutors and tutees did not share the same behaviors, "disharmony" was the result, and participants often reported feeling uncomfortable. Boudreaux recommended that tutors make their expectations for tutee involvement clear at the beginning of consultations or check frequently for tutee response: "I have a thing about being sure I'm getting across to you. So when you understand what I'm talking about, just say 'Umhmm' or look at me and nod your head. Otherwise, I'll think I'm not being clear, and I'll go on and on and bore us both to death" (p. 150).

GAZE. Boudreaux (1998) argued that eye gaze was an important indicator of "harmony" or "disfluency" in the tutoring session, although she mused that the difference or similarity in the use of eye gaze could be a contributing factor, "while the difference in gender and background of the participants may cause the particular nonverbal behavior" (p. 100). One dyad, Eleanor (tutor) and Brad (tutee), looked at each other infrequently, while another dyad, Eleanor (tutor) and Callie (tutee), frequently looked at the same thing, whether it was each other, the paper, or away. Brad's lack of eye gaze and backchanneling caused Eleanor to monologue or talk on and on, but her talk with Callie was well balanced. Boudreaux discovered that simultaneous eye gaze, whether between tutor or tutee or both at the paper, was indicative of rapport. She indicated the possibility that their similar age and gender could cause them to have similar nonverbal styles. Boudreaux wrote of one tutor who used her eye gaze and facial expression to keep the writer on the topic. If the writer strayed too far from the topic, the tutor looked at the writer and stopped smiling or talking. This technique was effective in returning the writer to the task.

GESTURE. Thompson (2009) was one of the first to study the formal meanings of gestures in tutoring sessions. For instance, in one episode in Thompson's research, she noted a tutor providing *direct instruction* by making a hand gesture to indicate the length of the writer's paper, comparing its current length to the desired length. *Cognitive scaffolding* was achieved by the use of gesture such as the tutor pausing and halting all movements until the student responded. *Motivational scaffolding* was achieved through a teasing gesture that helped to build rapport with the tutee as well as open-handed gestures motioning towards the tutee.

A recent conversation-analytic study of gestures in L2 conversational tutoring (Seo & Koshik, 2010) investigated how tutors signal the need for repair (correction). The researchers found that tutees understood two tutor gestures as signals for repair: (a) head poke and upper body movement forward, and (b) head turn, which prompted the tutee to self-correct an error, or (c) a combination of both. The researchers also noticed that "these gestures were held [unmoving] until the problem targeted by the repair initiator was resolved" (p. 2224). Seo and Koshik wondered whether these gestures were typical only of L1-L2 tutoring interactions or whether their results could be generalized to other contexts. We would be curious to replicate their study in the writing center.

PHYSICAL ORIENTATION. We uncovered only one study in the RAD literature on writing centers that addressed physical orientation (positioning) of tutor and tutee. Babcock (2011a) discussed her observations of "where to sit and whom to address" (p. 106) in interpreted writing center tutorials with deaf tutees. She found three possible seating arrangements: tutee and interpreter next to one another with the tutor opposite (the convention preferred by interpreters); tutor and tutee next to one another with the interpreter opposite; and tutor and tutee next to one another at a computer with the interpreter next to the computer. The second and third configurations, Babcock noted, allowed the tutor and tutee to interact in written English unaided by the interpreter—something the tutees seemed to prefer.

Recommendations for Practice

So much of the material in this chapter is descriptive in nature, and much of it, such as laughter, eye gaze, and overlap, is beyond conscious control. However, we are able to offer a few suggestions:

- Openly negotiate with the writer his or her goals for the session and what each of your roles will be (Hynds, 1989).
- Don't ask questions when a simple statement would do (Blau, Hall, & Strauss, 1998).
- Don't assume a collaborative frame (Kim, 2009). Be flexible, as the tutee may have other ideas for how the tutorial should proceed.
- Pay attention to nonverbal cues and possible differences in interaction styles (Boudreaux, 1998).
- Engage in teacher-research by video- or audio-taping your tutoring sessions, transcribing them, and reflecting on the details of interaction as explained in this chapter.

CHAPTER SEVEN

A Sample Research Question: What Is a Successful Tutorial?

"We can help you to be a better writer." This writing center slogan displayed on posters across a college campus implies a theory of development that writers can indeed become "better" and provides an assurance that the writing center is an environment that promotes such development (Carroll, 2002, p. xi).

Just what is a "successful" writing center tutorial? For many of us, the answer is, "We know it when we see it." Our knowledge is tacit. But we must have some idea since the multitude of tutoring manuals, workshop, and conference presentations exist for some purpose—and it is certainly *not* to fail at supporting writers, but rather to *succeed*. But succeed at what? Here are some conceivable (positive) outcomes:

- Satisfying the tutor, the writer, or both
- Satisfying the course instructor
- Engaging in meaningful interaction about writing with a peer
- Creating better writing
- Creating a better writer
- Helping the writer revise his/her project for the better
- Identifying writing skills that are transferable to future projects
- Helping the writer get a better grade on his/her project

- Creating incentives for a repeat visit by the writer
- Creating incentives for instructors to refer more students to the writing center

And certainly there are more.

A second important question: How many of these outcomes can be investigated empirically? And a third question: How many of these outcomes can be investigated within the ethical and institutional constraints within which writing centers operate? Boquet (1995) noted that writing centers have often used "documentation as information" as "documentation as justification" in arguing for their effectiveness (p. 62). Are there times that writing center administrators have "tweaked" that documentation to satisfy the whims of those that hold the purse strings?

Here is an (actual) example. A writing center director is asked by his supervisor to show how writing center use contributes to student retention and graduation, a key priority for the university. Unsurprisingly, the writing center director sees an opportunity to prove the writing center's worth and to possibly garner additional funding for the next fiscal year. The supervisor suggests that the director collaborate with the English Department's first- and second-year writing program. Students from selected sections of first-year composition would be monitored for writing center usage and for final portfolio grades. Ostensibly, those students who visited the writing center for support would earn higher course grades, raise their grade-point averages, and be retained as university students from first to second year. What could be simpler?

Unfortunately, nothing about this situation is simple. First of all, can writing center tutorial success be measured empirically? And if so, how? Satisfaction surveys? Discourse analyses of student paper revisions? Comparing mid-term with end-of-semester grades? Second, what definitions of "success" are implied in this project? The director's supervisor most probably defines writing center success as not only helping writers get better grades on their papers but also better grades in the course. The first- and second-year writing program defines writing center success as helping the writer revise his or her project for the better, which may or may not be reflected in an improved or passing course grade (e.g., grades could be as much about attendance as they are about writing quality). The writing program may also value a writing center that "satisfies" course instructors or at least one that avoids instructing students in a way contrary to instructors' goals. On the other hand, writing center definitions of "success" may rate none of these as important. Given the "hands off" relationship between the writing center and course instructors, writing center administrators may be agnostic about student revisions and grades. In fact, many writing centers have a policy of keeping students' writing center visits confidential, sharing information with course instructors only with the writers' permission.

For their part, writing centers are more prone to define "success" as "better writers," taking a long view of writing and writing development. Writing center participants should feel satisfied with the time spent, fulfilling the administrative (and pedagogical) goal of repeat visits by the writer. If the work done in the writing center consultation satisfies the course instructor, good; if it doesn't, so be it. Instructor referrals of future students to the writing center are seen as less important than meeting a particular writer's goals in individual sessions.

In this chapter, we aim to investigate all aspects of writing tutorial success, moving beyond individual writing centers' assessments to potentially more generalizable outcomes. Before doing so, however, we step back from the appraisal of academic writing tutoring to the appraisal of academic tutoring in general. In this way, we hope to find research questions, approaches, methods, and outcomes that will be instructive to those investigating writing centers.

Success in Academic Tutoring

Success in Developmental Education

Writing center scholars have taken great pains to characterize our work as nonremedial. In comparison, the field of developmental education has also wrestled with the definition and measurement of "success" for some time. Developmental education researchers Casazza and Silverman (1996), for example, echo our concern about the dearth of empirical research in writing center studies:

> It becomes clear that we need to strengthen the research component of our field. Our experiences are significant, and in order to ensure that they become part of the growing body of literature dedicated to learning assistance and developmental education, we need to validate them formally. One way to do so is by applying the process of scientific investigation more regularly to our practice. This will help make our accomplishments today a resource for tomorrow's practitioner. (p. 213)

One research outcome the authors envisioned was creating "the unifying framework that will be essential to our establishing a coherent professional identity" (p. 247).

Because developmental education studies are almost all grant funded (i.e., through the National Center for Developmental Education), qualitative and quantitative research methods have been used for some time. Based on empirical research, developmental educators know that "well trained tutors, as opposed to untrained or marginally trained tutors, is what separates successful tutoring programs from mediocre tutoring programs" (Boylan, 2002, pp. 49–50). Such educators also know that successful tutor training programs include study of "learning theory, metacognition, motivation, counseling/interviewing, group dynamics, and adult learning models" (p. 50). They also know that both group and individual tutoring can be effective, but the evidence is unclear whether peer or professional tutors produce better results (p. 49). Developmental educators, therefore, can draw a distinction between knowledge and lore in their field, between research findings and "tips" (Boylan, 2002).

Boylan and colleagues (1992) surveyed 150 institutions and uncovered five major criteria for individual "best practices":

1. It must have been cited in several scientific research studies of the effect of developmental education.
2. It must have been cited over time in the research on effective developmental education.
3. It must have been successfully replicated at several college or university campuses.
4. It must have been considered by expert professionals participating in the study as important for developmental education.
5. It must have had supporting research and evaluation data using sound methodology to validate its effectiveness at institutions where it has been applied. (Boylan, 2002)

Rarely do best practices in writing center work meet even one of these criteria. This suggests to us how far writing center researchers have yet to go in supporting our claims of effectiveness.

Success in Peer Education

The use of one-on-one tutoring (expert-novice) as a superior alternative to classroom teaching is well supported. Bloom (1984) demonstrated that students who participated in tutoring performed an average of two standard deviations better on assessments than those taught in traditional classroom settings. More recently, Graesser and Person (1994) showed that students asked questions 240 times as frequently in tutorials as they did in class, and that the quality of their questions increased with more tutoring sessions, leading to higher achievement. Further research uncovered even more positive outcomes when the tutor was a peer. We would do well to thoroughly investigate the peer-tutoring literature. "Of course!" writing center administrators and tutors exclaim: We've "known" that putting the "peer" into collaborative tutoring creates a superior learning environment from the outset. But have we "proven" it? Best practices in peer tutoring in education are heavily supported by RAD research, but empirical inquiry in writing center work is running approximately 20 years behind, as we will demonstrate in this review of the literature.

Peer education researchers, like writing center researchers, find their theoretical roots in collaborative learning (Bruffee, 1978, 1999) and cooperative learning (Slavin, 1996). Researchers have found collaborative/cooperative learning to be effective in a broad range of educational contexts (Johnson & Johnson, 1992; King, 1998). A well-known study by Yarrow and Topping (2001), for example, learned that Paired Writing, in which students wrote together and both students were trained in metacognitive prompting and scaffolding, produced better writing quality for students matched by gender and pre-experiment writing scores as compared with students who wrote alone. In the writing pairs, each student spent equal time as a "writer" and "helper," and each performed a self-analysis and peer analysis as part of their interaction. The fact that this study was conducted in an elementary-school class of 10- and 11-year-olds has not escaped us: We wonder whether the emphasis on "individual achievement" in secondary and tertiary education has denied writers of valuable formative experience.

Chi, Roy, & Hausmann (2008) hoped to link the effectiveness of tutoring with the effectiveness of collaboration by creating a new learning environment: Pairs of students collaboratively observed and discussed a videotape of another student being tutored in physics (by an expert). Three control conditions were also set: (a) A pair of students collaborating on a physics assignment; (b) two students being tutored individually by expert physics tutors; and (c) two students individually observing a videotape of another student being tutored. Results showed that collaborative vicarious learning was just as effective as one-on-one tutoring. Based on these findings, Chi and colleagues formulated the "active/constructive/interactive observing hypothesis" (p. 336): (a) Tutees who actively interacted with their tutors and constructed meaning based on tutor scaffolding were successful learners; (b) lone observers, if actively observing, learned just as much as those interacting one-on-one with a tutor; and (c) the more interactive collaborators became while observing others being tutored, the more they learned.

Note that Chi and colleagues are cognitive scientists whose goal is to create a computer-based learning interface as effective as person-to-person interaction (see also Graesser et al., 2004). Writing center professionals, of course, do not want to be replaced by machines. How can we design a study to test Chi and colleagues' hypotheses in a writing center setting? It would not be that difficult. For example, the results of their study suggest strong support for group tutoring in the writing center, as we detailed in Chapters 3 and 4. Comparing the effectiveness of collaborative one-on-one peer tutoring to collaborative peer group tutoring to *observa-*

tions of one-on-one peer tutoring to *observations* of group tutoring presents an important research goal for writing centers.

In sum, then, collaborative/cooperative learning is different from but not exclusive of peer tutoring, though some studies have shown that one-on-one peer tutoring continues to produce more effective outcomes (e.g., Pilkington & Parker-Jones, 1996). But what exactly is *peer tutoring*? Hock, Deshler, and Schumaker (1999) examined the polysemy of the term: *Tutoring* can mean one-on-one instruction, or it can mean "assignment assistance" (p. 102). Slavin (1996) proposed four definitions of *peer tutoring*: elaborated explanations, peer modeling, peer practice, and peer assessment and correction (p. 52). Topping (1996) proposed a 10-dimensional descriptive typology for tutoring, ranging from *curriculum content* to *place, time, tutor and tutee characteristics,* and *role continuity.* He theorized that pairings of each of these ten dimensions would result in a large number of different configurations, all of them termed "tutoring," some of them not yet in existence. By 2005, Topping had extended the descriptive typology to 13 "organizational variables of peer learning," adding dimensions including *voluntary/compulsory.* Accounts of writing centers and writing center tutoring have long suffered from a lack of a cross-institutional typology such as this; how useful one would be in any writing center research project, especially in a study of success!

The peer-tutoring research is brimming with meta-analyses of effectiveness. For example, Maheady (1998) traced the educational and collective advantages and disadvantages of peer tutoring programs based on 600 empirical studies (emphasis ours). While we stress that participants in most of these studies were elementary and secondary pupils, rather than university students, the results of the meta-analysis may apply to writing center tutoring at the university level. Peer tutoring advantages Maheady cited included

- Increased frequency of positive social interaction
- Improved self-concept and attitudes toward school
- Increased time on task
- Increased response opportunities
- Increased opportunity for and immediacy of error correction
- Increased remediation of learning difficulties and prevention of future academic failure. (pp. 49–52)

The only disadvantages Maheady noted that are relevant outside the classroom context were quality control of peer tutoring and the possibility of undue reliance on tutors (pp. 54–56).

Falchikov (2001) investigated academic, metacognitive, study skills, and non-academic outcomes in peer tutoring research over 30 years. The 1970s, she wrote, saw a focus on pragmatic aims such as "the need to improve learning without increased financial cost to universities" (p. 68). In the 1980s, the "experimental method" tested theoretical predictions; studies focused on problem-solving, improved student learning, and investigations of the tutoring process (p. 68). Reports of positive outcomes for tutors were also prominent. In the 1990s, research focused on the *effectiveness* of peer tutoring and its contribution to skills development and student retention (p. 69). During that decade, tutor and tutee outcomes dominated research reports. Falchikov's meta-analysis included studies on cross-level and unequal peer tutoring, and from there, we focused on her findings for same-level, equal-status peer tutoring. Outcomes in this category included improved "low-level cognitive skills" (learning definitions, memorizing concepts, vocabulary building) (p. 70) as well as better performance by students working with peers as opposed to working alone (p. 71). Study skills such as notetaking and affect and attitudes towards the subject matter also improved.

Gordon and colleagues (2007) asked, "Has tutoring worked?" Their meta-analysis of empirical research yielded findings that are applicable to writing center tutoring, specifically:

- The location of the tutoring sessions may maximize long-term student results.
- Use scaffolded instruction.
- Spend an adequate amount of time on tasks.
- Don't focus on narrow, isolated instructional activities.

Tutoring succeeds because of personal involvement between the tutor and tutee and provision of immediate and relevant feedback (pp. 166-176). Yet "personal involvement" is not the primary motivator of change, according to Cromley and Azevedo (2005), who researched the role of scaffolding in the tutoring of reading. While motivational scaffolding was evidenced by tutors' direct negative feedback to tutee errors and feedback such as "Try that again," cognitive scaffolding included "simplifying problems, hinting, asking open-ended questions...and prompting" (p. 89). Thus, more experienced tutors "used significantly more cognitive scaffolding and significantly less motivational scaffolding" than less experienced reading tutors (p. 83).

Individual studies have also demonstrated the ways in which peer tutoring affects educational outcomes, though not always in the ways hypothesized. Reinheimer and McKenzie (2011), for example, explored the relationship between peer tutoring and retention rates of 207 first-time, full-time undeclared freshmen in a four-year longitudinal study. Undeclared students often share these qualities: They are academically underprepared, unable to make long-term career decisions, and/or not ready to make a decision (yet). They found that tutoring had a significant impact on the retention and graduation rates of this demographic, though not conclusively on overall GPA. In earlier research, Roscoe and Chi (2007) studied how peer tutors could best benefit (or "learn") from tutorial interaction. They observed that the few tutors in this study who built up *reflective knowledge* through "self-monitoring of comprehension, integration of new and prior knowledge, and collaboration in construction of knowledge" benefited more from tutoring than those engaged in *knowledge-telling* (p. 534). Writing center research has yet to either quantify or qualify tutor learning in "successful" interactions.

Based on individual studies and meta-analyses of peer tutoring effectiveness, researchers have gathered what they term "best learning assistance practices." For instance, Arendale (2010) identified 50 best practices, several of which coincide with *de facto* writing center practices: "Offering drop in learning assistance centers" (p. 96); "using cooperative and collaborative learning activities to engage students in learning" (p. 98); "providing continuous professional development for all learning assistance positions" (p. 99); and "managing faculty and student expectations of learning assistance capabilities" (p. 103). Less consonant with writing center practices were "using rigorous qualitative and quantitative evaluation models" and "adopting national standards in specific areas related to learning assistance" (p. 101). In trying to distance ourselves from developmental and peer education, do writing centers overlook the very mechanisms that can only legitimate our work to the academy?

Two ongoing research programs have focused specifically on the peer tutoring of writing. The first is that of Strijbos, Narciss, and Dünnebier (2010). The researchers asked whether peer respondents' competence level affected perceptions of electronic peer feedback and how these perceptions related to writers' revisions of a text. Participants were 89 graduate psychology students in the Netherlands. Variables in the quantitative study were (a) what type of feedback writers received, concise or elaborated, and (b) who was providing it, a teacher or peer. Possible combinations of these variables created four groups plus a control group to which no feedback was offered. "Please revise the following text to enhance its comprehensibility," participants were asked (p. 295). Results showed that participants most often associated elaborated feedback as coming from respondents perceived as more competent. However, this condition did not lead to high-quality revisions. That is, the authors could find no significant correlation between perception of respondents' competence and the quality of revision. Implications of the study, according to Strijbos and colleagues (2010), were (a) that more "competent" feedback did not necessarily yield better writing revisions if writers decided a text did not need revision (!) and (b) that feedback from a peer perceived as less competent could be just as adequate in promoting revisions *if* revisions were perceived as necessary. For writing center researchers, this immediately calls to mind the question of what motivates writers to seek writing center assistance: Is it their own estimation of whether their texts require revision or their instructors' estimation, or both, that leads to writing center use? Also, how effective can tutorials be if the instructor believes the text requires revision but the writer does not agree?

The second peer tutoring research program is related to the development and testing of SWoRD (Scaffolded Writing and Rewriting in the Discipline) at the University of Pittsburgh. Funded by grants from the Andrew W. Mellon and National Science Foundations, SWoRD is a peer response web-based software, available to any instructor. Its developers, Kwangsun Cho and colleagues, have shown that feedback from peers can be just as valid and facilitative of revision as that of either writing or content instructors (Kaufmann & Schunn, 2011; Nelson & Schunn, 2009; Patchan, Charney, & Schunn, 2009). In fact, feedback from multiple peers using SWoRD has proven superior to that of either a single expert (= instructor) or single peer both in terms of perceived helpfulness and in effecting revisions that improve writing quality (Cho, Schunn, & Charney, 2006). Usability tests thus far have been positive. For example, while some instructors were worried that their students would refuse to use the software, they discovered that having once participated in peer review using SWoRD, students quickly gave up most of their objections to its efficacy.

At the University of Kansas, Thonus has worked with faculty members in the psychology and physics departments who have used and will continue to use SWoRD-facilitated peer revision in large (400+ student) classes. Why? SWoRD permits them to assign writing-to-learn activities and to develop general and disciplinary writing skills in large classes the same way they would in small classes. We have yet to discover whether web-based peer-response systems like SWoRD are equally effective across the disciplines, and more research is needed on their reliability and validity in varied educational contexts.

Definitions of Success in Writing Center Work

As we have shown, the study of tutoring, especially peer tutoring, is burgeoning in educational and cognitive science fields. Few writing center publications, however, have cited this research. Some may believe (a) that writing tutoring is so different from subject-matter tutoring that no transfer is possible, or (b) that "best practices" lack theoretical foundation and therefore lack integrity; or even (c) that studies of peer tutoring in elementary and secondary schools cannot be generalized to colleges and universities. We contest these beliefs, arguing that any and all comparisons with studies in the tutoring literature can only support the case for peer writing tutoring, and therefore all of writing center work.

In the same year (1984) that Bloom demonstrated that tutoring was the single most effective strategy in improving students' performance, both Stephen North and Kenneth Bruffee justified the program and curriculum of peer tutoring in a writing center setting. Even though North (1984b) called for studies of tutorial practices, little empirical research on the value of specific practices has been conducted (Jones, 2001). Rogers (2008) noted that "Most writing center claims of success are not evidence-based" (p. 33), and that "the word *successful* is often used interchangeably with the word *effective* in current literature on tutoring" (p. 115, italics original).

The few studies that do exist have been largely descriptive, comparing findings with writing center lore about how tutors *ought* to work. For example, Roberts (1988), in "A Study of Writing Center Effectiveness," contrasted classroom-based composition instruction with credit-bearing writing-center-based individualized writing instruction at two West Virginia community colleges. He found no significant differences in writing quality outcomes between the groups. Two years later, McClure (1990) asked, "Can seemingly under-qualified and underprepared first-semester college students be effective writing center tutors?" (p. 7). She measured "respect for writing tutors" through a "Student Evaluation of the Writing Center Tutorial." She collected tutors' reflections through questionnaires after individual sessions and at semester's end and transcribed 118 hours of consultations, which she analyzed for "idea units" and conversational moves. While McClure's presentation of individual tutor-writer cases was detailed, her discussion of these in terms of generalized "tutorial behaviors" was sketchy and appealed to lore categories such as tutor control and draft ownership. Perhaps the most promising finding of her study is this: Even though peer writing tutors did not have "the vocabulary of composition instructors" to meta-comment on writers' texts, they were able to act as readers and identify when they were confused.

In the few evidence-based studies we uncovered in the writing center literature, tutorial success has been assessed through tutor and/or writer satisfaction, good interaction, writing development, writer development, good revisions, or better grades and course completion.

Success as Tutor and/or Writer Satisfaction

Carino and Enders (2001) performed a quantitative study of the connection between student satisfaction and frequency of writing center visits. They wanted to substantiate the "dark knowledge" or lore that "the more times students visit the writing center, the more they like it" (p. 85). Carino and Enders asked instructors in four required English classes at Indiana State University to administer a writing center satisfaction survey to their students. Results showed that frequency of writing center use correlated with students' confidence as writers and perception of writing improvement. However, the authors discovered no statistical correlation between writing center use and satisfaction measures linked to *tutor* performance. We find this study fascinating in its argument for quantitative methodology yet its mitigation of that approach: The title of their *Writing Center Journal* article rephrases "statistical correlation" as "story," and the methodology section begins with "what we (actually the *statisticians*) did." In this sense, the authors' characterization of the study supports lore and the modes of inquiry that perpetuate it.

Informed by but not bound to lore, Thonus (2002) explored tutor and writer assessments of tutorial success using an interactional sociolinguistic approach that combined conversation-analytic and ethnographic methods to analyze features and sequences of talk. Her data sources were session transcripts and participant interviews. In her findings, she identified ten attributes of "successful" tutorials:

1. The tutor is a student, actively engaged in academic writing in his or her discipline.
2. The instructor "surrogate" role is declined by the tutor, and this abdication is welcomed by the student.
3. Tutor authority and expertise are not openly negotiated.
4. The tutor's diagnoses and the student's self-diagnoses [that is, session agendas] correspond and are agreed upon early in the session.
5. Turn structure more closely resembles that of "real" conversation rather than an ask-and-advise service encounter....
6. Average to high rates of interactional features (volubility, overlaps, backchannels, laughter) signal involvement of both parties....
7. The interactional features of the tutorial are markedly characterized by movements toward solidarity, including such features as simultaneous laughter, affiliative overlaps, and small talk.
8. Negotiation of acceptances and rejections of tutor evaluations and directives most often results in student acceptances....
9. Tutor mitigation [downplaying] of directives is frequent (for Native Speaker [L1] tutorials).
10. Symmetrical interpretations of discourse phases, directive forcefulness, and tutor and student behaviors contributing to success indicate that tutor and student have achieved some degree of intersubjectivity, the understanding of the other's intent. (pp. 126–129)

Thonus made no claims that her study was anything other than descriptive; clearly, perceptions of success may be quite different from actual success depending on audience and criteria.

Thompson, Whyte, Shannon, and colleagues (2009) looked at both lore- and research-based aspects of tutoring sessions. They found that session feedback linked to satisfaction supported the lore that the writing tutorial was a place to make students feel comfortable and have their questions answered. On the other hand, contrary to lore, Geither (2010) noticed that tutors' attention to lower-order concerns over higher-order concerns (per tutee wishes) and "directive" tutoring methods were judged more successful by L2 writers. But simply using tutor and student judgments to determine whether consultations are successful can be problematic. Kiedaisch and Dinitz (1993), for example, examined several tutorials that were rated highly by both students and tutors but were rated differently by faculty raters. Perhaps tutor and tutee perceptions alone are not wholly reliable means of judging tutorial effectiveness; nonetheless, these perceptions are definitely important at the local level if writing centers hope to continue to receive institutional funding and support.

Success as Meaningful Interaction

What is it about the peer-to-peer interaction in writing center tutorials that creates positive outcomes, also known as "success"? Researchers interested in interaction have most often studied tutorials between L1 tutors and L2 writers or sessions held online (see Chapters 4 and 6). Filling that gap, Flagel and Bell (2001) investigated details of an interaction between a graduate student tutor and a "mature student" over a first-year English paper. The case study was written as a critique of the tutor's enacted "ownership" of the writer's draft and assumption of responsibility for the correctness of revisions. The authors used transcript and text analysis as well as stimulated recall to get at tutor and student interpretations of their session. So long as the tutor continued to view the tutee as a *student* as opposed to a *writer*, Flagel and Bell argued that her contributions to the interaction would hinder rather than help the tutee. Another study that linked interactional features to less-than optimal tutorial outcomes is Thonus (1999b). She demonstrated how tutors' overuse of politeness strategies with L2 writers yielded confusion and poor uptake of suggestions (see a parallel in Person et al., 1995, for L1 algebra tutees).

Most researchers, however, have sought positive outcomes from tutorial interactions. Studying tutorials between graduate-student and faculty tutors and L2 writers, Cumming and So (1996) defined as "successful" the ability of the L2 writers to take "more proactive roles in identifying, negotiating, or resolving problems in their writing" (p. 207). They employed a 2 x 2 research design, yielding 4 combinations of variables. These were (a) the language used in the tutoring session (target or native) and (b) session focus, defined as either error correction or "procedural facilitation," a sort of self-questioning heuristic. Cumming and So found that shared tutor and writer vocabulary in the "procedural facilitation" prompts yielded a distinct benefit: Tutors activated previous knowledge attuned specifically to learners' needs for improved performance, informed writers of its nature, then unambiguously labeled it for future reference when encountering problems of a similar type. This meta-communication about students' text revisions, using a limited set of procedural facilitation prompts, countered the logical problems associated with ad hoc error correction. Cumming and So showed that instructors' corrections could backfire if writers had no way of linking content or language corrections to specific issues in their drafts and then using them to effect revisions.

Weigle and Nelson (2004) investigated tutoring sessions between L2 writers and graduate student tutors in a Master's program in Teaching English as a Second Language (MATESOL). They discovered that tutorials with the L2 writers were influenced by the participants' fluency in English. They also learned that the writers benefitted from sharing papers with their tutors in advance via email, that writers appreciated tutors' direct suggestions, and that both writers and tutors thrived on good rapport (though this was difficult to measure).

Writing center studies of interaction between and among *peers* are few. In an early study of tutorial interaction, Blau, Hall, and Strauss (1998) examined the transcript of one session between a graduate-student tutor and a graduate-student L2 writer and associated written questionnaires to explore what they called "the tutor/client conversation" (p. 18). They coded the transcript for rhetorical strategies in echoing, questions, and qualifiers. Generalizing their findings, the authors wrote:

> In a number of cases that we examined, an undue—or misdirected—emphasis on the collaborative approach resulted in tutorials that seemed to waste time and lack clear direction. This is not to suggest that collaboration should be discarded as a goal of tutorial relationships. But collaboration, like any other teaching/ learning mode, has to be used judiciously and appropriately (p. 38).

In 2002, Blau, Hall, and Sparks arrived at more specific guidelines for tutors to mitigate tendencies towards taking over the tutorial. Though minuscule by current RAD standards, these studies opened the door to the possibility that more interaction is not necessarily better interaction in terms of tutorial outcomes.

A foray into current studies of "cognitive tutors" (also known as computer-mediated "intelligent learning systems") reveals that researchers are struggling with some of the same questions about tutor-learner interaction as are writing center researchers and practitioners. For example, Koedinger and Aleven (2007) wrestled with "the assistance dilemma": How should (cognitive) tutors "balance information or assistance giving and withholding to achieve optimal student learning?" (p. 239). They discovered that tutors who initially withheld information, then revealed information at the point of need through techniques such as hinting and yes/no questioning, fostered greater student learning than those who "spilled the beans" when first consulted.

Some researchers have moved beyond "success" in writer or writing learning to questions of the social relations that result from writing center collaboration. Thonus (2008), for example, studied how laughter, especially coordinated laughter, contributed to the construction of affiliation and familiarity in writing center consultations. She established as an important research question whether quality of interaction improved quality of student writing (although that was not measured). While coordinated laughter was more frequent in interactions between tutors and writers who had previously worked together, it was also used as a resource in developing familiarity between unacquainted tutors and writers. Thonus also wondered how the relationship between acquaintanceship, familiarity, and coordinated laughter would play out in other educational situations.

More recent research on social relations is Godbee (2011), a mixed-methods study combining triangulated observation, interviews, and audio and video recordings. She posited that one-on-one writing center consultations could contribute to positive social change, especially around the issue of race. Godbee's dissertation is also an investigation of research approaches and methods: Sessions were transcribed using Conversation Analytic (CA) style, creating data that could be analyzed on the micro level, with attention not only to words but to gaze, body position, and gesture. In the interview data, Godbee coded for "potentials" for social change: raising critical consciousness, building affiliative relationships, and restructuring power relations (p. 96). In the transcript data, Godbee saw that intimacy and solidarity were created through troubles-telling and humor, which she interpreted as "one indication of the writers' willingness to sustain difficult discussions, to share personal experiences, to build relationships, and to challenge institutional structures" (p. 113). Further analysis led Godbee to focus on "epistemic rights: rights to experience, knowledge, and earned expertise...power associated with speaking and writing, in reclaiming one's voice, and in naming and affirming one's life" (p. 152). She connected these with intra- and interracial positioning and collaborative talk. Godbee's research pointed beyond tutees' writing quality and the "success "of individual writing center consultations to larger issues that have usually been dealt with in a theoretical/anecdotal way.

Success as Writing Development (a.k.a. Better Writing)

A good deal of RAD research exists on the impact of particular instructor and student practices on student writing development. For example, Dutch researchers Breetvelt, van den Bergh, and Rijlaarsdam (1994) investigated the relationship between writers' cognitive strategies and text quality. Writer strategies were analyzed at set times during the writing process through think-aloud protocols (writers' talking about their thinking while writing). Text quality was also measured at set times during the writing process by four criteria (goal orientation, structure and organization, audience awareness, language usage, or style). The researchers discovered that certain strategies were clearly associated with different points in the writing process as measured by the quality of students' drafts. For example, evaluating strategies were positively associated with text quality at the beginning of the writing process but not at the end. Interestingly, revision strategies were negatively associated with writing quality near the end of the writing process! Although the majority of these studies do not include research questions or findings about writing center usage, they provide a cornucopia of methods for studying and measures for analyzing writing development that can be applied to writing center outcomes.

The major methodological difficulty in studying writing quality is that few principled, consistent measures of the construct exist; most studies rely on either researcher-developed or post-hoc categories. For example, Haswell's (2000) longitudinal study of the development of 64 writers from first- to third-year writing classes employed a holistic rating plus nine specific measures, including idea elaboration and substantiation, establishment of logical boundaries, and fluency. Faigley and Witte's (1981) typology has been used across numerous studies of writing quality, including those conducted in writing center contexts. More recently, researchers at the Institute for Intelligent Systems at the University of Memphis (McNamara, Crossley, and McCarthy, 2010) created a computerized corpus of expert-graded student essays to generate a linguistic description of writing quality. They found that syntactic complexity (see also Beers & Nagy, 2009), lexical diversity, and word frequency were positively associated with writing quality. We are curious to see whether McNamara and colleagues' measures can be applied to writing development as an outcome of writing center tutorials, especially when *serial* (versus one-time) changes to writers' texts are made during sessions based on writers' (also *serial*) agendas.

The fact that little research exists on writing development per se in the writing center context may be directly attributed to the belief of many writing center professionals that the purpose of tutorials is not to create better *writing* but better *writers* (North, 1984a; Stahr, 2008). Jones (2001) problematized the relationship between *writing* as a general and generalizable ability (such as intelligence)—what North might have meant by *better writers*—as opposed to *writing* as a set of specialized skills. The latter construct was supported by Hayes and colleagues' (2000) study of variability in individual writers' performance across writing tasks. They realized that holistically scored, high-quality writing on one assignment did not predict the same level of quality on the next.

Nonetheless, some researchers have focused on "better writing" as a construct. As part of an institutional assessment at Indiana Wesleyan University, Henson and Stephenson (2009) performed an experimental study of writing quality improvement comparing writing center clients with non-clients in one section of elementary composition and one section of advanced composition. Writing center attendees self-selected, and the researchers controlled for other variables by administering the Daly-Miller Writing Apprehension Test and the Myers-Briggs Type Indicator. Results showed that the 23 writing center users showed statistically significant improvement (as measured by two raters) from first to final drafts as compared with 28 control group subjects. Henson and Stephenson admitted to flaws in their methodology; we believe the most egregious was analyzing all writing center clients' essays, regardless of whether they had actually worked on them with a writing center tutor. That is, they equated good writing with becoming a good writer, an equivalence we believe has yet to be established. Though much could be improved, this institutional assessment qualifies as RAD research and evidences the use of quantitative methods in writing center research.

Lunsford and colleagues' Stanford Study of Writing actually included survey questions regarding writing center use. Rogers (2008), who wrote his dissertation on writing centers using the Stanford data, noted that students got more out of their writing center visits (with either peer or writing instructor tutors) earlier in their college careers. Students reported less reliance on writing center support as their coursework and writing assignments became more discipline specific. Rogers concluded that writing center usage, along with opportunities for revision and teacher-student conferences, was important "in fostering development." However, he argued that "to ensure maximal development, attention must be paid by individual teachers to the ongoing development of individual students across the curriculum" (p. 292). No doubt because of this finding, in a later paper Rogers (2010) identified peer-to-peer talk as a factor contributing to the development of writing abilities but confined his analysis to in-classroom interaction alone. He argued that a review of writing development literature allows for few direct causal arguments; rather, longitudinal studies "have contributed to the generation of valuable hypotheses concerning how people learn to write and the impact of writing on learning, and they have provided a rich description of the multiple variables that contribute to the development of writing abilities" (p. 366). This conclusion provides little support for a direct correlation between writing center use and writing development at the university level.

In terms of writing development, what do writing center *tutors* stand to gain? While we could find no studies investigating this question in the writing center literature, the classroom peer-review literature offers some answers. New Zealand researchers Medcalf, Glynn, and Moore (2004) found that elementary-school reciprocal peer tutoring resulted in gains of "writing rate, accuracy, and audience ratings of clarity of message and enjoyment of writing" (p. 157). Researching university-level students, Lundstrom and Baker (2009) asked, "What are the benefits of peer review to the reviewers' own writing?" They created a classroom-based study in which 91 English L2 writing students engaged in peer review; half of the writers were trained to offer feedback while the other half were trained to receive feedback. The authors used an essay-scoring rubric that attended to both global and local writing issues. The writers who were trained to and only offered feedback to their peers showed significant gains in language as well as organization, development, and cohesion/ coherence.

Success as Writer Development (a.k.a. Better Writers)

The Council of Writing Program Administrators' *WPA Outcomes Statement for First-Year Composition* (2008) is one attempt at describing what it means to be a good writer, at least at one level of proficiency. The *Outcomes* were operationalized as learner actions, such as "Understand how genres shape reading and writing" or "Control such surface features as syntax, grammar, punctuation, and spelling." While laudable goals, and quite detailed at that, the *Outcomes* lack scalability and precision at the level of the individual composition, which is precisely what researchers may want to study and definitely what tutors and tutees are interested in.

Writing center professionals "know" that students who use our services become better writers, and we probably also assume that makes them more successful academically. But can we produce evidence to support this? The general tutoring literature contains numerous studies of attempts to do so. Kostecki and Bers (2008), for example, measured success by GPA, course grade, and persistence in a new community college population of 2,724 students. Using analysis of variance and regression analysis, they showed that, controlling for extraneous variables, "tutoring was associated with student success" (p. 6), a finding that suggested it should continue to be included in the "arsenal" of support services for community college students.

Something else that writing center professionals say we "know" is that the more times that a writer uses the writing center, the better writer he or she becomes. (We can't determine writing improvement, since we're not the arbiters of quality— instructors assign the grades.) But do we have the evidence? Again, we would do well to consult the general tutoring literature for published research studies. Cooper (2010), for example, followed two cohorts of freshmen at Western Washington University to see whether increased drop-in tutoring center attendance (comparing > 10 times/quarter, = 10 times/quarter, < 10 times/quarter) yielded better GPAs and higher persistence rates. Freshmen who visited the tutoring center did better on both measures than those who did not. Significant differences in both GPA and persistence were seen comparing freshmen who visited more than 10 times/quarter vs. less than 10 times/quarter, and these differences were noted across race/ethnicity, SAT score, and high school GPA.

One of the most obvious ways to investigate writer development is by studying *writer quality* as expressed in attitudes. Davis (1988) researched how writing center attendance affected students' attitudes towards writing. He administered Reigstad and McAndrew's Writing Attitude Scale to eight sections of a first-year composition course (totaling 121 students) at the beginning and end of the semester. He found that writing center clients improved their attitudes towards writing by an average of 124%, while those who were not writing center clients improved their attitudes toward writing by only 74%. Those who interacted with peer tutors in the writing center improved by a startling 181%, leading Davis to conclude that if the composition courses all included peer response, the writing center could be repurposed to serve students outside of these courses. His conclusion seems quaint now, since subsequent research has shown that classroom peer response and peer tutoring are somewhat distinct. Nonetheless, Davis's research is an interesting early example of a quantitative study of writer development related to the writing center.

Another learner characteristic that has been associated with development is *self-efficacy* (Bandura, 1986). This construct refers to individuals' abilities to learn new information and skills as a result of their beliefs about their possession of those abilities. Individuals' perceptions are influenced by interpretations of one's performance, or *mastery experience*; by observations of others performing tasks and comparing oneself with them; verbal and social *persuasion* from others; and apprehension, comprising anxiety and stress. A 25-year quantitative research literature exists on self-efficacy and writing outcomes conducted in K-12 and college settings (e.g., White & Bruning, 2005; Shell, Murphy, & Bruning, 1989). Self-efficacy research has led to the pedagogical recommendation that teachers spend as much time working with students on their perceptions of competence as on developing actual competence (see Hackett & Betz, 1989, on mathematics teaching). Multiple studies have shown that writerly self-efficacy is highly correlated with writing performance. Pajares and Johnson (1994), for example, argued that "the relationship between outcome expectations and performance is mediated by writing self-efficacy" (p. 325). And in a meta-analysis of the extant literature on self-efficacy and writing, Pajares (2003) demonstrated that the correlation between expectations and performance had developed into a predictive relationship: Writers with positive self-efficacy beliefs actually performed better on writing tasks.

We have found two recent studies in the writing center literature that applied self-efficacy to writing outcomes. The first is Williams and Takaku's (2011) longitudinal study, which examined the relationship between positive self-efficacy, help-seeking behavior (writing center use), and student grades in a third-year university composition course. Participants were 6 undergraduate cohorts studied over an 8-year period, for a total of 671 students. The researchers tested three hypotheses using quantitative methods: (a) International ESL students' levels of self-efficacy would be lower than those of domestic students; (b) participants with lower levels of self-efficacy would seek out writing center assistance more frequently than those with higher levels of self-efficacy; and (c) seeking writing center help would positively correlate with higher grades (p. 7). All three hypotheses were supported, especially for the international students: Despite their initially lower self-efficacy assessments, because of more frequent writing center usage they performed even better than the domestic students in composition classes. Given the robustness of their findings, Williams and Takaku argued that "such assessment [self-efficacy] could readily replace the common practice of merely tabulating the number of tutoring sessions or students served per academic year" (p. 13). We agree.

Even more recently, Schmidt and Alexander (in press) applied self-efficacy research to writing center assessment at Western Oregon University. The writing center was an ideal location for self-efficacy research, they proposed, because of the "self-evaluation, coaching, and repeated practice in action" that characterize this work. Their study differed from Williams and Takaku's in that student course grades were not part of the data set. Based on earlier self-efficacy scales, the researchers created a measure specific to writing, the Post-Secondary Writerly Self-Efficacy Scale (PSWSES). Carefully matching self-efficacy items to writing-related outcomes (based on Pajares, 2003), the 20-item PSWSES was administered to 505 writing center users. They then compared a subset of clients who had completed at least three writing center sessions in one term to a control group of writers who had never visited the writing center. Results showed that (a) tutors' and writers' assessments of writers' self-efficacy correlated, demonstrating construct validity; and (b) as measured by the PSWSES, writers' self-efficacy increased across multiple writing tutorial sessions when compared to the control group. The most interesting result was that writerly self-efficacy among the control group remained consistent over time, suggesting "the need for writing center services for all students, from the developmental to the expert student-writer."

Schmidt and Alexander's study offers a refreshing departure from extrinsic "competence indicators" to intrinsic "perceived competence development." Self-efficacy research removes the need to employ external measures such as student grades or even internal measures such as "satisfaction," placing agency for writing outcomes with those who most benefit from writing center sessions: writers. Schmidt and Alexander's research motivated tutors and administrators to "look beyond the paper and the student's writing development to something much larger: the student's beliefs about writerly success in the future."

Success as (Good) Revision

The most outcomes-based studies of writing center effectiveness ask about the text revisions tutors suggest during a session that are actually made by tutees during and after the session. Perhaps the earliest example of a study looking at writer revisions as a clue to tutorial success was Stay's "When Re-writing Succeeds: An Analysis of Student Revisions" (1983). Examining L2 writing tutorials, Williams (2004) discovered that writers were more likely to make revisions when their tutors offered direct suggestions. However, it was unclear that their revised drafts were any better, and the effectiveness of direct suggestions was questionable. Williams' research leads logically to this question: Is more revision as an outcome of writing center tutorials necessarily better revision? In a study conducted at a Canadian university writing center, Bell (2002) attempted to answer this question. He asked:

1. Do undergraduate university students who voluntarily visit trained, experienced peer tutors in the writing center make the talked-about types of revisions after the session is over?
2. Does voluntarily seeing a trained, experienced peer tutor about a draft help undergraduates produce better final products?
3. What tutoring methods do trained, experienced peer tutors employ with undergraduates who voluntarily bring drafts to thewriting center?

Bell used Faigley and Witte's (1981) typology to code student drafts for revisions and Reigstad's (1980) typology to describe tutoring methods. The results? He simply could not answer the first two questions because of the answer to (3): Because sessions were largely tutor-centered, almost all revisions were made *during* sessions rather than *after* them. Bell lamented that he had no way of discovering whether "students became noticeably better writers" because "they were generally too passive" (p. 13). He equated revisions as better "final products" with better writing without questioning the possibly more complex relationships among them. Note also that Bell used only Faigley and Witte's (1981) typology, without pairing it with Witte and Faigley's (1981) apparatus for coding revisions in coherence and cohesion, which we view as important since it includes categories such as micro- and macrostructure changes. In future studies that investigate revisions to students' texts, we recommend the use of more recent and sophisticated coding schemes such as those proposed by Haswell (2000) and by Borg and Deane (2011).

Synchronous and asynchronous tutorials held online offer another context in which to study writer revisions as a result of peer interaction. As mentioned in Chapter 3, we view Hewett's work as particularly credible because of its methodological rigor and internal consistency. It bears the signs of an ongoing *research program*, which is rare in writing center inquiry. Hewett (2006) examined virtual "whiteboard" interactions between tutors and writers in a synchronous online environment. She recruited 23 undergraduate students enrolled in first-year English classes and 14 "online instructors," yielding 52 interactions in the chat feature, where tutors and writers managed the work of the session. Hewett found that much of the chat dealt with "tutorial" rather than "writing interaction"; she saw this as attending to task: "When participant talk did not focus on the writing, the talk reflected interactions that were focused particularly on the tutorial process itself and not on social talk or outside activities—indicating a general seriousness of purpose" (p. 16). Regarding student revisions based on online interaction (the "gold standard" of efficacy), Hewett, like Bell (2002), used Faigley and Witte's typology to code changes in student texts before and after tutoring sessions. Unfortunately, she saw few substantive changes related to rhetorical effect. Nonetheless, she noticed that writers made choices among those that online instructors offered them, taking ownership over their writing. She admitted that instructor and writer interviews would have offered even greater insight into the revision process and its outcomes.

In a case study of nine undergraduate students at DePauw University, Stahr (2008) investigated writer revision as a result of feedback from instructor, classroom peer, and peer writing center tutors, all of whom she characterized as *readers*. Stahr uncovered no noticeable differences in writer revisions: "The amount of feedback and the source of that feedback do not necessarily impact the degree of revision" (p. 227). According to Stahr, the distinction between substantive and surface revisions seemed most closely related to the capacity of both writer and peer to take risks: "Rather than asking whether a text needs to be revised, tutorials should be occasions during which students and tutors grapple with what more the student's text can do, with the possibilities for revision that the draft itself presents" (p. 245). In fact, because "well-edited papers" often masked underlying conceptual and organizational weaknesses, respondents were less likely to offer revision advice, and, as a result, two of the nine writers who were L2 learners actually produced the most substantive revisions. One weakness of the study is that in an attempt to avoid quantitative measures of revision, Stahr failed to produce a descriptive typology; thus, "degree of revision"—ostensibly a quantitative measure—was neither a transparent nor a comparable category.

In a recent dissertation, Van Horne (2011), like Hewett, employed Faigley and Witte's (1981) revision typology to analyze the "revision sessions" writers held after their writing center tutorials. Using a social constructivist framework and a qualitative research design, he investigated how 11 writers and writing consultants viewed student revision and its relationship to the sessions. Of interest in Van Horne's selection of writers is that some were also peer tutors, participating in so-called "incestuous" consultations (p. 37). Van Horne triangulated data from close transcriptions of the tutorials (Gilewicz & Thonus, 2003), session report forms, interviews with instructors, and member checks. Data were coded and analyzed with a co-researcher to increase reliability. He found that students who did not have specific goals before their writing consultations bought into their consultants' descriptions of writing center activity, either taking away "corrected drafts" or "new conceptions of revision" (p. 242). In contrast, students who went to their sessions with specific goals created their own descriptions of writing center activity. As a result, they used their consultations to engage and make meaning, to "compose new sections of their text or receive feedback about certain aspects of their existing text" (p. 243). Surprisingly, writing consultants who engaged as tutees in "incestuous" consultations were more likely to produce the same conceptions of revision as writers who did not have specific goals for their consultations. Based on these results, Van Horne argued that one of tutors' principal goals when working with any writer is "to elicit the students' situation definitions of what a writing conference is for and what it means to meaningfully revise" (p. vi).

Success as Better Grades, Course Completion, Persistence, and Graduation

Writing centers, as described by Beth Boquet (2002), "are implicated in [a] distancing maneuver," desiring to be seen as "something other-than, something-more-than a remedial service" (p. 41). Boquet cited Nancy Grimm:

> [M]any writing centers distance themselves from a remedial classification by promoting writing centers as places for *all* writers, *not just* remedial writers. The *not just* qualifier was a defensive response to the lack of recognition accorded those who work in writing centers. Thus, the increased diversity of students in higher education is avoided twice—first by universities establishing programs like writing centers that distance faculty from students; and second by writing centers' distancing themselves from a remedial function. (1999, p. 10)

Boquet and Grimm's critique is well deserved: Writing centers, by avoiding direct involvement in student assessment, have tended to maintain a peripheral role in the university, above the fray of discussions about student outcomes. (At the same time, we have complained of being marginalized!) No longer. In today's environment of accountability, every department, every academic service, has come under scrutiny or soon will. How is the writing center contributing to student persistence and graduation, and how can that contribution be characterized quantitatively and qualitatively?

Even if writing center administrators and tutors have not been asking (or answering) that question, students have. For many writing center users, a "successful" consultation is one that yields a better assignment grade, period. In their case study of one psychology class, Morrison and Nadeau (2003) admitted from the outset that "grades did influence students' level of satisfaction with the writing center" (p. 26). Students were required to use the writing center. The authors' data sources were student pre- and post-grade evaluations of writing center tutorials as well as a survey administered one year after the class ended. Without exception, between pre-grade and post-grade evaluations, students lowered their ratings of writing tutorials: Students who received "A" grades in the course lowered their ratings slightly less than the rest. On the other hand, the survey administered one year later showed that "time appeared to heal most wounds": Ratings on this evaluation were similar to pre-grade evaluations (p. 32). Morrison and Nadeau attributed students' evaluations to a "self-serving bias" in which writers took credit for their achievements but held others accountable for their failures. "The writing center becomes another source for ascribing blame outside of the student-faculty relationship" (p. 33), they wrote. To combat this perception, they recommended that administrators maintain clear lines of communication with faculty, that faculty postpone due dates as an incentive for students to visit the writing center, and that tutors negotiate clear and attainable session goals with writers.

Pantoja (2010) wrote an especially stinging indictment of four community colleges' practices of assessing writing center "success" based, at least partially, on student grade outcomes. In a qualitative study employing a particularly thick description of the community college as a writing center research setting, she argued that institutions' definitions of success were often at odds with writing centers' definitions of success, and by buying into institutional definitions and failing to articulate their own definitions, writing centers were unsuccessful in doing either (cf. Lerner, 2003). Based on the theme of "meaning" that arose through a grounded theory analysis, Pantoja posited that "student learning" be the measure of writing tutorial and writing center success (p. 62). She quoted Warnock and Warnock's (1984) description of the writing center, where "writing is taught with a focus on meaning, not form; on process, not product; on authorial intention and audience expectation, not teacher authority or punitive measures; on holistic and human concerns, not errors and isolated skills" (p. 16). Unfortunately, since not all writing and content instructors taught writing as meaning-making, grades, she argued, were a poor measure of writing and writing center success.

We could find no other empirical studies linking writing center attendance with better assignment grades, course grades, persistence, or graduation. An actual RAD study of this question would require heroic measures:

- Implementation and continued assessment of writing tutorial practices directly linked to improved revisions;
- A clear definition of writing tutorial outcomes (including writer revisions) related to paper and course grades, which would necessitate instructor buy-in to writing center use in a way that motivates rather than discourages students;
- A statistical correlation between course grades and persistence and between persistence and graduation;
- The funding, researchers, time, and perseverance to investigate these questions across not one but many institutions.

Additionally, we could find no RAD research of any kind that studied *instructors'* satisfaction with their students' writing center sessions (except, tangentially, Kiedaisch & Dinitz, 1993 and Thonus, 2001). Hayward (1983) compared instructors' goals for writing center sessions with tutors' goals but satisfaction was not measured. Nor could we find any studies that researched instructors' evaluations of their students' revisions after writing center sessions other than using course grade or course completion data. The only study remotely related to this is Calfee (2007), detailed in the next section. Jones (2001) summarized some articles in the writing center literature describing instructors' largely negative reactions to the support their students received in the writing center. Unfortunately, because the articles were based on anecdotes collected in particular writing centers, we cannot determine whether the instructor attitudes reported by Jones are representative of all instructors across multiple contexts. Such "holes" in the writing center research literature are both distressing and exciting; there is still so much we do not know. And we will need to know because we will be asked to demonstrate how using writing center services directly affects students' success, not only as writers, but as students who persist and graduate.

Success as Repeat Visits to the Writing Center

Closely related to the study of writing center outcomes as better grades, course completion, persistence, and graduation is research on outcomes generated by repeat rather than one-time writing center usage. In fact, some university writing programs have paired writing centers with writing assessment efforts (Johnson-Shull & Kelly-Riley, 2001). In his dissertation, Van Dam (1985) researched the correlation between writing center usage and grades on narrative and expository essays at the beginning and end of a freshman composition course at the University of Southern California. He observed that the treatment group (frequent writing center users) scored an average of 7% higher than did those in the control group (who did not visit the writing center). He also found that 74% of the treatment group had been required to attend at least three times, and 95% of this group believed using the writing center had positively affected their grades.

Young and Fritzsche (2002) examined the relationship between procrastination tendency, peer feedback, and "student writing success" in a quantitative study of 206 undergraduates in writing-intensive courses at the University of Florida. The researchers began with the premise that students who procrastinate (either through tendency or actual behavior) on writing assignments are less likely to produce quality (or "successful") writing. Procrastination tendency was derived from participants' responses to the Procrastination Assessment Scale-Students (Solomon & Rothblum, 1984), and procrastination behaviors from the State-Trait Anxiety Inventory (Spielberger, 1983) and their own Writing Behaviors Assessment. "Successful" writing was measured by major paper grades, course grades, and overall GPA. They investigated three hypotheses:

1. Writing center use would be associated with reduced procrastination behavior, higher grades, greater satisfaction, and lower evaluation anxiety.
2. Writing center use would be more helpful for those with high procrastination tendency than for those with low procrastination tendency.
3. Writers with high procrastination tendency would be less likely to use the writing center, particularly when writing center use was not explicitly required by the instructor. (p. 47)

The researchers discovered that procrastination tendency and behaviors were pervasive problems among the participants. However, these did not always lead writers to seek feedback from writing center consultants, which they rated as less helpful than feedback from teachers. Hypotheses 1 and 3 were confirmed, while support for Hypothesis 2 was mixed: For students with high procrastination tendencies, "Writing center use was associated with less procrastination behavior and greater satisfaction with the writing process" (p. 51). The higher the procrastination tendency of the students, the more likely they were to benefit from writing center support—if they managed to get there. Young and Fritzsche discovered no relationship between feedback from any source and paper grades, course grades, or overall GPA. The only positive correlations they found were between high procrastination tendency, higher anxiety, and lower overall GPA, no single factor of which writing center use could directly influence.

Calfee (2007) examined the relationship between asynchronous online writing tutoring (provided by Smarthinking) and students' grades in community college developmental writing courses. In a particularly ambitious study, she collected data over three semesters from students who participated in online tutoring sessions

(267) and compared their outcomes (measured by summing A, B, and C grades and dividing the total by the number of grades) with a control group of 1,961 students who either participated in face-to-face sessions in the writing center or not at all. Results indicated that writers who participated in online sessions performed significantly better (75%) in the course than those in the control group (67%) who had never participated in writing tutoring. Statistical regression demonstrated that the more times a student used the online tutoring service, the better his or her grade. Certainly, these results may have been confounded by factors such as variable instructor grading rubrics, grade inflation, and/or the Pygmalion effect. If Calfee had separated non-participants from face-to-face session participants, creating two control groups, and run regression analyses on these, we believe her study would have been even more valid and informative, not to mention replicable.

Conclusion

There are two possible positive outcomes we identified at the beginning of this chapter about which we failed to find any empirical research:

- Identifying writing skills that are transferable to future projects
- Creating incentives for instructors to refer more students to the writing center

The first should be fairly easy to investigate *if* tutors have been trained to explicitly summarize skills identified and learned when they close the consultation. (Theodori, 2011 is an attempt to gauge effectiveness according to learning outcomes.) A revised draft could be collected from the writer, and, if that writer returns to the writing center, tutors could look for evidence of transfer, collecting the writer's draft as evidence. Writing center administrators might be uncomfortable with such direct assessment of student writing, but we would argue that this evidence may be exactly what those who hold the purse strings require for continued funding of our efforts.

The second outcome, whether "success" directly affects instructors' willingness to refer more students to the writing center, would be more difficult to investigate. First of all, what constitutes a "referral"? We return to Chapter 3, in which we summarized research on requiring writing center use. Are there differences in writers' satisfaction, grades, or other outcomes depending on whether their instructors refer them as part of a course requirement, for extra credit, or for another reason? In addition, what sorts of motivation might instructors cultivate in their students depending on the role of writing in their writing-intensive WAC/WID courses versus content-oriented lecture classes? And how much improvement in student writing, or student attitudes towards writing, would instructors qualify as "success"? So many variables emerge from attempting to answer this question that we suggest it initially be tackled in a descriptive, qualitative research study. From those results, individual findings can be teased out and investigated cross-institutionally.

A final uninvestigated outcome is how *tutors'* writing improves as they provide feedback to fellow academic writers in the writing center. This question has been investigated in classroom peer tutoring for improvements in English learners' writing ability (Lundstrom & Baker, 2009). The authors discovered that students who were on the "giving" end of peer feedback made greater gains than those who were on the "receiving" end, all other variables being equal. This study cries out for replication in the writing center setting. Can the received hypothesis that working as a writing tutor translates into better academic writing for writing consultants as compared to their academic peers be supported by empirical evidence?

As important as institutional continuity is in tough budget times, it is our hope that empirical research about "success," however defined, whether qualitative or quantitative, can do even more than encourage the continued support and maintenance of physical and human writing center resources. Our goal is that research will become so much a part of the fabric of writing center work that all administrative and pedagogical decisions will be founded upon it. While publishing "how we do things in my/our writing center" may make sense locally, investigating a single research question like this one across many writing centers will yield more comparable and, thus, more trustworthy results. This evidence, while never incontrovertible, can inform our administrative and tutoring practice in ways that anecdote and lore simply cannot.

CHAPTER EIGHT

An Agenda for Writing Center Research

Defined originally as service rather than research units, writing centers and the professionals who work in them have struggled over the years to find ways to incorporate research systematically into already daunting instructional and administrative loads and sometimes fiscally uncertain futures. (Kail, 2002, p. 315)

We conclude this volume by discussing research questions about writing center practice that have yet to be investigated, selected from each chapter of the book. We propose approaches, methods, and data analysis possibilities for each of these questions. We discuss how continuing to develop a coherent empirical research agenda will prepare writing center researchers to sit at the academic "head table" (Harris, 2000) and to engage in evidence-based practice in the writing center.

Research Basics in Evidence-Based Practice

Research questions arising from our discussion of approaches and methods in RAD research are not so much empirical as they are visionary. Following Drake (2009), we asked them in Chapter 2 but in the opposite order:

1. **Who gets to decide what counts as evidence?**

   The "who," we believe, will increasingly be fellow writing center researchers, conference organizers, and publication editors. No longer will professionals in this field remain satisfied with "comparing notes" about "our writing centers" at conferences; instead, we will want to hear about research that is aggregable, replicable, and data driven, inquiry that leads to new paradigms in writing center theory and practice. As we approach the academic "head table," writing center publications will become clearer about their purposes and more rigorous in their methodological review of submissions. Writing center researchers will understand the contributions that scholars in fields in addition to composition and rhetoric can make to our work, and writing center research will be cited as it applies to parallel fields such as teaching, tutoring, and counseling—a trend we have yet to notice.

2. **What types of evidence should be developed and how should they be weighted? How restrictive should the definition of evidence be?**

   Definitions of *evidence* will vary, of course, depending on the research questions and expected outcomes of inquiry. We have been clear in our argument that both quantitative and qualitative methods and data analysis are essential to writing center research, and no one type of evidence need be privileged above another unless that evidence is tangential to the particular study. This stance values both the aggregate and the individual, meeting postmodern criteria. We have also been clear that any writing center research must find evidence for its validity in actual writing center practice. This argument parallels the "clinical decision-making" in evidence-based practice (or practice-based evidence!) in medical and health professions discussed in Chapter 2. Researchers are the clinicians, and they make the decisions about what evidence is needed to best confirm or disconfirm hypotheses about best practices in patient treatment. We see an even more immediate parallel in teacher research and action research in evidence-based education. Finally, we have been clear that research based on empirical evidence always leads to meta-analyses: Findings from comparable studies are examined, conclusions are drawn, and research questions become ever more focused and specific. As individual researchers, we stand on the shoulders of giants[1]; we need not reinvent the wheel with each research study, and "our" writing centers, at root, are not all that different from any others when it comes to inquiry about our theory and practice.

The Contexts of Tutoring

How does the institutional context of a writing center affect its effectiveness? As the educational accountability movement reaches higher education, this question will become ever more important as writing center directors and those who hold the purse strings demand ever more detailed explanations. This question is also the logical extension of the benchmark inquiry of the Writing Centers Research Project. Each of the four WCRP questions could be investigated in a variety of research projects:

1. **What do writing centers look like?**

   Research question: How do writing centers design their spaces to support *identification, pathos,* and *ethos* (Bemer, 2010)? Are there differences between writing centers designed from scratch as compared with those housed in "borrowed spaces"?

   Research approach and methodology: a cross-institutional qualitative study involving at least six writing centers, three of which are housed "in their own spaces" and three of which are housed in "borrowed spaces." Methodology would be largely ethnographic, focusing on staff, tutor, and writer characterization of the spaces gathered through detailed interviews and participant observation. Emergent themes could be connected to identification, pathos, and ethos and submitted to participants for member checks.

2. **Whom do writing centers serve?**

   Research question: Are there demonstrated differences in usage patterns among writing centers located, for example, in English departments, learning centers, or libraries?

   Research approach and methodology: a cross-institutional quantitative study, with researchers at universities or colleges with comparable student bodies but with different institutional contexts for writing center work collecting usage data comprising student academic level, course, or other purpose for which assistance was requested, and frequency of use. Such data could also be mined for information on gender, ethnicity, GPA, etc. Follow-up qualitative studies could focus on users' experiences, including questions about how they first heard about the writing center, how they accessed the writing center, how their instructors incorporated writing center use into instruction, how their consultations with writing tutors affected them and their texts, and why they would choose to use the writing center again or not. Data could be collected through surveys, e-mails, and/or interviews.

Research question: Are there demonstrated differences in usage patterns among writing centers with multiple satellites, for example, in residence halls, academic departments, or in the wider community, and those with a single location?

Research approach and methodology: a cross-institutional quantitative study, with researchers at universities or colleges with comparable student bodies and institutional contexts but with either single locations or multiple satellites collecting usage data comprising student academic level, course or other purpose for which assistance was requested, and frequency of use. Follow-up qualitative studies could focus on users' experiences as detailed above.

Research question: Does including the writer in the "feedback loop" of constructing tutorial reports (Larrance & Brady, 1995) stimulate repeat writing center usage or greater reported satisfaction with writing center consultations?

Research approach and methodology: a mixed-methods inquiry at a single institution followed by replication at sites with similar and different audiences and purposes for tutorial reports. Are reports available to writers? To writing consultants? To writing center administrators? To instructors? For documentation only? For assessment purposes? For student evaluation and grading? An experimental design might involve assigning half of writing center users to the treatment condition (users prompted to contribute to reports) and assigning half of writing center users to the control condition (users unable to contribute to reports). Data on repeat visits could be collected and satisfaction surveys distributed. Qualitative inquiry could involve content or discourse analyses of writer contributions to the reports and interviews focusing on tutor and staff responses to these.

3. **Who are the consultants?**

Research question: Does tutors' satisfaction with their work as writing consultants vary with the number of hours worked? The wages paid? The length of tutoring sessions? The students helped?

Research approach and methodology: a cross-institutional mixed-methods study combining consultant responses to an index such as the Job Satisfaction Survey or the Minnesota Satisfaction Questionnaire and a standardized survey specific to writing center tutoring. Follow-up structured interviews could provide qualitative data to create predictive statements that could influence how tutors are recruited, trained, scheduled, and remunerated.

Research question: What experiences do peer tutors take away with them from their time as writing center consultants? What are the long-range effects of the skills they have learned and developed?

Research approach and methodology: aggregation of the data already collected by the Peer Tutor Alumni Research Project. We recommend widespread distribution of the PTARP survey, possibly through the National Conference on Peer Tutors in Writing, adding even more data (we're reminded of Jane Cogie's 1997 article, "Theory Made Visible: How Tutoring May Affect the Development of Student-Centered Teachers"). Once surveys are collected, focus groups could be held around the U.S. to provide additional insights and richness to the data. A large report could be published that includes recommendations for tutor training, hiring, and outplacement based on the results.

4. **Who are the directors?**

Research question: What backgrounds do writing center directors have? Do those who have written theses and dissertations on writing centers become directors? If so, how and why? If not, why not?

Research approach and methodology: an update of the Writing Centers Research Project, coupled with more extensive follow-up studies to Babcock, Carter-Tod, and Thonus (forthcoming).

Research question: What training is available for new writing center directors? What role does the International Writing Centers Association Summer Institute play in this training? What is the role of WCenter, a listserv sponsored by Texas Tech University, in informal mentoring and training? How committed are writing center directors to assessment and research?

Research approach and methodology: a survey of IWCA Summer Institute alumni and of WCenter users (eliminating duplicates). Coordination with the WCRP to cross-code data, offering a qualitative as well as quantitative overview of writing center directors and their work. Publications could update recent research by Babcock, Ferrel, and Ozias (2011) and by Salem and Eodice (2010).

Tutoring "Different" Populations

Research questions focus on populations of basic writers, writers with disabilities, L2 writers, and graduate-student writers as well as issues of how tutoring these populations challenges the received "methodology as mythology" (Plummer & Thonus, 1999).

Research Question: Do basic (or developmental) writers respond better to individual or to group tutoring? What are the writing and larger educational outcomes of each approach?

Research Approach and Methodology: an experimental study with comparable writers (ACT/SAT score, gender, age, etc.) assigned to either the treatment (group tutoring) or the control group (individual tutoring). This could be followed up by qualitative analysis of writer revisions and interviews with writers and course instructors. Possible connection with course grades, persistence, and overall GPA could also be investigated.

Research Question: What tutoring methods are effective with deaf writers? Are ASL interpreters necessary, or can sessions be conducted entirely in (written) English? Are there differences in outcomes if deaf tutees are tutored in sign language only, as Wood (1995) claimed?

Research Approach and Methodology: a cross-institutional study using the qualitative research approach and data collection methods of Babcock (2005, 2008a, 2009, 2011a). Babcock's "Outlaw Tutoring" policies could be applied in a variety of writing center contexts and outcomes examined. The researcher should be fluent in ASL and contact sign in order to conduct research on tutoring sessions in ASL, but the work of Cumming and So (1996) implies that using the native language in tutoring does not affect outcomes.

Research Question: Most studies of L2 writers have focused on tutees. What about tutors? What are tutors' knowledge about and attitudes toward working with L2 writers? How can tutors be better prepared to help these writers?

Research Approach and Methodology: a qualitative study using tutor interviews, logs/journals, observations of tutoring sessions and tutor training sessions and analyses of written training materials. The study could also be conducted as an action research project, involving the tutors themselves in the data collection and write-up.

Research Question: Should graduate-level writers be tutored by graduate-level tutors?

Research Approach and Methodology: a quantitative, quasi-experimental approach in which graduate students visiting the writing center are randomly paired with either undergraduate or graduate level tutors. Session satisfaction surveys could be compared, especially items reflecting the competence of the tutor.

Tutoring Activities

Research Question: Is there an overall pattern to tutorial discourse?
Research Approach and Methodology: meta-analysis or meta-synthesis of the various studies that have attempted to categorize tutorial discourse in order to determine a model. The resulting framework could be investigated in actual tutoring session transcripts using Conversation Analysis or discourse analysis.

Research Question: What are the listening behaviors of tutees in tutoring sessions?
Research Approach and Methodology: a qualitative study using stimulated recall, in which tutoring sessions are videotaped and then played back to the participant, and the researcher asks the participant to pause the tape and reflect at significant moments. The researcher could also take notes on his or her perceptions of the listening behavior of the tutee as well as ask the tutee to complete a log or journal entry immediately following the session.

Research Question: Is there a preferred method for reading in tutoring sessions, and if so, what is it?
Research Approach and Methodology: a combined qualitative and quantitative study in which a large number of tutoring sessions are observed and the resulting drafts are collected. Reading activities could be analyzed, categorized, and compared with changes writers made in subsequent drafts. The research could interview participants about their feelings and reactions concerning the reading activity. This study would attempt to make sense of the various (sometimes conflicting) results found by previous studies.

Research Question: What is the role of writing in tutoring? How often do tutors and tutees write, and what do they write?
Research Approach and Methodology: ethnographic or participant-observer approach, resulting in a case study of the writing activities of a particular writing center. The researcher could engage in participant observation in a writing center for a semester or year, observing tutoring sessions and taking notes on writing behaviors observed. Any writing done during the tutoring sessions could be compiled for later analysis. The researcher could interview tutors and tutees that were observed to determine the use of writing, the reason for it, and their attitudes toward it. The researcher could then establish further categories for research.

Research Question: How do tutors use meta-discourse in tutoring sessions? How do writers use it?

Research Approach and Methodology: a descriptive, qualitative study in an attempt to establish categories for further investigation. The researcher could use an existing corpus or develop a corpus of tutoring transcripts and mine it for features of meta-discourse to be categorized, explained, and analyzed using a discourse analysis approach. The resulting write-up would be a descriptive analysis of use for practitioners and future researchers.

The Details? They Matter

Research Question: Is there a preferred type of consultation? Writing center theory and lore prefer a student-centered consultation, but these are fairly rare in the data. What does this mean? What types of consultations do students prefer, and which kinds result in better learning outcomes?

Research Approach and Methodology: a qualitative or quasi-experimental study. The researcher could determine categories of conferences from trancript data and then train tutors to engage in one of two or three different types of tutoring sessions with specific tutees. The researcher could also make videos of sample tutoring sessions and show these in turn to tutors, tutees, writing center directors, and instructors and ask them to rate the sessions based on what and how much they thought the tutee learned. For naturalistic or quasi-experimental data, the researcher could interview the tutor and tutee and also collect "before" and "after" drafts. If the same tutor and tutee could engage in different types of sessions, this would allow the researcher to control for other factors such as age, race, and gender.

Research Question: Studies of affect are sorely lacking in the literature on tutoring. Babcock (2011a) noted (in an extremely small sample) that male-male tutoring dyads were less likely to show affect than all-female dyads. Since this avenue of research is totally open, the research question could be "What is the role of affect or feelings in the writing center tutorial?"

Research Approach and Methodology: a qualitative study resulting in a grounded theory analysis. The researcher could observe, transcribe, and analyze tutoring sessions, looking for open displays of affect, and then attempt to categorize and explain them. Stimulated recall could also be used, especially in instances where the researcher was not sure what the participant was feeling, or to determine feelings that were not displayed in the tutoring session. Member checking would be crucial in a study such as this, so the researcher should present study participants with drafts of the research study report in order to confirm the analyses.

Research Question: Most of the current research on negotiation has focused on L2 writers. What about L1 writers? How are session goals negotiated with L1 writers?
Research Approach and Methodology: a fairly straightforward descriptive study and analysis might be done using grounded theory or discourse analysis. The researcher could use tutoring sessions from a corpus of previously collected data. The write-up could compare findings from studies of L2 writers.

Research Question: How can the linguistic work on directives, suggestions, and politeness be used to directly improve tutoring?
Research Approach and Methodology: tutor-research or action research program. In training, tutors could be introduced to the frameworks of Ritter (2002), Thonus (1998; 1999b), and Zdrojkowski (2007). Tutors could then record and transcribe their own sessions, paying special attention to the linguistic forms they use and reflecting on student uptake and reaction. Tutors could plan to modify the features and structures of their discourse accordingly. As was done in *At the Point of Need* (Nelson, 1991), tutors could assemble their results into a conference presentation, journal article, or training materials for future tutors.

Research Question: What is the role of pauses in the tutoring session?
Research Approach and Methodology: an application of Conversation Analysis. Detailed transcriptions with accurate measurement of pauses would be crucial. The researcher could combine CA with Critical Discourse Analysis (see Ritter, 2002) to see if issues of dominance or institutional hierarchy are evidenced in pauses. For instance, does the tutor exhibit power by asking a question and then waiting an extremely long time for an answer?

Generating More Research Topics

If none of the future research topics we have proposed are appealing, we suggest some ways of generating more:

- Examine your own tutoring or that of others. Ask questions about your practice and its effectiveness. Decide on a research approach and data-gathering methods that would generate answers to these questions.
- Examine assessments done in your own writing center. Select an interesting finding or theme, and create a research question or questions from it.
- Examine writing center theory for ideas and concepts that can be researched empirically. Scan the writing center literature for challenges to a theory and imagine a research question and possible sites for inquiry.

- Examine writing center lore and ask a question that might dispute it. Consider approaches and methods of inquiry to find answers.

Conclusion

> No one ever died from an unanswered question (Yiddish proverb).

There will always be more to research about writing center practice. And we researchers can take our time, narrowing our topics and selecting methodologies carefully so that our work is RAD—replicable, applicable, and data-driven— and therefore generalizable beyond "our" writing centers. A good many of the references in this book are to unpublished dissertations and theses, many of them of excellent quality. We call for journal editors and book publishers to encourage writing center dissertation authors to submit all or part of their studies for publication. This "grey literature" contains important information for writing center professionals and researchers, and it should be ignored no longer. These thousands of document pages are an untapped treasure, one that will definitely enrich our understanding of writing center work and challenge our theorizing as we move forward as a field.

Note

1. We allude to the title of Stephen Hawking's (2002) book, *On the Shoulders of Giants* (Philadelphia, PA: Running Press).

KU Writing Center

Research Information
Statement/Oral Consent

Approved by the Human Subjects Committee University of Kansas, Lawrence Campus (HSCL) on 1/24/2012. Approval expires one year from 2/6/2012 HSCL# 17819

The KU Writing Center at the University of Kansas supports the practice of protection for human subjects participating in research. The following information is provided for you to decide whether you wish to participate in the present study. You should be aware that even if you agree to participate in this study, you are free to withdraw at any time without penalty. At that time, any data collected that could be associated with your participation will be destroyed.

We are conducting this study to better understand conversations in writing center consultations and to use this knowledge to improve writing consultant practice. We ask, "What features of writing center talk—conversational moves by consultants and writers, including questions, restatements, and suggestions—best facilitate student learning and revision?" To answer this question, we will make an audiorecording of your consulting session today. To follow up, we may conduct a 10-minute interview with you and/or ask you to complete a brief online questionnaire. This questionnaire will take less than 10 minutes to complete.

The content of the questionnaire or interview should cause no more discomfort than you would experience in your everyday life. Although participation may not benefit you directly, we believe that the information obtained from this study will help us gain a better understanding of conversations in writing center consultations, knowledge we will use to improve writing consultant practice. Audio recordings, records of consultations, and transcripts will be stored on password-protected staff computers inaccessible to the public.

Your participation is solicited, although strictly voluntary. Your name will not be associated in any way with the research findings. If you would like additional information concerning this study before or after it is completed, please feel free to contact us by phone or mail.

If you have any additional questions about your rights as a research participant, you may call (785) 864-7429 or (785) 864-7385 or write the Human Subjects Committee Lawrence Campus (HSCL), University of Kansas, 2385 Irving Hill Road, Lawrence, Kansas 66045-7563.

Sincerely,
Terese Thonus, Ph.D
University of Kansas
Lawrence, KS 66045
(785) 864-2398
tthonus@ku.edu

Application for Project Approval

TITLE: DATE:

1. Name of Investigator(s)
2. Department Affiliation
3. Mailing Address
4. Phone Number(s)
5. Name of Faculty Member Responsible for Project
6. Type of investigator and nature of activity. (Check appropriate categories)
   - ☐ Faculty or staff of The University of Texas of the Permian Basin
     - ☐ Project to be submitted for extramural funding;
       Agency _____
     - ☐ Project to be submitted for intramural funding;
       Source _____
     - ☐ Project unfunded
     - ☐ Other
   - ☐ Student at The University of Texas of the Permian Basin
     - ☐ Graduate   ☐ Undergraduate   ☐ Special
     - ☐ Senior Thesis   ☐ Master's Thesis or Project
     - ☐ Class project (number and title of class) _____
     - ☐ Independent study (name of faculty supervisor) _____
     - ☐ Other (please explain) _____
7. Qualification for exempt status: Research described in the proposal is (check those which apply)
   - ☐ Research conducted in commonly accepted educational settings using normal educational practices.
   - ☐ Research using educational tests, survey, interview or observation tech-

niques which do not expose subjects to risk of identification which could include negative personal consequences.

☐ The data being collected is from elected or appointed officials or candidates.

☐ Research uses secondary data and subjects cannot be identified.

☐ Research is conducted in cooperation with a public service department or agency for program evaluation purposes.

NOTE: The qualification for exempt status is determined by UTPB ACHE. All information requested in this form is required for processing.

8. **Are individuals other than faculty, staff, or students of UTPB involved in the research? Please identify investigators and research group**

9. **Certifications**

ALL STUDENT APPLICATIONS SUBMITTED TO ACHE FOR REVIEW MUST BE SIGNED BY ALL INVESTIGATORS INCLUDING THE FACULTY MEMBER SUPERVISING THE RESEARCH ACTIVITY.

I have received and read the policies and procedures of The University of Texas of the Permian Basin regarding human subjects in research as outlined in the Handbook of Operating Procedures, Section 7. I subscribe to the standards and will adhere to the policies and procedures of the review board.

AND

I am familiar with the published guidelines for the ethical treatment of students associated with my particular field of study (as published by the American Psychological Association, American Sociological Association, American Marketing Association, etc.).

Signature _____   Signature _____
First Investigator   Date   Faculty Supervisor   Date
                                          (If Investigator is Student)

Signature _____   Signature _____
Other Investigator/s   Date   Department Chair or Dean   Date

Office use only: Based upon the information provided in the application, the undersigned committee designee has determined that

1. The proposal is exempt from further review and may proceed according to procedures submitted (NOTE: Changes must be resubmitted) or that

2. The proposal requires changes as noted and further committee review.

_____
Reviewer   Date

Title:

10. **Please answer the following questions with regard to the research activity proposed:**
   Does the research involve: YES NO

   a. drugs or other controlled substances? ☐ ☐
   b. payment of subjects for participation? ☐ ☐
   c. access to subjects through a cooperating institution? ☐ ☐
   d. substances taken internally by or applied externally to the subjects? ☐ ☐
   e. mechanical or electrical devices (electrodes) applied to the subjects? ☐ ☐
   f. fluids (blood) or tissues removed from the subjects? ☐ ☐
   g. subjects experiencing stress (physiological or psychological)? ☐ ☐
   h. deception of subjects concerning any aspect of purposes or procedures? (misleading or withheld information) ☐ ☐
   i. subjects who would be judged to have limited freedom of consent (minors, mentally retarded, ill, or aged)? ☐ ☐
   j. any procedure or activities that might place the subjects at risk psychological, physical, or social)? ☐ ☐
   k. use of interviews, survey, questionnaires, audio or video recordings? ☐ ☐
   l. data collection over a period greater than one year? ☐ ☐
   m. a copy of the consent form will be given to the subjects (THIS IS MANDATORY, a copy must be attached to this form) ☐ ☐

11. **Approximate number of subjects to be involved in the research:**

12. **Project Purpose(s):**

13. **Describe the proposed subjects (age, sex, race, or other special characteristics):**

14. **Describe how the subjects are to be selected:** see above

15. Summary of the proposed procedures in the project (must be complete on this page, see instructions):

ITEMS 16-SUPPLEMENTARY APPENDIX, 17-CONSENT FORM, AND 18-QUESTIONNAIRES OR RESEARCH INSTRUMENTS MUST BE ATTACHED AS PART OF THE COMPLETE APPLICATION

References

"Action research: Transforming the generation and application of knowledge." Retrieved from http://www.uk.sagepub.com/journals/Journal201642?siteId=sage-uk&prodTypes=any&q=action+research+manifesto&fs=1. Retrieved March 24, 2012 from the *Action Research Journal* website.

Alonso, A. (2009). Clinician's love/hate relationship with clinical research. In R. A. Levy & J. S. Ablon (Eds.), *Handbook of evidence-based psychodynamic psychotherapy: Bridging the gap between science and practice* (pp. 385-388). New York: Humana Press.

American Heritage Dictionary of the English Language (4th ed.). (2006). New York: Houghton Mifflin Company. Retrieved from 22 February 2011 at http://dictionary.reference.com/help/ahd4.html.

American Psychological Association (2005). *Policy statement on evidence-based practice in psychology.* Retrieved from http://www2.apa.org/practice/ebpstatement.pdf

Anglada, L. B. (1999). *Online writing center responses and advanced EFL students' writing: An analysis of comments, students' attitudes, and textual revisions.* (Doctoral dissertation, Texas Tech University). ProQuest Dissertations & Theses, 9925612.

Arendale, D. R. (2010). Access at the crossroads: Learning assistance in higher education. *ASHE Higher Education Report, 35*(6). San Francisco: Jossey-Bass.

Austin, J. L. (1962). *How to do things with words.* New York: Oxford University Press.

Babcock, R. D. (2005). *Tutoring deaf students in the writing center.* (Doctoral dissertation, Indiana University of Pennsylvania.) ProQuest Dissertations & Theses, 3167231.

Babcock, R. D. (2008a). Tutoring deaf college students in the writing center. In C. Lewiecki-Wilson & B. J. Brueggemann (Eds.), *Disability and the teaching of writing.* (pp. 28–39). Boston: Bedford/St. Martin's.

Babcock, R. D. (2008b). Outlaw tutoring: Editing and proofreading revisited. *Journal of College Reading and Learning, 38,* 63–70.

Babcock, R. D. (2009). Research-based tutoring tips for working with deaf students. *Kansas English,* 93(1), 73–98.

Babcock, R. D. (2011a). Interpreted writing center tutorials with college-level deaf students. *Linguistics and Education,* 22(2), 95–117.

Babcock, R. D. (2011b). When something is not quite right: Pragmatic impairment and compensation in the college writing tutorial. *Writing Lab Newsletter, 35*(5–6), 6–10.

Babcock, R. D. (forthcoming). *The intersection of learning disability, pragmatics and speech acts in the college writing tutorial.* Manuscript submitted for publication.

Babcock, R. D., Carter-Tod, S., & Thonus, T. (forthcoming). *After the writing center dissertation: What's next?* Manuscript submitted for publication.

Babcock, R. D., Ferrel, T., & Ozias, M. (2011). The Summer Institute for Writing Center Directors and Professionals: A narrative bibliography. *Composition Forum, 23.* http://composition forum.com/issue/23/summer-institutebibliography.php

Babcock, R. D., Manning, K., & Rogers, T., with McCain, A., & Goff, C. (in press.) *A synthesis of qualitative studies of writing centers, 1983–2006.* New York: Peter Lang.

Bandura, A. (1986). *Social foundations of thought and action: A social cognitive theory.* New York: Prentice Hall.

Barnett, K. E. (2007). *Leading college writing centers into the future: Strategies for survival and sustainability.* (Doctoral dissertation, Johnson & Wales University) ProQuest Dissertations & Theses, 3315138.

Barnett, R. W., & Blumner, J. S. (Eds.)(1999), *Writing centers and writing across the curriculum programs: Building inter disciplinary partnerships* (pp. 105–118). Westport, CT: Greenwood Press.

Barnett, R. W., & Blumner, J. S. (Eds.) (2001). *The Allyn and Bacon guide to writing center theory and practice.* Boston: Allyn and Bacon.

Barnett, R. W., & Blumner, J. S. (Eds.) (2008). *The Longman guide to writing center theory and practice.* New York: Longman.

Baruch, Y. (1999). Response rate in academic studies: A comparative analysis. *Human Relations,* 52(4), 421–438.

Baxter Magolda, M. B., & Rogers, J. L. (1987). Peer tutoring: Collaborating to enhance intellectual development. *College Student Journal,* 21(3), 288–296.

Bean, J. P. (1998). *Conversation and gender in a university composition program.* (Doctoral dissertation, University of North Carolina at Greensboro) ProQuest Dissertations & Theses, 9919173.

Bean, J. (1999). Feminine discourse in the university: The writing center conference as a site of linguistic resistance. In J. Addison & S. J. McGee (Eds.), *Feminist empirical research: Emerging perspectives on qualitative and teacher research* (pp. 127–144). Portsmouth, NH: Boynton/Cook.

Beaumont, P. A. (1978). *A descriptive study of the role of the tutor in a conference on writing.* (Master's thesis, University of San Diego).

Beers, S. F., & Nagy, W. E. (2009). Syntactic complexity as a predictor of adolescent writing quality: Which measures? Which genre? *Reading & Writing,* 22, 185–200.

Bell, D. C., & Elledge, S. R. (2008). Dominance and peer tutoring sessions with English language learners. *Learning Assistance Review,* 13, 17–30. ERIC document EJ818224.

Bell, D. C., Arnold, H., & Haddock, R. (2009). Linguistic politeness and peer tutoring. *Learning Assistance Review, 14*(1), 37–54.

Bell, D. C., & Hübler, M. T. (2001). The virtual writing center: Developing ethos through mailing lists discourse. *Writing Center Journal, 21*(2), 57–78.

Bell, D. C., & Youmans, M. (2006). Politeness and praise: Rhetorical issues in ESL (L2) writing center conferences. *Writing Center Journal, 26*(2), 31–47.

Bell, J. H. (1989). *Tutoring in a writing center.* (Doctoral dissertation, University of Texas at Austin.) ProQuest Dissertations & Theses, 9005528.

Bell, J. H. (1999). Tutoring a provisional student in composition. *Journal of College Reading and Learning, 29*(2), 194–208.

Bell, J. H. (2000). When hard questions are asked: Evaluating writing centers. *Writing Center Journal, 21*(1), 7–28.

Bell, J. H. (2002). Research report: Better writers: Writing center tutoring and the revision of rough drafts. *Journal of College Reading and Learning, 33*, 5–20. Retrieved from http://find articles.com/p/articles/mi_hb3247/ is_1_33/ ai_n28966211/?tag=mantle_skin;content

Bemer, A. N. (2010). *The rhetoric of space in the design of academic computer writing locations.* (Doctoral dissertation, Utah State University) ProQuest Dissertations & Theses, 3423992.

Berg, B. L. (2009). *Qualitative research methods for the social sciences* (7th ed.). New York: Pearson.

Bisson, L. (2007). A tutee's tears. *Writing Lab Newsletter, 32*(4), 14–15.

Bizzell, P. (1986). What happens when basic writers come to college? *College Composition and Communication, 37*(3), 294–301.

Blalock, S. (1997). Negotiating authority through one-to-one collaboration in the multicultural writing center. In C. Severino, J. Guerra, & J. Butler (Eds.), *Writing in multicultural settings* (pp. 79–93). New York: Modern Language Association.

Blau, S. R., Hall, J., Davis, J., & Gravitz, L. (2001). Tutoring ESL students: A different kind of session. *Writing Lab Newsletter, 25*(10), 1–4.

Blau, S., Hall, J., & Sparks, S. (2002). Guilt-free tutoring: Rethinking how we tutor non-native English-speaking students. *Writing Center Journal, 23*(1), 23–44.

Blau, S., Hall, J., & Strauss, T. (1998). Exploring the tutor/client conversation: A linguistic analysis. *Writing Center Journal, 19*(1), 19–48.

Block, R. (2010). *Reading aloud in the writing center: A comparative analysis of three tutoring methods.* (Doctoral dissertation, University of Louisville) ProQuest Dissertations & Theses, 3415200.

Blom, B. (2009). Knowing or un-knowing? That is the question in the era of evidence-based social work practice. *Journal of Social Work, 9*(2), 158–77.

Blomfield, R., & Hardy, S. (2000). Evidence-based nursing practice. In L. Trinder (Ed.), *Evidence-based practice: A critical appraisal* (pp. 111–137). Oxford: Blackwell.

Bloom, B. S. (1984). The 2 sigma problem: The search for methods of group instruction as effective as one-to-one tutoring. *Educational Researcher, 13*, 4–16.

Bloome, D. (2004). *Discourse analysis and the study of classroom language and literacy events.* Mahwah, NJ: Lawrence Erlbaum.

Bokser, J. A. (2005). Pedagogies of belonging: Listening to students and peers. *Writing Center Journal, 25*(1), pp. 43–59.

Boquet, E. H. (1995). Writing centers: History, theory, and implications. (Doctoral dissertation, Indiana University of Pennsylvania) ProQuest Dissertations & Theses, 9531331.

Boquet, E. H. (2002). *Noise from the writing center*. Logan: Utah State University Press.

Boquet, E. H. (2007). More than a claim of faith: If Darwin ran the writing center. In J. Griffin, C. Mattingly, & M. Eodice (Eds.), *Writing at the Center: Proceedings of the 2004 Thomas R. Watson conference*. Emmitsburg, MD: International Writing Centers Association Press.

Boquet, E. H., & Lerner, N. (2008). Reconsiderations: After "The Idea of a Writing Center." *College English, 71*(2), 170–189.

Borg, E., & Deane, M. (2011). Measuring the outcomes of individualized writing instruction: A multilayered approach to capturing changes in students' texts. *Teaching in Higher Education, 16*(3), 319–331.

Bormann, E. (1985). Symbolic convergence theory: A communication formulation. *Journal of Communication, 35*(4), 128–138.

Boudreaux, M. A. (1998). *Toward awareness: A study of nonverbal behavior in the writing conference.* (Doctoral dissertation, Indiana University of Pennsylvania) ProQuest Dissertations & Theses, 9828752.

Boylan, H. R. (2002). *What works: research-based practices in developmental education*. Boone, NC: National Center for Developmental Education.

Boylan, H. R., Bonham, B. S., & Bliss, L. B. (1992). *National study of developmental education: Students, programs and institutions of higher education*. Boone, NC: National Center for Developmental Education.

Breetvelt, I., van den Bergh, H., & Rijlaarsdam, G. (1994). Relations between writing processes and text quality: When and how? *Cognition and Instruction, 12*(2), 103–123.

Briggs, L. C. (1991). *Writing center talk in a long-term writer-consultant relationship.* (Doctoral dissertation: Syracuse University). ProQuest Dissertations & Theses, 9204493.

Briner, R. (2000). Evidence-based human resource management. In L. Trinder (Ed.), *Evidence-based practice: A critical appraisal* (pp. 184–211). Oxford: Blackwell.

Broder, P. F. (1981). Such good friends: Cooperation between the English department and the writing lab. *Writing Program Administration, 5*(2), 7–11.

Brown, G. & Yule, G. (1983). *Discourse analysis*. Cambridge: Cambridge University Press.

Brown, K. (2008). *Breaking into the tutor's toolbox: An investigation into the strategies used in writing center tutorials.* (Doctoral dissertation, University of Louisville) ProQuest Dissertations & Theses, 3333805.

Brown, P. & Levinson, S. (1987). *Politeness*. Cambridge: Cambridge University Press.

Brown, P., & Levinson, S. (1978). Universals in language use: Politeness phenomena. In E. Goody (Ed.), *Questions and politeness* (pp. 56–289). Cambridge: Cambridge University Press.

Bruffee, K. A. (1984). Peer tutoring and the "conversation of mankind." In G. A. Olson (Ed.), *Writing centers: Theory and administration* (pp. 3–15). Urbana, IL: National Council of Teachers of English.

Bruffee, K. A. (1978). "The Brooklyn Plan": Attaining intellectual growth through peer-group tutoring. *Liberal Education, 64*(4), 447–468.

Bruffee, K. A. (1999). *Collaborative learning: Higher education, interdependence, and the authority of knowledge* (2nd ed.) Baltimore: Johns Hopkins University Press.

Bushman, D. (1991). Past Accomplishments and current trends in writing center research. In R. Wallace and J. Simpson (Eds.), *The writing center: New directions.* (pp. 27–38). New York: Garland.

Calfee, J. (2007). Online tutoring and student success in developmental writing courses. *Journal of Applied Research in the Community College, 15*(1), 77–80.

Callaway, S. (1993). *Collaboration, resistance and the authority of the student writer.* (Doctoral dissertation: University of Wisconsin-Milwaukee) ProQuest Dissertations & Theses, 9400702.

Camps, A., & Milian, M. (Eds.) (2000). *Metalinguistic activity in learning to write.* Amsterdam: Amsterdam University Press.

Cardenas, D. (2000). *The conversation of the consultation: Describing collaborations.* (Doctoral dissertation, Texas A&M University) ProQuest Dissertations & Theses, 9994219.

Carino, P. (2002). Reading our own words: Rhetorical analysis and institutional discourse of writing centers. In P. Gillespie, A. Gillam, L. F. Brown, & B. Stay, (Eds.), *Writing center research: Extending the conversation* (pp. 91–110). Mahwah, NJ: Erlbaum.

Carino, P., & Enders, D. (2001). Does frequency of visits to the writing center increase student satisfaction? A statistical correlation study—or story. *Writing Center Journal, 22*(1), 83–102.

Carroll, L. A. (2002). *Rehearsing new roles: How college students develop as writers.* Carbondale: Southern Illinois University Press.

Carter-Tod, S. L. (1995). *The role of the writing center in the writing practice of L2 students.* (Doctoral dissertation, Virginia Polytechnic Institute) ProQuest Dissertations and Theses, 9606230.

Casazza, M. E., & Silverman, S. L. (1996). *Learning assistance and developmental education: A guide for effective practice.* San Francisco: Jossey-Bass.

CCCC Committee on Part-Time/Adjunct Issues. (2001). Report on the coalition on the academic workforce/CCCC survey of faculty in freestanding writing programs for fall 1999. *College Composition and Communication, 53*(2), 336–348.

Chi, M., Roy, M., & Hausmann, R. G. M. (2008). Observing tutorial dialogues collaboratively: Insights about human tutoring effectiveness from vicarious learning. *Cognitive Science, 32,* 301–241. doi: 10.1080/0364021070863396

Childers, P. B. (1999). Writing center or experimental center for faculty research, discovery, and risk taking? R. W. Barnett & J. S. Blumner (Eds.), *Writing centers and writing across the curriculum programs: Building interdisciplinary partnerships* (pp. 177–186). Westport, CT: Greenwood Press.

Chiseri-Strater, E., & Sunstein, B. S. (2006). *What works? A practical guide for teacher research.* Portsmouth, NH: Heinemann.

Chiu, S. C.-H. (2011). *Negotiating linguistic certainty for ESL writers in the writing center.* (Doctoral dissertation, Michigan State University). ProQuest Dissertations & Theses, 3444496.

Cho, K., & MacArthur, C. (2010). Student revision with peer and expert reviewing. *Learning and Instruction, 20,* 328–338.

Cho, K., Schunn, C. D., & Charney, D. (2006). Commenting on writing: Typology and perceived helpfulness of comments from novice peer reviewers and subject matter experts. *Written Communication, 23*(3), 260–294.

Clark, I. L. (1985). Leading a horse to water: The writing center and the required visit. *Writing Center Journal, 5*(2), 31–35.

Clark, I. L. (1988). Preparing future teachers of composition in the writing center. *College Composition and Communication, 39*(3), 347–350.

Clark, I. L. (2001). Perspectives on the directive/non-directive continuum in the writing center. *Writing Center Journal, 22*(1), 34–58.

Coelho, F. de O. (2011). Academic writing development through dialogues between tutors and second-language learners. (Master's thesis, San José State University) ProQuest Dissertations & Theses, 1495036.

Cogie, J. (1997). Theory made visible: How tutoring may affect the development of student-centered teachers. *Writing Program Administration, 21*(1), 7684.

Cogie, J. (1998). In defense of conference summaries: Widening the reach of writing center work. *Writing Center Journal, 18*(2), 4970.

Cogie, J. (2006). ESL student participation in writing center sessions. *Writing Center Journal, 26*(2), 4866.

Cogie, J., Strain, K., & Lorinskas, S. (1999). Avoiding the proofreading trap: The value of the error correction process. The *Writing Center Journal, 19*(2), 6–32.

Commission on English Language Program Accreditation (2010). *Accreditation overview.* Retrieved from http://www.cea-accredit.org/accreditation.html

Connor, U. (1996). *Contrastive rhetoric: Cross-cultural aspects of second-language writing.* Cambridge: Cambridge University Press.

Coogan, D. (1999). *Electronic writing centers: Computing the field of composition.* Stamford, CT: Ablex.

Cook-Gumperz, J. (1993). Dilemmas of identity: Oral and written literacies in the making of a basic writing student. *Anthropology and Education Quarterly, 24*(4), 336–356.

Cooper, E. (2010). Tutoring center effectiveness: The effect of drop-in tutoring. *Journal of College Reading and Learning, 40*(2), 21–34.

Corbett, S. J. (2011). Using case study multi-methods to investigate close(r) collaboration: Course-based tutoring and the directive/nondirective instructional continuum. *Writing Center Journal, 31*(1), 55–81.

Corbin, J., & Strauss, A. L. (2008). *Basics of qualitative research* (3rd ed.). Los Angeles: Sage.

Cordingley, P. (2004). Teachers using evidence: Using what we know about teaching and learning to reconceptualize evidence-based practice. In G. Thomas & R. Pring (Eds.), *Evidence-based practice in education* (pp. 77–90). New York: Open University Press.

Corrigan, J. (1997). A guide for writing tutors working with dyslexic students. *Writing Lab Newsletter 21*(10), 1–3, 10.

Cosgrove, C. (1993). Conferencing for the "learning disabled": How we might really help. In T. Flynn & M. King (Eds.). *Dynamics of the writing conference* (pp. 95–102). Urbana, IL: National Council of Teachers of English.

Council for Exceptional Children (2008). *Classifying the state of evidence for special education professional practices: CEC practice study manual.* Retrieved from http://www.cec.sped.org/Content/NavigationMenu/ProfessionalDevelopment/

Council of Writing Program Administrators (2008). *WPA Outcomes Statement for First-Year Composition.* Retrieved from http://wpacouncil.org/positions/outcomes.html

Courtney, J. P. (2009). *Performing student, teacher, and tutor of writing: Negotiating ideas of writing in a first-year writing course and writing center tutorials.* (Doctoral dissertation, University of North Carolina at Charlotte) ProQuest Dissertations & Theses, 3360423.

Craig, D. V. (2009). *Action research essentials.* San Francisco: Jossey-Bass.

Cromley, J. G., & Azevedo, R. (2005). What do reading tutors do? A naturalistic study of more and less experienced tutors in reading. *Discourse Processes, 40*(2), 83–113.

Cumming, A., & So, S. (1996). Tutoring second language text revision: Does the approach to instruction and the language of communication make a difference? *Journal of Second Language Writing, 5*(3), 197–225.

Currie, L., & Eodice, M. (2005). Roots entwined: Growing a sustainable collaboration. In J. K. Elmborg & S. Hook (Eds.), *Centers for learning: Writing centers and libraries and collaboration* (pp. 42–60). Chicago: Association of College and Research Libraries.

Curzan, A., & Adams, M. (2006). *How English works: A linguistic introduction.* New York: Longman.

Davies, A. (1991). *The native speaker in applied linguistics.* Edinburgh: Edinburgh University Press.

Davies, A. (2003). *The native speaker: Myth and reality.* Clevedon, UK: Multilingual Matters.

Davis, K. (1988). Improving students' writing attitudes: The effects of a writing center. *Writing Lab Newsletter, 12*(10), 3–5.

Davis, K. (1993). What the faculty know about what we do: Survey results. *Writing Lab Newsletter, 17*(4), 6–7.

Davis, K., Hayward, M., Hunter, K., & Wallace, D. L. (1988). The function of talk in the writing conference: A study of tutorial conversation. *Writing Center Journal, 9* (1), 45–51.

DeCiccio, A., Ede, L, Lerner, N., Boquet, B., & Harris, M. (2007). Work in progress: Publishing writing center scholarship. *Writing Lab Newsletter, 31*(7), 1–6.

Delpit, L. (1988). The silenced dialogue: Power and pedagogy in educating other people's children. *Harvard Educational Review, 58,* 280–98.

Denny, H. (2010). *Facing the center: Toward an identity politics of one-to-one mentoring.* Logan: Utah State University Press, 2010.

Denzin, N. K., & Lincoln, Y. S. (2005). *The Sage handbook of qualitative research* (3rd ed.). Thousand Oaks, CA: Sage Publications.

DePiero, D. L. (2007). *An empirical study of students' expectations of writing centers.* (Doctoral dissertation, University of Rhode Island) ProQuest Dissertations & Theses, 327-6979.

Dettman, D. M. (2006). *Perspectives, priorities, and professionalism: A case study of the Charles Mills Writing Center at Nazareth College of Rochester.* (Doctoral dissertation, University of Rochester) ProQuest Dissertations & Theses, 3220550.

Devet, B., & Gaetke, K. (2007). Three organizations for certifying a writing lab. *Writing Lab Newsletter, 31*(7), 7–12.

Dinitz, S., & Kiedaisch, J. (2003). Creating theory: Moving tutors to the center. *Writing Center Journal, 23*(2), 63–76.

DiPardo, A. (2003). "Whispers of coming and going": Lessons from Fannie. In C. Murphy and S. Sherwood (Eds.), *The St. Martin's sourcebook for writing tutors* (2nd ed.) (pp. 101–117). Boston: Bedford/St. Martin's.

Directives for human experimentation. Regulations and ethical guidelines. Office of Human Subjects Research. National Institutes of Health. Retrieved from http://ohsr.od.nih.gov/guidelines/nuremberg.html. Reprinted from Trials of War Criminals before the Nuremberg Military Tribunals under Control Council Law No. 10, Vol. 2, pp. 181-182.. Washington, D.C.: U.S. Government Printing Office, 1949.

Drake, D. B. (2009). Evidence is a verb: A relational approach to knowledge and mastery in coaching. *International Journal of Evidence Based Coaching and Mentoring, 7,* 1–12.

Driscoll, D. L., & Wynn-Perdue, S. (2010, November). *RAD research in the center: An analysis of research* in the Writing Center Journal, 1980–2009. Paper presented at the International Writing Centers Association Conference, Baltimore.

Ede, L. (1996). Writing centers and the politics of location: A response to Terrance Riley and Stephen M. North. *Writing Center Journal, 16*(2), 111–130.

Edgington, A. (2008). Becoming visible: Tutors discuss reading and listening to student papers. *Writing Lab Newsletter, 33*(3), 9–13.

Elbow, P., & Belanoff, P. (2003). *Being a writer: A community of writers revisited.* Boston: McGraw-Hill.

Elmborg, J. K., & Hook, S. (Eds.). (2005). *Centers for learning: Writing centers and libraries in collaboration.* Chicago: Association of College and Research Libraries.

Emerson, R. J., & Records, K. (2008). Today's challenge, tomorrow's excellence: The practice of evidence-based education. *Journal of Nursing Education, 47,* 359–370.

Emerson, R. M., Fretz, R. I., & Shaw, L. L. (2007). Participant observation and field notes. In P. Atkinson, A. Coffey, S. Delamont, J. Lofland & L. Lofland (Eds.), *Handbook of ethnography.* (pp. 352–368). Los Angeles: Sage.

Enders, D. (2005). Assessing the writing center: A qualitative tale of a quantitative study. *Writing Lab Newsletter, 29*(10), 6–9.

Engstrom, E. U. (2005). Reading, writing, and assistive technology: An integrated developmental curriculum for college students. *Journal of Adolescent and Adult Literacy, 49(1),* 30–39.

Eraut, M. (2004). Practice-based evidence. In G. Thomas & R. Pring (Eds.), *Evidence-based practice in education* (pp. 91–115). New York: Open University Press.

Ervin, C. (2002). The Writing Centers Research Project survey results, AY 2000–2001. *Writing Lab Newsletter, 27*(1), 1–4.

Faerm, E. (1992). Tutoring Anne: A case study. *Writing Lab Newsletter, 16*(7), 9–10.

Faigley, L., & Witte, S. P. (1981). Analyzing revision. *Computers and Composition, 32(4),* 400–414.

Fairclough, N. (1989). *Language and power.* New York: Longman.

Fairclough, N. (1995). *Critical discourse analysis: The critical study of language.* London: Longman.

Falchikov, N. (2001). *Learning together: Peer tutoring in higher education.* London: Routledge Falmer.

Fallon, B. J. (2010). *The perceived, conceived, and lived experiences of 21st-century peer writing tutors.* (Doctoral dissertation, Indiana University of Pennsylvania) ProQuest Dissertations & Theses, 3433440.

Farrell, J. T. (1994). Some of the challenges to writing centers posed by graduate students. *Writing Lab Newsletter, 18*(6), 3–5.

Ferris, D., Pezone, S., Tade, C., & Tinti, S. (1997). Teacher commentary on student writing: Descriptions and implications. *Journal of Second Language Writing, 6*(2), 155–182.

Fetterman, D. M. (2009). *Ethnography step-by-step.* (3rd ed.). Thousand Oaks, CA: Sage.

Fischer, Fred H. (1989). *The effect of the tutorial writing center on underprepared community college students.* (Doctoral dissertation, Northern Arizona University) ProQuest Dissertations & Theses, 3119003.

Fischer, K. M., & Harris, M. (2001). Fill 'er up, pass the band-aids, center the margin, and praise the Lord: Mixing metaphors in the writing lab. In J. V. Nelson & K. Evertz (Eds.), *The politics of writing centers* (pp. 23–36). Portsmouth, NH: Boynton/Cook.

Fitzgerald, S., Mulvihill, P., & Dobson, R. (1991). Meeting the needs of graduate students: Writing support groups in the center. In R. Wallace & J. Simpson (Eds.), *The writing center: New directions* (pp. 133–144). New York: Garland.

Flagel, P., & Bell, J. H. (2001). "I will probably still do it my way": Is this the outcome of a successful tutorial session? *Journal of College Reading and Learning, 31*(2), 233–243.

Fletcher, D. C. (1993). On the issue of authority. In T. Flynn & M. King (Eds.), *Dynamics of the writing conference: Social and cognitive interactions* (pp. 41–50). Urbana, IL: NCTE.

Fox, C. M. (2003). *Writing across cultures: Contrastive rhetoric and a writing center study of one student's journey.* (Doctoral dissertation, University of Rhode Island) ProQuest Dissertations & Theses, 3141842.

Fox, J. (1989). Interactional differences in writing conferences. *Carleton Papers in Applied Language Studies, 6,* 1–30.

Frank, L. (1983). The writing lab at work: Two case studies. In M. Harris & T. Baker (Eds.), *New directions, new connections: Proceedings of the Writing Centers Association Fifth Conference.* West Lafayette, IN: Department of English, Purdue University.

Freed, A., & Ehrlich, S. (2010). *Why do you ask?: The function of questions in institutional discourse.* New York: Oxford University Press.

Fulkerson, R. (1990). Composition theory in the 1980s: Axiological consensus and paradigmatic diversity. *College Composition and Communication, 41*(4), 409–429.

Gallagher, C. W. (2011). Being there: (Re)making the assessment scene. *College Composition and Communication, 62*(3), 450–476.

Gardner, P. J., & Ramsey, W.M. (2005). The polyvalent mission of writing centers. *Writing Center Journal, 25*(1), 25–42.

Gars, S. M. & Neu, J. (2006). *Speech acts across cultures: Challenges to communication in a second language.* Berlin: Mouton de Gruyter.

Gee, J. P. (2005). *An introduction to discourse analysis.* (2nd ed.) New York: Routledge.

Geither, E. J. B. (2010). *Exploring success in tutoring the non-native English speaker at university writing centers.* (Doctoral dissertation, Cleveland State University) ProQuest Dissertations and Theses, 3437849.

Geller, A., Eodice, M, Condon, F., Carroll, M., & Boquet, E. (2006). *The everyday writing center.* Logan: Utah State University Press.

Georgetown University Writing Center. http://writingcenter.georgetown.edu/

Gere, A. R., & Abbott, R. D. (1985). Talking about writing: The language of writing groups. *Research in the Teaching of Writing, 19*(4), 362–381.

Giacomini, M. (2009). Theory-based medicine and the role of evidence: Why the emperor needs new clothes, again. *Perspectives in Biology and Medicine, 52,* 234–251.

Gilewicz, M. (2004). Sponsoring student response in writing center group tutorials. In B. J. Moss, N. P. Highberg, & M. Nicolas (Eds.), *Writing groups inside and outside the classroom* (pp. 63–78). Mahwah, NJ: Erlbaum.

Gilewicz, M., & Thonus, T. (2000, November). *Descriptive and evaluative language in group tutorials.* Paper presented at the National Writing Centers Association Conference, Baltimore, MD.

Gilewicz, M., & Thonus, T. (2003). Close vertical transcription in writing center training and research. *Writing Center Journal, 24*(1), 40–55.

Gillespie, P., Gillam, A., Brown, L. Falls & Stay, B. (Eds.) (2002). *Writing center research: Extending the conversation.* Mahwah, NJ: Erlbaum.

Gillespie, P., Hughes, B., & Kail, H. (2011). Nothing marginal about this writing center experience: Using research about peer tutor alumni to educate others. In N. Mauriello, W. J. Macauley, Jr., & R. T. Koch (Eds.), *Before and after the tutorial: Writing centers and institutional relationships* (pp. 35–52). New York: Hampton Press.

Gillespie, P., & Lerner, N. (2008). *The Longman guide to peer tutoring* (2nd ed). New York: Pearson Longman.

Glaser, B. G., & Strauss, A. L. (1967). *Discovery of grounded theory: Strategies for qualitative research.* Chicago: Aldine.

Godbee, B. (2011). *Small talk, big change: Identifying potential as for social change in one-with-one talk about writing.* (Doctoral dissertation, University of Wisconsin-Madison)

Goody, E. N. (1978). (Ed.). *Questions and politeness.* New York: Cambridge University Press.

Gordon, B. L. (2008). Requiring first-year writing classes to visit the writing center: Bad attitudes or positive results? *Teaching English in the Two-Year College, 36*(2), 154–163.

Gordon, E. E., Morgan, R. R., O'Malley, C. J., & Ponticell, J. (2007). *The tutoring revolution: Applying research for best practices, policy implications, and student achievement.* Lanham, MD: Rowman & Littlefield Education.

Gordon, T., Holland, J., & Lahelma, E. (2007). Ethnographic research in educational settings. In P. Atkinson, A. Coffey, S. Delamont, J. Lofland, & L. Lofland (Eds.), *Handbook of ethnography.* (pp. 188–203). Los Angeles: Sage.

Graesser, A. C., & Person, N. K. (1994). Question asking during tutoring. *American Educational Research Journal, 31*(1), 104–137.

Graesser, A. C., D'Mello, S. K., Craig, S. D., Witherspoon, A., Sullins, J., McDaniel, B., & Gholson, B. (2008). The relationship between affective states and dialog patterns during interactions with AutoTutor. *Journal of Interactive Learning Research, 29*(2), 293–312.

Graesser, A. C., Lu, S. Jackson, G. T., Mitchell, H. H., Ventura, M., Olney, A., & Louwerse, M. M. (2004). AutoTutor: A tutor with dialogue in natural language. *Behavior Research Methods, Instruments, & Computers, 36*(2), 180–192.

Gramley, S., & Pätzold, K.-M. (2004). *A survey of Modern English* (2nd ed.). London: Routledge.

Greer, R. D. (2002). *Designing teaching strategies: An applied behavior analysis systems approach.* New York: Academic Press.

Greer, R. D., & Keohane, D.-D. (2004). A real science and technology of education. In D. J. Moran & R. W. Malott (Eds.), *Evidence-based educational methods* (pp. 23–43). Amsterdam: Elsevier Academic Press.

Grice, [H.] P. (1991). *Studies in the way of words.* Cambridge: Harvard University Press.

Griffin, J. (2008). *Distance learning technologies and writing center conferences: A comparative analysis of two methods for delivering consultations at a distance.* (Doctoral dissertation, University of Louisville) ProQuest Dissertations & Theses,, 3333811.

Griffin, J. A., Mattingly, C., & Eodice, M. (2007). (Eds.). *Writing at the center: Proceedings of the 2004 Thomas R. Watson Conference, 7–9 October.* CD-ROM. Emmitsburg, MD: IWCA Press.

Grimm, N. M. (1999). *Good intentions: Writing center work for postmodern times.* Portsmouth, NH: Boynton/Cook.

Grimm, N. (2003). In the spirit of service: Making writing center research a "featured character." In M. A. Pemberton & J. Kinkead (Eds.), *The center will hold: Critical perspectives on writing center scholarship* (pp. 41-57). Logan, UT: Utah State University Press.

Grinnell, C. K. (2003). *The effect of a writing center on developmental student writing apprehension and writing performance.* (Doctoral dissertation, Grambling State University) ProQuest Dissertations & Theses, 3119003.

Guiora, A., Acton, W., Erard, R., & Strickland, F., Jr. (1980). The effects of Benzodiazepine (Valium) on permeability of language ego boundaries. *Language Learning, 30*, 351–361.

Guiora, A., Beit-Hallahmi, B., Brannon, R., Dull, C., & Scovel, T. (1972). The effects of experimentally induced changes into ego states on pronunciation ability in a second language: An exploratory study. *Comprehensive Psychiatry, 13*, 421–428.

Haas, T. S. (1986). *A case study of peer tutors' writing conferences with students: Tutors' roles and conversations about composing.* (Doctoral dissertation, New York University) ProQuest Dissertations & Theses, 8706315.

Hackett, G., & Betz, N. E. (1989). An exploration of the mathematics self-efficacy/ mathematics performance correspondence. *Journal for Research in Mathematics Education, 20*, 261–273.

Hammersley, M. (2000). Evidence-based practice in education and the contribution of educational research. In L. Trinder. (Ed.), *Evidence-based practice: A critical appraisal* (pp. 163–183). Oxford: Blackwell.

Hammersley, M. (2004). Some questions about evidence-based practice in education. In G. Thomas & R. Pring (Eds.), *Evidence-based practice in education* (pp. 133–149). New York: Open University Press.

Han, Z. (2004). To be a native speaker means not to be a nonnative speaker. *Second Language Research, 20*(2), 166–187.

Hancock, D. R., & Algozzine, R. (2006). *Doing case study research: A practical guide for beginning researchers.* New York: Teachers College Press.

Harklau, L., Losey, K. M., & Siegal, M. (Eds.). (1999). *Generation 1.5 meets college composition: Issues in the teaching of writing to U.S.-educated learners of ESL.* Mahwah, NJ: Lawrence Erlbaum.

Harris, M. (1986). *Teaching one-to-one: The writing conference.* Urbana, IL: National Council of Teachers of English.

Harris, M. (1999a). A writing center without a WAC program: The de facto WAC center/writing center. In R.W. Barnett & J. S. Blumner (Eds.), *Writing centers and writing across the curriculum programs: building interdisciplinary partnerships* (pp. 89–103). Westport, CT.: Greenwood Press.

Harris, M. (1999b). Diverse research methodologies at work for diverse audiences: Shaping the writing center to the institution. In S. K. Rose & I. Weiser (Eds.), *The writing program administrator as researcher: Inquiry in action and reflection* (pp. 1–17). Portsmouth, NH: Boynton/Cook.

Harris, M. (2000). Preparing to sit at the head table: Maintaining writing center viability in the twenty-first century. *Writing Center Journal, 20*(2), 13–22.

Haswell, R. H. (2000). Documenting improvement in college writing: A longitudinal approach. *Written Communication, 17*(3) 307–352.

Haswell, R. H. (2005). NCTE/CCCC's recent war on scholarship. *Written Communication, 22*(2), 198–223.

Hawthorne, J. (2006). Approaching assessment as if it matters. In C. Murphy & B. L. Stay (Eds.), *The writing center director's resource book* (pp. 237–245). Mahwah, NJ: Erlbaum.

Haviland, C. P., & Stephenson, D. (2002). Writing centers, writing programs, and WPAs: Roles by any other names? In S.C. Brown & T. Enos (Eds.), *The writing program administrator's resource: A guide to reflective institutional practice* (pp. 377–392). Mahwah, NJ: Lawrence Erlbaum.

Haviland, C. P., Notarangelo, M., Whitley-Putz, L., & Wolf, T. (Eds). (1998). *Weaving knowledge together: Writing centers and collaboration.* Emmitsburg, MD: National Writing Centers Association Press.

Haviland, C. P., & Trianosky, M. (2006). Tutors speak: What do we want from our writing center directors? In C. Murphy & B. L. Stay (Eds.), *The writing center director's resource book* (pp. 311–320). Mahwah, NJ: Erlbaum.

Hawkes, L. (2006). When compassion isn't enough: Providing fair and equivalent access to writing help for students with disabilities. In C. Murphy & B. L. Stay (Eds.), *The writing center director's resource book* (pp. 371–377). Mahwah, NJ: Lawrence Erlbaum.

Hawthorne, J. (2006). Approaching assessment as if it matters. In C. Murphy & B. L. Stay (Eds.), *The writing center director's resource book* (pp. 237–245). Mahwah, NJ: Erlbaum.

Hayes, J. R., Hatch, J. A., & Silk, C. M. (2000). Does holistic assessment predict writing performance? Estimating the consistency of student performance in holistically scored writing assignments. *Written Communication, 17*(1), 3–26.

Hayward, M. (1983). Assessing attitudes towards the writing center. *Writing Center Journal, 3*(2), 1–10.

Healy, D. (1995). In the temple of the familiar: The writing center as church. In B. Stay, C. Murphy, & E. H. Hobson (Eds.), *Writing center perspectives* (pp. 12–25). Emmitsburg, MD: NWCA Press.

Hedges, L. V. (2000). Using converging evidence in policy formation: The case of class size research. *Evaluation and Research in Education, 14*, 193–205.

Henson, R., & Stephenson, S. (2009). Writing consultations can effect quantifiable change: One institution's assessment. *Writing Lab Newsletter, 33*(9), 1–5.

Hess, K. J. (2008). *"Making sense" in the center: In support of writing center-based collaborative writing groups.* (Master's thesis, California State University, Fresno) ProQuest Dissertations & Theses, 1460356.

Hewett, B. L. (2000). Characteristics of interactive computer-mediated peer group talk and its influence on revision. *Computers and Composition, 17*(3), 265–288.

Hewett, B. L. (2004–2005). A synchronous online instructional commentary: A study of student revision. *Readerly/Writerly Texts: Essays in Literary, Composition, and Pedagogical Theory, 11 & 12*(1), 47–67.

Hewett, B. L. (2006). Synchronous online conference-based instruction: A study of whiteboard interactions and student writing. *Computers and Composition, 23*(1), 4–31.

Hewett, B. L. (2010). *The online writing conference: A guide for teachers and tutors.* Portsmouth, NH: Boynton/Cook Heinemann.

Hey, P., & Nahrwold, C. (1994). Tutors aren't trained—they're educated: The need for composition theory. *Writing Lab Newsletter, 18*(7), 4–5.

Hinds, J. (1987). Reader vs. writer responsibility: A new typology. In U. Connor & R. B. Kaplan (Eds.), *Writing across languages: Analysis of L2 texts* (pp. 141–152). Reading, MA: Addison-Wesley.

Hirose, K. (2003). Comparing L1 and L2 organizational patterns in the argumentative writing of Japanese EFL students. *Journal of Second Language Writing, 12*(2), 181–209.

Hobson, E. (1992). *Where theory and practice collide: Beyond essentialist descriptions of the writing center.* (Doctoral dissertation, University of Tennessee) ProQuest Dissertations & Theses, 9306642.

Hobson, E. H. (1995). Writing center practice often counters its theory. So what? In J. A. Mullin & R. Wallace (Eds.), *Intersections: Theory-practice in the writing center* (pp. 1–10). Urbana, IL: NCTE.

Hobson, E. H. (1997). Forms and functions of formative assessment. *Clearing House, 71*(2), 68–70.

Hobson, E. H. (1998). *Wiring the writing center.* Logan: Utah State University Press.

Hobson, E. H., & Lerner, N. (1999). Writing centers/WAC in pharmacy education: A changing prescription. In R.W. Barnett & J. S. Blumner (Eds.), *Writing centers and writing across the curriculum programs: Building interdisciplinary partnerships* (pp. 155–175). Westport, CT: Greenwood Press.

Hock, M. F., Deshler, D. D., & Schumaker, J. B. (1999). Tutoring programs for academically underprepared college students: A review of the literature. *Journal of College Reading and Learning, 29*(2), 101–114.

Hood, P. D. (2003). *Scientific research and evidence-based practice.* Retrieved from http://www.wested.org/online_pubs/scientific.research.pdf

Horner, A., & Jacobson, K. H. (1985). *An action research proposal: Identifying and addressing problems related to RACC's writing laboratory.* (ERIC Document No. 261718).

Horner, B., & Lu, M.-Z. (2000). Expectations, interpretations, and contributions of basic writing. *Journal of Basic Writing, 19*(9), 43–52.

Horner, R. H., Carr, E. G., Halle, J., McGee, G., Odom, S., & Wolery, M. (2005). The use of single-subject research to identify evidence-based practice in special education. *Exceptional Children, 71*, 165–179.

Hunter, K. R. (1993). *Tutor talk: A study of selected linguistic factors affecting tutor-writer interaction in a university writing center.* (Doctoral dissertation, Indiana University of Pennsylvania) ProQuest Dissertations & Theses, 9407522.

Hunzer, K. M. (1997). Misperceptions of gender in the writing center: Stereotyping and the facilitative tutor. *Writing Lab Newsletter, 22*(2), 6–10.

Huot, B. (1988). Working with Charlotte: A close look at tutoring the special learner. *Writing Lab Newsletter, 13*(3), 9–12.

Hutchings, C. (2006). Researching students: Lessons from a writing centre. *Higher Education Research & Development, 25*, 247–261. Retrieved October 19, 2009 from Academic Search Complete.

Hyland, K. (2003). *Second language writing.* Cambridge: Cambridge University Press.

Hynds, S. (1989). Perspectives on perspectives in the writing center conference. *Focuses, 2*(2), 77–90.

Ianetta, M., & Fitzgerald, L. (2010). *Writing Center Journal*: An alternative history. *Writing Center Journal, 30(1),* 9–11.

Ianetta, M., McCamley, M., & Quick, C. (2007). Taking stock: Surveying the relationship of the writing center and TA training. *WPA: Writing Program Administration, 31* (1–2), 104–123.

Inman, J. A., & Sewell, D. N. (Eds.) (2000). *Taking flight with OWLS: Examining electronic writing center work.* Mahwah, NJ: Lawrence Erlbaum.

International Writing Centers Association (2011). *IWCA Year in Review*. Retrieved from http://writingcenters.org/2011/02/iwca-year-in-review/

International Writing Centers Association. *2012 Summer Institute*. Retrieved from http://writingcenters.org/links/2012-summer-institute/

Jacoby, J. (1994). "The use of force": Medical ethics and center practice. In J. A. Mullin & R. Wallace (Eds.), *Intersections: Theory-practice in the writing center* (pp. 132–147). Urbana, IL: National Council of Teachers of English.

Jefferson, G. (2004). Glossary of transcript symbols with an introduction. In G. Lerner (Ed.), *Conversation analysis: Studies from the first generation* (pp. 13–31). Amsterdam: John Benjamins.

Job Satisfaction Survey. Retrieved from http://shell.cas.usf.edu/~pspector/scales/jsspag.html

Johanek, C. (2000). *Composing research: A contextualist paradigm for rhetoric and composition.* Logan: Utah State University Press.

Johnson Black, L. (1998). *Between talk and teaching: Reconsidering the writing conference.* Logan: Utah State University Press.

Johnson, D. W., & Johnson, R. T. (1992). Positive interdependence: Key to effective cooperation. In R. Hertz-Lazarowitz & N. Miller (Eds.), *Interaction in cooperative groups: The theoretical anatomy of group learning* (pp. 174–199). Cambridge, UK: Cambridge University Press.

Johnson, T. J. C. (1997). *In search of status: An empirical study of writing centers in four academic settings.* (Doctoral dissertation, West Virginia University) ProQuest Dissertations & Theses, 9727680.

Johnson-Shull, L., & Kelly-Riley, D. (2001). Writes of passage: Conceptualizing the relationship of writing center and writing assessment practices. In R. H. Haswell (Ed.), *Beyond outcomes: Assessment and instruction within a university writing program* (pp. 83–91). Westport, CT: Ablex.

Johnson-Shull, L., & Wyche, S. (2001). An assessment office within a writing center: The butterfly effect. In R. H. Haswell (Ed.), *Beyond outcomes: Assessment and instruction within a university writing program* (pp. 25–35). Westport, CT: Ablex.

Jones, C. (2001). The relationship between writing centers and the improvement of writing ability: A review of the literature. *Education, 122*, 3–20.

Jones, R.H., Garralda, A., Li, D. C. S., & Lock, G. (2006). Interactional dynamics in on-line and face-to-face peer-tutoring sessions for second language writers. *Journal of Second Language Writing, 15*(1), 1–23.

Jordan, K. S. (2003). *Power and empowerment in writing center conferences.* (Doctoral dissertation: Louisiana State University Agricultural & Mechanical College.)

Jordan-Henley, J. (1995). A snapshot: Community college writing centers in an age of transition. *Writing Lab Newsletter, 20*(1), 1–7.

Kail, H. (2000). Writing center work: An ongoing challenge. *Writing Center Journal, 20* (2), 25–28.

Kail, H. (2002). [Review of the book *Writing Center Research: Extending the Conversation* by P. Gillespie, A. Gillam, L. Falls Brown, & B. Stay (Eds.)]. *College Composition and Communication, 54*(2), 315–318.

Kane, E. (2011.) *Making quality contact in the writing center: A collective case study of the connection between writing consultants' discourse community knowledge and genre knowledge.* (Doctoral dissertation, University of Alabama) ProQuest Dissertations & Theses, 3422960.

Kaufman, J. H., & Schunn, C. D. (2011). Students' perceptions about peer assessment for writing: Their origin and impact on revision work. *Instructional Science, 39*, 387–406.

Kelly, M. S., Raines, J. C., Stone, S., and Frey, A. (2010). *School social work: An evidence-informed framework for practice.* New York: Oxford University Press.

Kiedaisch, J., & Dinitz, S. (1991). Learning more from the students. *Writing Center Journal, 12*(1), 90–100.

Kiedaisch, J., & Dinitz, S. (1993). Look back and say "so what": The limitations of the generalist tutor. *Writing Center Journal, 14*(1), 63–74.

Kiedaisch, J., & Dinitz, S. (2007). Changing notions of difference in the writing center: The possibilities of Universal Design. *Writing Center Journal, 27*(2), 39–59.

Kim, Y. J. (2007). A discourse analysis of writing tutorials with reference to the dominance in nonnative tutors and nonnative tutees. *Seoul National University Working Papers in English Linguistics and Language, 6*, 14–34.

Kim, Y.-K. (2009). *Frame analysis of writing center interactions: Discourse analysis of writing center tutorials with NS and NNS students: Volubility and questions.* Saarbrücken, Germany: VDM Verlag.

King, A. (1998). Transactive peer tutoring: Distributing cognition and metacognition. *Educational Psychology Review, 10*(1), 57–74.

Kinkead, J. A. (1993). The scholarly context: A look at themes. In J. A. Kinkead & J. G. Harris (Eds.), *Writing centers in context: Twelve case studies* (pp. 238–247). Urbana, IL: National Council of Teachers of English.

Kinkead, J. A. (1996). The National Writing Centers Association as mooring: A personal history of the first decade. *Writing Center Journal, 16*(2), 131–143.

Kinkead, J. A., & Harris, J. G. (1993). *Writing centers in context: Twelve case studies.* Urbana, IL: National Council of Teachers of English.

Kirsch, G. (1992). Methodological pluralism: Epistemological issues. In G. Kirsch & P. Sullivan (Eds.), *Methods and methodology in composition research*, (pp. 247–269). Carbondale & Edwardsville: Southern Illinois University Press.

Konstant, S. B. (1992). Multisensory tutoring for multisensory learners. *Writing Lab Newsletter, 16*(9–10), 6–8.

Koedinger, K. R., & Aleven, V. (2007). Exploring the assistance dilemma in experiments with cognitive tutors. *Educational Psychology Review, 19*, 239–264.

Kostecki, J., & Bers, T. (2008). The effect of tutoring on student success. *Journal of Applied Research in the Community College, 16*(1), 6–12.

Kovarsky, D. (2008). Representing voices from the life-world in evidence-based practice. *International Journal of Language and Communication Disorders, 43*, 47–57.

Kuriloff, P. C. (1999). Writing centers as WAC centers: An evolving model. In R. W. Barnett & J. S. Blumner (Eds.), *Writing centers and writing across the curriculum programs: Building interdisciplinary partnerships* (pp. 105–118). Westport, CT: Greenwood Press.

Kutz, E. (1997). *Language and literacy.* Portsmouth, NH: Boynton/Cook.

Labov, W., & Fanshel, D. (1977). *Therapeutic discourse.* New York: Academic Press.

Lamb, M. (1981). Evaluation procedures for writing centers: Defining ourselves through accountability. In T. Hawkins & P. Brooks (Eds.), *New directions for college learning assistance: Improving writing skills* (pp. 69–82). San Francisco: Jossey Bass.

Lape, N. (2008). Training tutors in emotional intelligence: Toward a pedagogy of empathy. *Writing Lab Newsletter, 33*(2), 1–6.

Larrance, A. J., & Brady, B. (1995). A pictogram of writing center conference follow-up. *Writing Lab Newsletter, 20*(4), 5–7.

Lauby, J. (1985). Understanding the dyslexic writer. *Writing Lab Newsletter, 9*(5), 7–9.

Law, J., & Murphy, C. (1997). Formative assessment and the paradigms of writing center practice. *The Clearing House, 72*, 106–108.

Leitch, R., & Day, C. (2000). Action research and reflective practice: Towards a holistic view. *Education Action Research, 8*(1), 179–194.

Leki, I., Cumming, A. H., & Silva, T. (Eds.). (2008). *A synthesis of research on second language writing in English.* New York: Taylor & Francis.

Lerner, N. (1996). *Teaching and learning in a university writing center.* (Doctoral dissertation, Boston University) ProQuest Dissertations & Theses, 9622601.

Lerner, N. (1997). Counting beans and making beans count. *Writing Lab Newsletter, 22*(1), 1–4.

Lerner, N. (2001). Choosing beans wisely. *Writing Lab Newsletter, 26*(1), 1–5.

Lerner, N. (2003). Writing center assessment: Searching for proof of our effectiveness. In M. Pemberton & J. Kinkead (Eds.), *The center will hold: Critical perspectives on writing center scholarship* (pp. 58–73). Logan: Utah State University Press.

Lerner, N. (2005). Internal outsourcing of academic support: The lessons of supervised study. *WPA: Writing Program Administration, 29*(1–2), 81–95.

Lerner, N. (2006). Time warp: Historical representations of writing center directors. In C. Murphy & B. L. Stay (Eds.), *The writing center director's resource book* (pp. 3–11). Mahwah, NJ: Erlbaum.

Lerner, N. (2007). Rejecting the remedial brand: The rise and fall of the Dartmouth writing clinic. *College Composition and Communication, 59*(1), 13–35.

Lerner, N. (2009a). *The idea of a writing laboratory.* Carbondale: Southern Illinois University Press.

Lerner, N. (2009b). Introduction to a list of dissertations and theses on writing centers, 1924–2008. *Writing Lab Newsletter, 33* (7), 6–9.

Lerner, N. (2010, November). *Whose ideas count the most? A study of citation practices in the Writing Center Journal.* Paper presented at the International Writing Centers Association Conference, Baltimore, MD.

Lerner, N., & Kail, H. (2004). *Writing center assessment bibliography.* Retrieved from http://api.ning.com/files/dT-20GNOJNMPA6aW8O-yxWaFo73qQpBbnKrnYNbYNkGtJUsSO85OTkLXYORdi79ronT5*SBGFYSDlA5*4ND-o-OP*mSVwoT2/WCAssessmentBib.pdf

Leverenz, C. S. (2001). Graduate students in the writing center: Confronting the cult of (non)expertise. In J. V. Nelson & K. Evertz (Eds.), *The politics of writing centers* (pp. 50–61). Portsmouth, NH: Heinemann/Boynton-Cook.

Levin, K. (2007). *More things than dreamt of in our philosophy: Tutoring, administration, and other peculiarities of writing center work.* (Doctoral dissertation, Indiana University) ProQuest Dissertations & Theses, 3243798.

Li, H., & Hamel, C. M. (2003). Writing issues in college students with learning disabilities: A synthesis of the literature from 1990 to 2000. *Learning Disability Quarterly, 26*(1), 29–46.

Liggett, S., Jordan, K., & Price, S. (2011). Mapping knowledge-making in writing center research: A taxonomy of methodologies. *The Writing Center Journal, 31*(2), 50–88.

Lockett, S. K. (2008). *Rethinking "the orthodoxy of current practice" in the writing center: Working with non-native, deaf, and learning disabled writers.* (Master's thesis, University of Houston, Clear Lake) ProQuest Dissertations & Theses, 1462811.

Lu, M.-Z. (1992). Conflict and struggle: The enemies and preconditions of basic writing. *College English, 54*(8), 887–913.

Lundstrom, K., & Baker, W. (2009). To give is better than to receive: The benefits of peer review to the reviewer's own writing. *Journal of Second Language Writing, 18*, 30–43.

Lunsford, A. (1979). Cognitive development and the basic writer. *College English, 41*(1), 38–46.

Lunsford, A. (2003). Collaboration, control, and the idea of a writing center. In C. Murphy (Ed.), *The St. Martin's sourcebook for writing tutors* (2nd ed.) (pp. 46–53). Boston: Bedford/St. Martin's.

Macauley, W. J., Jr., & Mauriello, N. (Eds.) (2007). *Marginal words, marginal work? Tutoring the academy in the work of writing centers.* Cresskill, NJ: Hampton Press.

MacDonald, R. B. (1991). An analysis of verbal interaction in college writing tutorials. *Journal of Developmental Education, 15*(2–4), 6–12.

Mackiewicz, J. (1999). Power in discourse frames: The use of politeness strategies to balance hierarchy and equality in writing center tutoring. *Crossroads of Language, Interaction, and Culture, 1*, 77–93.

MacLean, M. S., & Mohr, M. M. (1999). *Teacher-researchers at work.* Berkeley, CA: National Writing Project.

Magnotto, J. N. (1991). *The constructions of college writing in a cross-disciplinary, community college writing center: An analysis of student, tutor and faculty representations* (Doctoral dissertation, University of Pennsylvania) ProQuest Dissertations & Theses, 9200269.

Maheady, L. (1998). Advantages and disadvantages of peer-assisted learning strategies. In K. Topping & S. Ehly (Eds.), *Peer-assisted learning* (pp. 45–66). Mahwah, NJ: Lawrence Erlbaum.

Manguson, R. (1986). Preventing wrecks: The role of the writing lab in teacher preparation. *Writing Lab Newsletter, 10*(8), 11–14.

Marek, M.-R. (1991/1992). Right brain processing and learning disabilities: Conclusions not to reach in the writing center. *Writing Lab Newsletter, 16* (4–5), 14–18.

Marron, P. (1993). Tutoring a deaf student: Another view. *Writing Lab Newsletter, 17*(5), 15–16.

Marshall, M. J. (2001). Sites for (invisible) intellectual work. In J. V. Nelson & K. Evertz (Eds.), *The politics of writing centers* (pp. 74–84). Portsmouth, NH: Boynton/Cook.

Massey, L. (2006). Learning to write, program design, and the radical implications of context. [Review of *The end of composition studies*, by D. W. Smith]. *Pedagogy: Critical Approaches to Teaching Literature, Language, Composition, and Culture, 6*, 179–188.

Matsuda, P. K. (1997). Contrastive rhetoric in context: A dynamic model of L2 writing. *Journal of Second Language Writing, 6*(1), 45–60.

Mauriello, N., Macauley, Jr., W. J., & Koch, R. T. (Eds.). (2007). *Before and after the tutorial: Writing centers and institutional relationships.* Cresskill, NJ: Hampton Press.

Mausehund, J. A. (1993). *An analysis of the relationship of writing ability, writing apprehension, and the interrelationship of peer-review activities in business communication classes.* (Doctoral dissertation, Northern Illinois University) ProQuest Dissertations & Theses, 9400654.

Maxwell, M. (1994). Does tutoring help? A look at the literature. In M. Maxwell (Ed.), *From access to success* (pp. 109–116). Clearwater, FL: H & H Publishing.

McClure, S. H. (1990). *An observational study of the behavior of first semester college students as tutors in a writing center.* (Doctoral dissertation, Indiana University of Pennsylvania) ProQuest Dissertations & Theses, 9022651.

McInerney, K. H. (1998). *A portrait of one writing center through undergraduate tutors' talk: Themes of home, heart, and head.* (Doctoral dissertation, University of Iowa) ProQuest Dissertations & Theses, 9904322.

McKinney, J. G. (2005). Leaving home sweet home: Towards critical readings of writing center spaces. *Writing Center Journal,* 25(2), 6–20.

McNamara, D. S., Crossley, S. A., & McCarthy, P. M. (2010). Linguistic features of writing quality. *Written Communication,* 27(1), 57–86.

McQuiggan, S. W., Robison, J. L., & Lester, J. C. (2010). Affective transitions in narrative-centered learning environments. *Educational Technology & Society,* 13(1), 40–53.

Medcalf, J., Glynn, T., & Moore, D. (2004). Peer tutoring in writing: A school systems approach. *Educational Psychology in Practice,* 20(2), 157–178.

Melnick, J. F. (1984). The politics of writing conferences: Describing authority through speech act theory. *Writing Center Journal,* 4(2), 9–21.

Merbitz, C. T., Vieitez, D., Merbitz, N. H., & Binder, C. (2004). Precision teaching: Applications in education and beyond. In D. J. Moran & R. Malott (Eds.), *Evidence-based education methods* (pp. 63–78). San Diego: Academic Press.

Meyer, E., & Smith, L.Z. (1987). *The practical tutor.* New York: Oxford University Press.

Michaels, S. (1986). Narrative presentations: An oral preparation for literacy with first graders. In J. Cook-Gumperz (Ed.), *The social construction of literacy* (pp. 110–137) Cambridge: Cambridge University Press.

Mick, C. S. (1999). "Little teachers," big students: Graduate students as tutors and the future of writing center theory. *Writing Center Journal,* 20(1), 33-50.

Mindess, A. (2006). *Reading between the Signs.* 2nd edition. Boston: Intercultural Press.

Minnesota Satisfaction Questionnaire. Retrieved from http://www.psych.umn.edu/psylabs/vpr/msqinf.htm

Montgomery, N. (1994). Facilitating talk about student texts in small writing groups. *Focuses,* 7(2), 79–88.

Moore, R. H. (1950). The writing clinic and the writing laboratory. *College English,* 11, 388–393.

Moran, D. J., & Malott, R. W. (Eds.). (2004). *Evidence-based educational methods.* Amsterdam: Elsevier Academic Press.

Moridis, C. N., & Economides, A. A. (2009). Prediction of student's mood during an online test using formula-based and neural network-based method. *Computers & Education,* 54, 644–652.

Morrison, J. B., & Nadeau, J.-P. (2003). How was your session at the writing center? Pre-and post-grade student evaluations. *Writing Center Journal,* 23(2), 25–42.

Moser, A. H. (2002). *Theories, techniques, and the impacts of computer-mediated conferencing in a university writing center: Toward a model for training programs.* (Doctoral dissertation, Virginia Polytechnic Institute and State University) ProQuest Dissertations & Theses, 3157770.

Moser, J. (1993). Crossed currents: ESL students and their peer tutors. *Research & Teaching in Developmental Education,* 9(2), 37–43.

Mota de Cabrera, C. R. (2004). *Teaching, tutoring, and revision: The experiences of two ESL students in a rhetoric class.* (Doctoral dissertation, University of Iowa) ProQuest Dissertations & Theses, 3114463. Available at http://ir.uiowa.edu/etd/123

Mullin, A. (1994). Improving our abilities to tutor students with learning disabilities. *Writing Lab Newsletter,* 19(3), 1–4.

Mullin, A. (2002). Serving clients with learning disabilities. In B. B. Silk (Ed.), *The writing center resource manual* (pp. IV.1.1–IV.1.8). Emmitsburg, MD: IWCA Press.

Mullin, J. A., & Wallace, R. (Eds.). (1994). *Intersections: Theory-practice in the writing center.* Urbana, IL: National Council of Teachers of English.

Murphy, C., & Law, J. (1995). *Landmark essays on writing centers.* New York: Routledge.

Murphy, C., Law, J., & Sherwood, S. (1996). *Writing centers: An annotated bibliography.* Westport, CT: Greenwood Press.

Murphy, C., & Sherwood, S. (Eds.) (2011). *The St. Martin's sourcebook for writing tutors* (4th ed). Boston: Bedford/St. Martin's.

Murphy, C., & Stay, B. (2006). *The writing center director's resource book.* Mahwah, NJ: Lawrence Erlbaum.

Nakamaru, S. (2010). Lexical issues in writing center tutorials with international and and US-educated multilingual writers. *Journal of Second Language Writing, 19*(2), 95–113.

Nash, G. (2006). Politeness in the writing center: An analysis of NS tutor and NNS student discourse. *Writing Lab Newsletter, 31*(4), 1–6.

National Conference on Peer Tutoring in Writing. Retrieved from http://www.ncptw.org/

Neff, J. (1994/2008). Learning disabilities and the writing center. In R. W. Barnett & J. S. Blummer (Eds.), *The Longman guide to writing center theory and practice.* (pp. 376–390). New York: Pearson. (Reprinted from J. A. Mullin & R. Wallace (Eds.) (1994.) *Intersections: Theory-practice in the writing center* (pp. 81–95). Urbana, IL: National Council of Teachers of English).

Nelson, J. V., & Evertz, K. (2001). *The politics of writing centers.* Portsmouth, NH: Boynton/Cook.

Nelson, M. M., & Schunn, C. D. (2009). The nature of feedback: How different types of peer feedback affect writing performance. *Instructional Science, 37*, 375–401.

Nelson, M. W. (1991). *At the point of need: Teaching basic and ESL writers.* Portsmouth, NH: Boynton/Cook.

Neuleib, J. W. (1984). Research in the writing center: What to do and where to go to become research oriented. *Writing Lab Newsletter, 9*(4), 10–13.

Neuleib, J. W., & Scharton, M. A. (1995). Writing others, writing ourselves: Ethnography and the writing center. In J. A. Mullin & R. Wallace (Eds.), *Writing center perspectives* (pp. 54–67). Urbana, IL: NCTE.

New York University Writing Center. Retrieved from http://www.nyu.edu/cas/ewp/html/writing_center.html

Newton, J. (1990). Electronic tutoring and ESL students' writing. In M.-L. Craven, R. Sinyor, & D. M. Paramskas (Eds.), *CALL: Papers and reports.* (pp. 87–89). La Jolla, CA: Athelstan.

Nicolas, M. (2002). *Re-telling the story: An exploration of the feminization of the writing center narrative.* (Doctoral dissertation: Ohio State University) ProQuest Dissertations & Theses, 3059306.

Nicolas, M. (2005). Writing centers as training wheels: What message are we sending our students? *Praxis: A Writing Center Journal, 3*(1). Retrieved from http://projects.uwc.utexas.edu/praxis/?q=node/46

Norris, B. L. (2010). *On the practices of writing centers: A comparative case analysis of two writing centers.* (Doctoral dissertation, University of Washington) ProQuest Dissertations & Theses, 3443203.

North, S. M. (1984a). The idea of a writing center. *College English, 46*(5), 433–446.

North, S. M. (1984b). Writing center research: Testing our assumptions. In Olsen, G. A. (Ed.), *Writing centers: Theory and administration* (pp. 24–35). Urbana, IL: NCTE.

North, S. M. (1985). Designing a case study method for tutorials: A prelude to research. *Rhetoric Review, 4*, 88–99.

North, S. M. (1987). *The making of knowledge in composition: Portrait of an emerging field.* Upper Montclair, NJ: Boynton/Cook.

O'Hare, T. (2005). *Evidence-based practices for social workers: An interdisciplinary approach.* Chicago: Lyceum.

O'Leary, C. E. (2008). It's not what you say, but how you say it (and to whom): Accommodating gender in the writing conference. *Young Scholars in writing: Undergraduate research in writing and rhetoric 6,* 60–72. Retrieved from http://cas.umkc.edu/english/publications/young scholarsinwriting/documents/ItsNotWhatYouSay.pdf

Oliver, V. J. (2009). *Writing center location and physical environment: The relevance of tutor and tutee perceptions.* (Master's thesis, Southern Illinois University, Carbondale) ProQuest Dissertations & Theses, 1473971.

Olsen, G. A. (Ed.) (1984). *Writing centers: Theory and administration* (pp. 24-35). Urbana, IL: NCTE.

Osman, G. D. (2007). *Student perceptions of the effectiveness of a mandatory remedial program at a historically Black university.* (Doctoral dissertation, Alabama State University) ProQuest Dissertations & Theses, 3286867.

Owens, D. (2008). Hideaways and hangouts, public squares and performance sites: New metaphors for writing center design. In K. Dvorak & S. Bruce (Eds.), *Creative approaches to writing center work* (pp. 71–83). Cresskill, NJ: Hampton Press.

Ozias, M., Hartz, J., McElhaney, S., Donnelli-Sallee, E., Garrison, K., Allen, I., & Fallon, B. (2008), October. *Learning "downstream": Exploring the outcomes of writing center cultures and conditions.* Paper presented at the meeting of the International Writing Centers Association, Las Vegas, NV.

Pajares, F. (2003). Self-efficacy beliefs, motivation, and achievement in writing: a review of the literature. *Reading & Writing Quarterly, 19,* 139–158.

Pajares, F., & Johnson, M. (1994). Confidence and competence in writing: The role of self-efficacy, outcome expectancy and apprehension. *Research in the Teaching of English, 28,* 313–331.

Pantoja, M. V. (2010). *An analysis of writing tutoring assessment in four community college writing centers.* (Doctoral dissertation, University of Arizona) ProQuest Dissertations & Theses, 3410759.

Patchan, M. M. (2011). *Peer review of writing: learning from revision using peer feedback and reviewing peers' texts.* (Doctoral dissertation, University of Pittsburgh) ProQuest Dissertations & Theses, 3471914.

Patchan, M. M., Charney, D., & Schunn, C. D. (2009). A validation study of students' end comments: Comparing comments by students, a writing instructor, and a content instructor. *Journal of Writing Research, 1*(2), 124–152.

Peer Tutor Alumni Research Project. Retrieved from http://www.writing.wisc.edu/pwtarp/

Peguesse, C. L. (2000). *Writing centers professionalize: Visions and version of legitimacy.* (Doctoral dissertation, University of Arizona) ProQuest Dissertations & Theses, 9983920.

Pemberton, M. A. (1998). Writing center ethics: "Special needs" students and writing centers. *Writing Lab Newsletter, 23* (4), 12–13.

Pemberton, M. A. (2011). Revisiting "Tales Too Terrible to Tell": A survey of graduate coursework in writing program and writing center administration. In N. Mauriello, W. J. Macauley, Jr., & R. T. Koch (Eds.), *Before and after the tutorial: Writing centers and institutional relationships* (pp. 255–274). New York: Hampton Press.

Pemberton, M. A., & Kinkead, J. (Eds.) (2003). *The center will hold: Critical perspectives on writing center scholarship.* Logan: Utah State University Press.

Person, N. K., Kreuz, R. J., Zwann, R. A., & Graesser, A. C. (1995). Pragmatics and pedagogy: Conversational rules and politeness strategies may inhibit effective tutoring. *Cognition and Instruction, 13*(2), 161–188.

Pilkington, R., & Parker-Jones, C. (1996). Interacting with computer-based simulation: The role of dialogue. *Computers and Education, 27*, 1–14.

Plummer, L., & Thonus, T. (1999, April). *Methodology as mythology: Tutors' directive instruction.* Paper presented at the National Writing Centers Association, Bloomington, IN.

Position Statement on Disability and Writing Centers. Retrieved from ProfessionalStandards/Practice_Studies_Manual_1_25.pdf

Powers, J. K, & Nelson, J. V. (1995). L2 writers and the writing center: A national survey of writing center conferencing at graduate institutions. *Journal of Second Language Writing, 4*(2), 113–138.

Pridham, F. (2001). *The language of conversation.* London: Routledge.

Protecting human research participants. NIH Office of Extramural Research. Retrieved from http://phrp.nihtraining.com/users/login.php

Purdue Online Writing Lab. Retrieved from http://owl.english.purdue.edu/

Putman, M., & Walker, C. (2010). Motivating children to read and write: Using informal learning environments as contexts for literacy instruction. *Journal of Research in Childhood Education, 24*(2), 140–151.

Purves, A. C. (Ed.). (1988). *Writing across languages and cultures: Issues in contrastive rhetoric.* Newbury Park, CA: Sage.

Rafoth, B. (2005). *A tutor's guide: Helping writers one to one* (2nd ed.). Portsmouth, NH: Boynton/Cook.

Rafoth, B., & Bruce, S. (Eds.). (2009). *ESL writers: A guide for writing tutors* (2nd ed.). Portsmouth, NH: Boynton/Cook.

Rafoth, B., Macauley, B., Stoltenberg, K., Housenick, S., Brown, J., & Baran, B. (1999). Sex in the center: Gender differences in tutorial interactions. *Writing Lab Newsletter, 24*(3), 1–5.

Ramey, H. L., & Grubb, S. (2009). Modernism, postmodernism and (evidence-based) practice. *Contemporary Family Therapy, 31*(2), 76–86.

Reason, P., & Bradbury-Huang, H. (Eds.) (2007). *The Sage handbook of action research: Participative inquiry and practice.* London: Sage.

Reigstad, T. J. (1980). *Conferencing practices of professional writers: Ten case studies.* (Doctoral dissertation, State University of New York at Buffalo) ProQuest Dissertations & Theses, 8104233.

Reilly, S. (2004). The move to evidence-based practice within speech pathology. In S. Reilly, J. Douglas, & J. Oates (Eds.), *Evidence-based practice in speech pathology* (pp. 3–17). London: Whurr.

Reinheimer, D., & McKenzie, K. (2011). The impact of tutoring on the academic success of undeclared students. *Journal of College Reading and Learning, 41*(2), 22–36.

Ritter, J. J. (2002). *Negotiating the center: An analysis of writing tutorial interactions between ESL learners and native-English speaking writing center tutors.* (Doctoral dissertation, Indiana University of Pennsylvania) ProQuest Dissertations & Theses, 3056649.

Roberge, M., Siegal, M., & Harklau, L. (Eds.). (2009). *Generation 1.5 in college composition: Teaching academic writing to U.S.-educated learners of ESL.* New York: Routledge.

Roberts, D. H. (1988). A study of writing center effectiveness. *Writing Center Journal* 9(1), 53–60.

Robertson, K. S. (2005). *Technology and the role of peer tutors: How writing center tutors perceive the experience of online tutoring.* (Doctoral dissertation, University of Massachusetts, Amherst) ProQuest Dissertations & Theses, 3163699.

Robinson, H. M. (2009). Writing center philosophy and the end of basic writing: Motivation at the site of remediation and discovery. *Journal of Basic Writing, 28,* 70–92.

Rodby, J. (2002). The subject is literacy: General education and the dialectics of power and resistance in the writing center. In P. Gillespie, A. Gillam, L. Falls Brown, & B. Stay (Eds.), *Writing center research: Extending the conversation* (pp. 221–234). Mahwah, NJ: Lawrence Erlbaum.

Rogers, P. M. (2008). *The development of writers and writing abilities: A longitudinal study across and beyond the college-span.* (Doctoral dissertation, University of California, Santa Barbara) ProQuest Dissertations & Theses, 3319795.

Rogers, P. M. (2010). The contributions of North American longitudinal studies of writing in higher education to our understanding of writing development. In C. Bazerman et. al. (Eds.), *Traditions of writing research* (pp. 365–377). New York: Routledge.

Rogers, R. (2004). *An introduction to critical discourse analysis in education.* Mahwah, NJ: Lawrence Erlbaum.

Roscoe, R. D., & Chi, M. T. H. (2007). Understanding tutor learning: knowledge-building and knowledge-telling in peer tutors' explanations and questions. *Review of Educational Research, 77,* 534–574.

Roswell, B. S. (1992). *The tutor's audience is always a fiction: The construction of authority in writing center conferences* (Doctoral dissertation, University of Pennsylvania) ProQuest Dissertations & Theses, 9308651.

Ryan, L., & Zimmerelli, L. (2010). *The Bedford guide for writing tutors* (5th ed.). New York: Bedford/St. Martin's.

Sackett, D. L., Rosenberg, W., Gray, J. A. M., Haynes, R. G., & Richardson, W. S. (1996). Evidence-based medicine: What it is and what it isn't. *British Medical Journal, 312,* 71–72.

Sackett, D. L., Straus, S. E., Richardson, W. S., Rosenberg, W., & Haynes, R. B. (2000). *Evidence-based medicine: How to practice and teach EBM* (2nd ed.). Edinburgh: Churchill Livingstone.

Sacks, H., Schegloff, E., & Jefferson, G. (1974). A simplest systematics for the organization of turn-taking for conversation. *Language, 50,* 696–753.

Sadoshima, S., & Turner, A. (2008, April). *Writing centers, language acquisition, and global contexts.* Paper presented at the International TESOL Convention, New York, NY.

Salem, L. A., & Eodice, M. (2010, November). *A rising tide lifts all boats: Alliances and professional development in writing center work.* Paper presented at the International Writing Centers Association Conference, Baltimore, MD.

Schiffrin, D. (1996). Interactional sociolinguistics. In S. McKay & N. H. Hornberger (Eds.), *Sociolinguistics and language teaching* (pp. 307–328). Cambridge: Cambridge University Press.

Schmidt, K. M., & Alexander, J. E. (in press). Writing center assessment: The development of an instrument to measure writerly self-efficacy. *Journal of Writing Assessment.*

Schumann, J. H., Holroyd, J., Campbell, R. N., & Ward, F. A. (1978). Improvement of foreign language pronunciation under hypnosis: A preliminary study. *Language Learning, 28*, 143–148.

Scott, T. (2009). *Dangerous writing: Understanding the political economy of composition.* Logan: Utah State University Press.

Searle, J. R. (1969). *Speech acts: An essay in the philosophy of language.* Cambridge, Cambridge University Press.

Seckendorf, M. H. (1986). *Writing center conferences: An analysis.* (Doctoral dissertation, State University of New York at Albany) ProQuest Dissertations & Theses, 8625994.

Seo, M.-S., & Koshik, I. (2010). A conversation analytic study of gestures that engender repair in ESL conversational tutoring. *Journal of Pragmatics, 42*(8), 2219–2239.

Settlement reached in suit over radioactive oatmeal experiment. (1998, January 1). *The New York Times*, p. A19. Retrieved from http://www.nytimes.com/

Severino, C. (1992). Rhetorically analyzing collaboration(s). *Writing Center Journal, 13*(1), 52–64.

Severino, C. (1993a). ESL and native-speaking writers and pedagogies: The issue of difference. *Writing Center Journal, 13*(2), 63–70.

Severino, C. (1993b). The "doodles" in context: Qualifying claims about contrastive rhetoric. *The Writing Center Journal, 14*(1), 44–62.

Severino, C. (1994). The writing center as site for cross-language research. *Writing Center Journal, 15*(1), 51–61.

Severino, C. (2002). Writing centers as contact zones. In J. Wolff (Ed.), *Professing in the contact zone* (pp. 230–239). Urbana, IL: NCTE.

Severino, C. (2009). Avoiding appropriation. In S. Bruce & B. Rafoth (Eds.), *ESL writers: A guide for writing tutors* (2nd ed.) (pp. 51–66). Portsmouth, NH: Heinemann/Boynton Cook.

Severino, C., & Deifell, E. (2011). Empowering L2 tutoring: A case study of a second language writer's vocabulary learning. *Writing Center Journal, 31*(1), 25–54.

Severino, C., Swenson, J., & Zhu, J. (2009). A comparison of online feedback requests by non-native English-speaking and native English-speaking writers. *Writing Center Journal, 29*(1), 36–57.

Shaughnessy, M. (1977). *Errors and expectations: A guide for the teacher of basic writing.* Oxford: Oxford University Press.

Shell, D. F., Murphy, C. C., & Bruning, R. H. (1989). Self-efficacy and outcome expectancy mechanisms in reading and writing achievement. *Journal of Educational Psychology, 81*(1), 91–100.

Silk, B. B. (1998). *The Writing Center Resource Manual.* Emmitsburg, MD: IWCA Press.

Silk, B. B. (2002). *The Writing Center Resource Manual* (2nd ed.). Emmitsburg, MD:IWCA Press.

Silva, T., & Matsuda, P. K. (Eds.). (2010). *Practicing theory in second language writing.* West Lafayette, IN: Parlor Press.

Sinclair, J. and Coulthard, R. M. (1975). *Toward an analysis of discourse.* Oxford, Oxford University Press.

Slavin, R. E. (1996). Research on cooperative learning and achievement: What we know, what we need to know. *Contemporary Educational Psychology, 21*, 43–69.

Sloan, P. J. (2007). *Contextualizing writing centres: Theory vs. practice.* (Doctoral dissertation, Carleton University) ProQuest Dissertations & Theses, MR26967.

Smarthinking. http://www.smarthinking.com

Smith, A.E. (2010). *Writing in/on the borderlands: (Basic) writers in the writing center.* (Doctoral dissertation, University of Louisville) ProQuest Dissertations & Theses, 3437642.

Smith, V. (2007). Ethnographies of work and the work of ethnographers. In P. Atkinson, A. Coffey, S. Delamont, J. Lofland, & L. Lofland (Eds.), *Handbook of ethnography*. (pp. 220–233). Los Angeles: Sage.

Smitherman, C. E. (2007). *Oral histories of the national writing centers association: A look at group dynamics.* (Doctoral dissertation, University of Louisville) ProQuest Dissertations & Theses, 3293567.

Sniveley, H. (2008). A writing center in a graduate school of education: Teachers as tutors, still in the middle. In M. Nicolas (Ed), *(E)Merging identities: Graduate students in the writing center.* (pp. 89–102). Southlake, TX: Fountainhead Press.

Snively, H., Freeman, T., & Prentice, C. (2006). Writing centers for graduate students. In C. Murphy & B. Stay (Eds.), *The writing center director's resource book* (pp. 153–163). Mahwah, NJ: Lawrence Erlbaum.

Soliday, M.S., & Gleason, B. (1997). From remediation to enrichment: Evaluating a mainstreaming project. *Journal of Basic Writing, 16*(1), 64–78.

Solomon, L. J., & Rothblum, E. D. (1984). Academic procrastination: Frequency and cognitive-behavioral correlates. *Journal of Counseling Psychology, 31,* 503–509.

Sosnoski, J. J. (1991). Postmodern teachers in their postmodern classrooms. In P. Harkin & J. Schilb (Eds.), *Contending with words: Composition and rhetoric in a postmodern age* (pp. 198–219). New York: Modern Language Association.

Spielberger, C. D. (1983). *State-trait anxiety inventory.* Redwood City, CA: Mind Garden.

Staben, J. E. (2005). *Not just chairs and tables: New peer tutors' negotiations with identity, literacy, and difference in a community college writing center.* (Doctoral dissertation, Indiana University of Pennsylvania) ProQuest Dissertations & Theses, 3194575.

Stachera, S. A. (2003). *Tongue tied: Coming to terms with our writing center practice.* (Doctoral dissertation, New Mexico State University) ProQuest Dissertations & Theses, 3115670.

Stahr, M. L. (2008). As if through another's eyes: A study of peer tutoring and first-year students' revision behaviors. (Doctoral dissertation, University of Pittsburgh) ProQuest Dissertations & Theses, 3335833.

Stake, R. E. (1995). *The art of case study research.* Thousand Oaks, CA: Sage.

Stalinski, S. (2003). Developing stronger practitioner certification in coaching-related professions: A USA perspective. *International Journal of Evidence Based Coaching and Mentoring, 1,* 6–8.

Stanford Study of Writing. Retrieved from http://www.sssw.stanford.edu

Starr, M., & Chalmers, I. (2003). *The evolution of the Cochrane Library, 1988–2003.* Retrieved from http://www.update-software.com/history/clibhist.htm

Stay, B. (1983). When re-writing succeeds: An analysis of student revisions. *Writing Center Journal, 4*(1), 15–28.

Stay, B., Murphy, C., & Hobson, E. (Eds.) (1995). *Writing center perspectives.* Emmitsburg, MD: National Writing Centers Association Press.

Stenström, A. (1994). *An introduction to spoken interaction.* London: Longman.

Stober, D. R., Wildflower, L., & Drake, D. B. (2006). Evidence-based practice: A potential approach for effective coaching. *International Journal of Evidence Based Coaching and Mentoring, 4,* 1–8.

Stonerock, K. H. (2005). *From training to practice: The writing center as a setting for learning to tutor.* (Doctoral dissertation, The Ohio State University) ProQuest Dissertations & Theses, 3176904. Retrieved from http://etd.ohiolink.edu/view.cgi?acc%5fnum=osu1117636352

Strijbos, J.-W., Narciss, S., & Dünnebier, K. (2010). Peer feedback content and sender's competence level in academic writing revision tasks: Are they critical for feedback perceptions and efficiencies? *Learning and Instruction, 20,* 291–303.

Stubbs, M. (1983). *Discourse analysis.* Chicago: University of Chicago Press.

Swain, M. (2006). Languaging, agency, and collaboration in advanced second language proficiency. In H. Byrnes (Ed.), *Advanced language learning* (pp. 95–108). London: Continuum.

Swan, M., & Smith, B. (2001). *Learner English: A teacher's guide to interference and other problems* (2nd ed.). Cambridge: Cambridge University Press.

Swift, P. W. (1986). *The effect of peer review with self-evaluation on freshman writing performance, retention, and attitude at Broward Community College (Florida).* (Doctoral dissertation, Florida Atlantic University) ProQuest Dissertations and Theses, 8770237.

SWoRD. Retrieved from https://sites.google.com/site/swordlrdc/

Taylor, V. G. (2007). *The balance of rhetoric and linguistics: A study of second language writing center tutorials.* (Doctoral dissertation, Purdue University) ProQuest Dissertations & Theses, 3340684.

Ten Have, P. (2007). *Doing conversation analysis.* (2nd ed.). Los Angeles, CA: Sage.

TESOL Standards Committee. (2002). *Policies and procedures.* Retrieved from http://www.tesol.org/s_tesol/bin.asp?CID=230&DID=1392&DOC=FILE.PDF

Theodori, A. (2011, February). Connecting the dots: Using our data for meaningful assessment and research. Paper presented at the meeting of the South Central Writing Centers Association, Houston, TX.

Thompson, I. (2006). Writing center assessment: Why and a little how. *Writing Center Journal 26*(1), 33–61.

Thompson, I. (2009). Scaffolding in the writing center: A microanalysis of an experienced tutor's verbal and nonverbal tutoring strategies. *Written Communication, 26*(4), 417–453.

Thompson, I., Whyte, A., Shannon, D., Muse, A., Miller, K., Chappell, M., et al. (2009). Examining our lore: A survey of students' and tutors' satisfaction with writing center conferences. *Writing Center Journal, 29*(1), 78–105.

Thonus, T. (1998). *What makes a writing tutorial successful: An analysis of linguistic variables and social context.* (Doctoral dissertation, Indiana University) ProQuest Dissertations & Theses, 9919428.

Thonus, T. (1999a). Dominance in academic writing tutorials: Gender, language proficiency, and the offering of suggestions. *Discourse and Society, 10*(2), 225–248.

Thonus, T. (1999b). How to communicate politely and be a tutor, too: NS-NNS interaction and writing center practice. *Text, 19*(2), 253–279. ERIC Document 419 414. 1–10.

Thonus, T. (2001). Triangulating the key players: Tutors, tutees, instructors, and collaboration in the writing center. *Writing Center Journal, 22*(1), 57–82.

Thonus, T. (2002). Tutor and student assessments of academic writing tutorials: What is "success"? *Assessing Writing, 8*(2), 110–134.

Thonus, T. (2003a). Serving Generation 1.5 learners in the university writing center. *TESOL Journal, 12*(1), 17–24.

Thonus, T. (2003b, April). *From dyad to group: Writing tutorials and NS-NNS interaction.* Paper presented at the California TESOL Conference, Pasadena, CA.

Thonus, T. (2004). What are the differences? Tutor interactions with first- and second-language writers. *Journal of Second Language Writing, 13*(3), 227–242.

Thonus, T. (2007). Listener responses as a pragmatic resource for learners of English. *CATESOL Journal, 19*(1), 132–145.

Thonus, T. (2008). Acquaintanceship, familiarity, and coordinated laughter in writing tutorials. *Linguistics and Education, 19*(4), 333–350.

Thonus, T. (2009, November). *Rules on the fly: Writing center tutors as "grammar" instructors.* Paper presented at the Symposium on Second Language Writing, Tempe, AZ.

Thonus, T. (in press). Languaging in L2 academic writing tutorials. In A. Mackey & K. McDonough (Eds.), *Interaction in diverse educational settings.* Amsterdam: John Benjamins.

Thonus, T., & Gilewicz, M. (2001, December). *Native-nonnative interaction in academic writing tutorials.* Paper presented at the Modern Language Association Conference, New Orleans, LA.

Threatt, T. (2009). *Gender and the writing center: How students' problems in writing fall into gendered categories of difference.* (Doctoral dissertation, University of Nevada, Reno) ProQuest Dissertations & Theses, 3375367.

Topping, K. J. (1996). The effectiveness of peer tutoring in further and higher education: A typology and review of the literature. *Higher Education, 32*(3), 321–345.

Topping, K. J. (2005). Trends in peer tutoring. *Educational Psychology, 25*(6), 631–645.

Torrance, H. (2004). Using action research to generate knowledge about educational practice. In G. Thomas & R. Pring (Eds.), *Evidence-based practice in education* (pp. 187–200). Maidenhead, UK: Open University Press.

Trinder, L. (Ed.) (2000). *Evidence-based practice: A critical appraisal.* Oxford: Blackwell.

Vallejo, J. F. (2004). *ESL writing center conferencing: A study of one-on-one tutoring dynamics and the writing process.* (Doctoral Dissertation, Indiana University of Pennsylvania) ProQuest Dissertations & Theses, 2120717.

Van Dam, D. C. (1985). *Effects of writing center usage and motivation on academic writing performance.* (Doctoral dissertation, University of Southern California) ProQuest Dissertations and Theses, 0556925.

Van Horne, S. A. (2011). *An activity-theory analysis of how college students revise after writing center conferences.* (Doctoral dissertation, University of Iowa) ProQuest Dissertations & Theses, 3473254.

Van Maanen, J. (1988). *Tales of the field: On writing ethnography.* Chicago, IL: University of Chicago Press.

Vandenberg, P. (1999). Lessons of inscription: Tutor training and the "professional conversation." *Writing Center Journal, 19*(2), 59–83.

Vazquez, L. (2008). *What motivational factors influence community college students' tendency to seek help from the writing center?* (Doctoral dissertation, University of Southern California) ProQuest Dissertations & Theses, 3325231.

Waite, S., & Davis, B. (2006). Developing undergraduate research skills in a faculty of education: Motivation through collaboration. *Higher Education Research and Development, 25*(4), 403–419.

Wallace, R., & Simpson, J. (Eds.) (1991). *The writing center: New directions.* New York: Garland.

Waring, H. Z. (2005) Peer tutoring in a graduate writing centre: Identity, expertise, and advice resisting. *Applied Linguistics, 26*(2), 141–68.

Waring, H. Z. (2007a). Complex advice acceptance as a resource for managing asymmetries. *Text and Talk, 27*(1), 107–137.

Waring, H. Z. (2007b). The multi-functionality of accounts in advice giving. *Journal of Sociolinguistics, 11*(3), 367–369.

Warnock, T., & Warnock, J. (1984). Liberatory writing centers: Restoring authority to writers. In G. A. Olson (Ed.), *Writing centers: Theory and administration* (pp. 16–23). Urbana, IL: NCTE.

Watkins-Goffman, L. F. (1986). *A case study of the second language writing process of a sixth-grade writing group.* (Doctoral dissertation, New York University) ProQuest Dissertations & Theses, 8625662.

Watts, R. J. (2003). *Politeness.* Cambridge, UK: Cambridge University Press.

WCenter. Retrieved from http://writingcenters.org/resources/join-the-wcenter-listserv/

Weaver, B. T. (1978). *The learning resources center: Individualized instruction in basic writing.* (Master's thesis, Ball State University).

Weaver, M. E. (1996). Transcending "conversing": A deaf student in the writing center. *JAC: A Journal of Composition Theory, 16*(2), 241–251.

Weigle, S. C., & Nelson, G. L. (2004). Novice tutors and their ESL tutees: Three case studies of tutor roles and perceptions of tutorial success. *Journal of Second Language Writing, 13*(3), 203–225.

Welch, N. (1995). Migrant rationalities: Graduate students and the idea of authority in the writing center. *Writing Center Journal, 16*(1), 5–23.

Wells, G., & Haneda, M. (2009). Extending instructional conversation. In L. Yamauchi (Ed.), *Human behavior and change: Theory, research, and practical application.* Retrieved from http://people.ucsc.edu/~gwells/Files/Papers_Folder/IC.pdf

Wenger, E. (1998). *Communities of practice: Learning, meaning, and identity. Learning in doing.* Cambridge, U.K.: Cambridge University Press.

Wewers, J. (1999). Writing tutors and dyslexic tutees: Is there something special we should know? In L. A. Podis and J. M. Podis (Eds.), *Working with student writers* (pp. 229–237). New York: Peter Lang.

White, M. J., & Bruning, R. H. (2005). Implicit writing beliefs and their relation to writing quality. *Contemporary Educational Psychology, 30*, 166–189.

Wilder, M. (2009). A quest for student engagement: A linguistic analysis of writing conference discourse. *Young Scholars in Writing, 8*, 94–105. Retrieved from http://cas.umkc.edu/english/publications/youngscholarsinwriting/documents/11%20-%20WILDER%20-%20WRITING%20BOOK%202010.pdf

Williams, J. (2004). Tutoring and revision: Second language writers in the writing center. *Journal of Second Language Writing, 13*(3), 173–201.

Williams, J. (2005). Writing center interaction: Institutional discourse and the role of peer tutors. In K. Bardovi-Harlig & B. Hartford (Eds.), *Interlanguage pragmatics: Exploring institutional talk* (pp. 37–66). Mahwah, NJ: Erlbaum.

Williams, J. (2008, April). *Tutoring L2 writers: Insights from SLA research.* Paper presented at the International TESOL Convention, New York, NY.

Williams, J., & Severino, C. (2004). The writing center and second language writers. *Journal of Second Language Writing, 13*(3), 165–172.

Williams, J. D., & Takaku, S. (2011). Help seeking, self-efficacy, and writing performance among college students. *Journal of Writing Research, 3*(1), 1–18.

Wilson, L., & LaBouff, O. (1986). Going beyond remedial: the writing center and the literature class. *Writing Center Journal, 6*(2), 19–29.

Wing Institute. (2011). *What is evidence-based education?* Retrieved from http://www.winginstitute.org/Evidence-Based-Education/what-is-evidence-based-education/

Witte, S. P., & Faigley, L. (1981). Coherence, cohesion, and writing quality. *College Composition and Communication, 32*(2), 189–204.

Wolcott, W. (1989). Talking it over: A qualitative study of writing center conferencing. *Writing Center Journal, 9*(2), 15–29.

Wolff-Murphy, S. (2001). *Politeness and self-presentation in writing center discourse.* (Doctoral dissertation, Texas A&M University) ProQuest Dissertations & Theses, 3033843.

Wood, G. F. (1995). Making the transition from ASL to English: Deaf students, computers, and the writing center. *Computers and Composition, 12*(2), 219–226.

Woolbright, M. (1992). The politics of tutoring: Feminism within the patriarchy. *Writing Center Journal, 13*(1): 16–30.

Woolley, M. E., Bowen, G. L., & Bowen, N. K. (2004). Cognitive pretesting and the developmental validity of child self-report instruments: Theory and applications. *Research on Social Work Practice, 14*, 191–200.

Wright, S. (1994). Mapping diversity: Writing center survey results. *Writing Lab Newsletter, 18*(2), 1–4.

Writing Centers Research Project. (2004). *Local practices, institutional positions.* http://coldfusion.louisville.edu/webs/a-s/wcrp/reports/analysis/index.cfm

Yarrow, F., & Topping, K. J. (2001). Collaborative writing: The effects of metacognitive prompting and structured peer interaction. *British Journal of Educational Psychology, 71*, 261–282.

Young, B. R., & Fritzsche, B. A. (2002). Writing centers users procrastinate less: The relationship between individual differences in procrastination, peer feedback. *Writing Center Journal, 23*(1), 45–58.

Young, V. H. (1992). *Politeness phenomena in the university writing conference.* (Doctoral dissertation, University of Illinois at Chicago) ProQuest Dissertations & Theses, 9310163.

Youngs, B. L., & Green, A. (2001). A successful peer writing assistant program. *Foreign Language Annals, 34*(6), 550–558.

Zdrojkowski, M. R. T. (2007). *Laughter in interaction: The discourse function of laughter in writing tutorials.* (Doctoral dissertation, Michigan State University) ProQuest Dissertations & Theses, 3264258.

Index

Speech therapy, evidence-based practice in, 27
Speech-to-text interface, 36
Spelling *see also* Mechanics, 94, 120, 128, 159
Spielberger, Charles D., 167
Staben, Jennifer E., 60
Stachera, S. Alison, 112–113, 116, 122, 136
Stahr, Margaret L., 157, 163
Stake, Robert E., 40–41
Stalinski, Sheryll, 29
Stance, 112
  Authoritative, 122, 124
  Passive, 124
Standards, writing center, 30, 58–59, 84–85, 150
Stanford Study of Writing, 158
Starr, Mark, 25
Statistical Package for the Social Sciences (SPSS), 36
Statistics, 42, 59, 79, 166
  Study results, 89, 153, 158, 168
Stay, Byron, 13, 15, 17, 118, 162
Stenström, A., 138
Stephenson, Denise, 67
Stephenson, Sharon, 158
Stimulated recall, 154, 176–177
Stober, Dianne R., 29
Stonerock, Krista H., 87–88, 92
Strain, Kim, 102
Strauss, Anselm L., 43
Strauss, Tracy, 47, 56, 130, 132, 138, 142, 155
Strickland, Fred W., Jr., 33
Strijbos, Jan-Willem, 150
Stubbs, Michael, 46
Student(s) *see* Tutee(s) or Writer(s)
Study skills, 148–149
Subjects, research *see* Participants
Success, 47, 88, 114, 129, 139, 143–169
  In academic tutoring, 145–154
  As better grades, 165, 167–168
  In developmental education, 145–146
  Groups, 91
  Interaction, 147, 150
  L2 tutoring, 127
  As meaningful interaction, 154–156
  Online tutoring, 98

  In peer education, 146–151
  As repeat visits, 166–168
  As revision, 150, 162–164
  As satisfaction, tutor/writer, 152–154
  As writer development, 159–161
  As writing development, 156–159
Suggestions, 50, 53, 55
  Explicit, 55, 104, 119, 133, 155, 162
    Tutee preference for, 123, 155
  And gender, 134
  Illocutionary force indicating devices, 105
  Implicit, 55, 154
  Offering of accounts, 109
  In online tutoring, 79–80
  As opposed to demands, 90
  For revision, 78, 79, 108, 117, 120, 123, 162
  Sequences, 112–113, 127–128, 132–134
  Suggestions for research, 178
  Tutees resisting/rejecting, 49, 120, 126, 134–135
  Types, 125, 131–134
Summer Institute for Writing Center Directors and Professionals, IWCA, 5, 7–8, 174
Sunstein, Bonnie S., 37
Survey(s) *see also* Questionnaires, 39, 42, 91, 146
  Of faculty, 70
  As research tool, 47
  Of students, 69–70, 74–75, 125, 131, 152–153, 158, 165
    Basic writers, 88–89, 103
    Graduate students, 106
    Post-consultation, 88, 100
    On writing center expectations, 80–81
  Suggestions for research, 172–175
  Of tutors, 19, 73, 94, 116, 125, 131
  Of writing centers, 59–66, 74, 107, 108
Swan, Michael, 101
Swift, Patricia W., 37
SWoRD (Scaffolded Writing and Rewriting in the Discipline), 151
Symbolic convergence theory, 83
Syntax *see also* Grammar, 82, 159
Synthesis, syntheses, 13, 94, 125, 176